About this book

This unique contribution to global educational debate and policy-making by the UN Special Rapporteur on the right to education highlights adverse impacts of denials and abuses of education. Millions are victimized by the denial of education, but the problem is attributed to poverty rather than misrule. Abuse of education exposes children and young people to indoctrination in the name of education. Reviewing the history of global commitment to education as a human right, the author traces the global split between rights-based and lottery-based approaches. Current problems are examined through the human rights perspective. This shifts the debate from sheer numbers of pupils and the recent preoccupation with market forces to a deeper discussion about what education should really comprise. Governments are obliged, collectively and individually, to make education available, accessible, acceptable and adaptable.

The book is an indispensable *tour d'horizon* of the problems encountered in the emerging global quest for rights-based education. It highlights examples of exposing and opposing abuses of power that this quest has involved and what needs to be done through examples of effective mobilization for change.

Katarina Tomasevski is Professor of International Law and International Relations at Lund University and External Lecturer at the Centre for African Studies of Copenhagen University. Educated at the University of Zagreb and Harvard Law School, her teaching experience spans all regions and includes professional training courses in human rights mainstreaming.

She is currently Special Rapporteur on the right to education of the United Nations Commission on Human Rights. This role has involved conceptualizing the right to education, carrying out human rights missions to individual countries to assess problems and prospects, investigating alleged violations of the right to education, and promoting rights-based education at all levels (from the local to the global) of policy-making.

Katarina Tomasevski has conducted major cross-national research projects, including on the fate of imprisoned children, the human rights dimensions of HIV/AIDS, and the application of international human rights safeguards for women in different regions and countries.

She has published extensively in English and Spanish and her books have been translated into French, Japanese and Chinese. Her books include:

Responding to Human Rights Violations 1946–1999 (Kluwer Law International, 2000), *Between Sanctions and Elections* (Pinter Publishers/Cassell, 1997), *Foreigners in Prison* (HEUNI, 1994), *Human Rights in Population Policies* (SIDA, 1994), *Women & Human Rights* (UN/NGLS and Zed Books, 1993).

EDUCATION DENIED

COSTS AND REMEDIES

Katarina Tomasevski

Zed Books
LONDON & NEW YORK

University Press Ltd
DHAKA

White Lotus Co. Ltd
BANGKOK

David Philip
CAPE TOWN

Education Denied was first published by
Zed Books Ltd, 7 Cynthia Street, London N1 9JF, UK and
Room 400, 175 Fifth Avenue, New York, NY 10010, USA.
www.zedbooks.demon.co.uk

In Bangladesh: The University Press Ltd,
Red Crescent Building, 114 Motijheel C/A,
PO Box 2611, Dhaka 1000.

In Burma, Cambodia, Laos, Thailand and Vietnam:
White Lotus Co. Ltd, GPO Box 1141, Bangkok 10501, Thailand

In South Africa: David Philip, an imprint of New Africa Books,
PO Box 23408, Claremont 7753
Tel: 2721 674 4136   Fax: 2721 674 3358

Distributed in the USA exclusively by Palgrave, a division of
St Martin's Press, LLC, 175 Fifth Avenue, New York, NY 10010

Copyright © Katarina Tomasevski, 2003

Cover designed by Andrew Corbett
Typeset in 10/12 pt Baskerville by Long House, Cumbria, UK
Printed and bound in the United Kingdom
by Biddles Ltd, Guildford and King's Lynn

A catalogue record for this book
is available from the British Library

ISBN   1 84277 250 3 Hb
       1 84277 251 1 Pb

Library of Congress Cataloging-in-Publication Data
has been applied for

This book has been published and distributed in the South
with the support of the Raoul Wallenberg Institute of Human Rights,
with funding from the Swedish International Development Co-operation Agency (Sida)

Contents

List of Boxes   viii

List of Figures   ix

List of Tables   ix

List of Credits   xi

Preface and Anti-acknowledgments   xiii

Introduction   1

PART I • WHY THE RIGHT TO EDUCATION?   7

1 Why Do We Need Safeguards Against Denials
and Abuses of Education by Governments?   9

'We only need to increase aid to governments of poor countries'   9

'Education is a taxpayer-funded government monopoly'   15

2 The Economics of the Right to Education   22

Why primary education was made free and compulsory   24

Blaming poverty rather than policy choices   27

Making policy choices: why people are not human capital   32

3 The Promise of the 1948 Universal Declaration of
Human Rights   36

Whose rights? Which rights? The initial intergovernmental blueprint   36

Enter the right to education   41

Safeguards against the denial of education   42

Preventing abuse of education   44

Sources of inspiration   44

    Continental European models   46

    The Anglo-American model   47

4 The Core Contents of the Right to Education   51

Free and compulsory education   53

Parental freedom of choice 55

Non-discrimination 57

Aims and purposes of education 60

Divided world: West/East, North/South 64

PART II • RUPTURING THE GLOBAL CONSENSUS 67

5 Enter the World Bank: Changing the Parameters of
the Debate 69

In its own words: the World Bank's approach to education 69

School fees: trial-and-error in Malawi 72

The message of street protests 77

6 The Impoverishment of Public Education and its Cost 83

The plunge in public finance 85

A race towards the bottom line 86

The educational price of the end of the Cold War 89

7 Unwilling, Unable or Unlike-minded?
Creators of Global Education Strategy 93

Who or what is the 'international community' in education? 93

Consensus as a recipe for inaction 97

Fuzzy vocabulary and governance to match 99

Can impoverished basic education help eliminate poverty? 101

8 Painfully Visible Loss of the Right to Education:
Transfigured University 108

From free public service to freely traded service 111

What is today's price of a university? 115

Brain-drain and brain-gain 118

PART III • PUTTING HUMAN RIGHTS BACK IN 123

9 Exposing and Opposing Exclusion 125

Exposing exclusion: asking the big Why? 125

Opposing exclusion: pinpointing government obligations 128

Rupturing global inaction 132

Rescuing education from debt bondage 133

Uganda's success story 136

Will it work in Tanzania? 139

10 Revisiting Segregated Education 143

Mobilization against colonialism and racism 143

Religious and secular schooling 148

The ripple effects of the 1979 Islamic revolution in Iran 149

Creationism *versus* evolutionism in the United States 150

Overcoming the heritage of *defectology* 151

11 Rights-based Education as a Pathway to Gender Equality 158

Why basic education for all girls may not make much difference on its own 158

Two faces of gender disparity 163

Child-mothers 165

Countering denials of women's rights 166

Adapting education to girls' equal rights 169

12 Human Rights Safeguards in Education 172

The medium is the message: the language of instruction 174

Shooting the messengers? Obstacles to teachers' rights 177

Censorship of textbooks 181

13 Summing Up: Human Rights through Education 187

A look back 188

Recognizing human rights violations in education 190

Violence and education, violence in education 193

Confronting the transmission of discrimination through education 195

INDEX 200

List of Boxes

1.1	The educational cost of corruption in Nigeria	10
1.2	Why Pakistan cannot afford schools for girls	13
1.3	Where has the money for children's education gone?	14
1.4	Re-education in China	16
1.5	Why was compulsory education in Turkey prolonged in 1997?	17
1.6	Denied rights: language, culture, identity	19
1.7	Killing schoolchildren: Emperor Bokassa's shameful legacy	20
2.1	The economic rationale for education in South Korea	22
2.2	When is education relevant?	29
2.3	The costs of ill-chosen models of education in Sierra Leone	30
3.1	Negotiating the Universal Declaration, fighting the Cold War	40
3.2	Huckleberry Finn, the most famous truant in history	43
4.1	Key treaty provisions on free and compulsory education	52
4.2	Dragged back to school	54
4.3	Guarantees for parental freedom of choice	55
4.4	Key treaty provisions on non-discrimination in education	58
4.5	Key treaty provisions on the orientation and purpose of education	61
4.6	The UN: splitting the right to education to fit the divided world	63
5.1	The World Bank's recipe for curbing demand for primary education in Banda's Malawi	73
5.2	Dialogue between the Special Rapporteur on the right to education and the World Bank	74
5.3	Why is the World Bank popular with G-7?	79
6.1	From economic optimism to consecutive economic crises	83
6.2	What young Europeans learned about the defeat of socialism	88
7.1	Words worth $300 million: outcomes of Jomtien and Dakar compared	98
7.2	What changes would human rights have made?	100
8.1	Casualties in battles between gown and gun in Nigeria, 1978–95	109
8.2	'Schools are for kids, not for sale'	113
8.3	Tiananmen Square, 4 June 1989	116
8.4	The cost of corporate sponsorship	119
9.1	Exclusion from education from A to W	126
9.2	What a difference a rights-based campaign can make: Shiksha Yatra in India	129
9.3	Mobilization of shame in creditor countries: 'Haven't we taken enough?'	134
9.4	Excerpts from PRSPs on alleviating the educational cost of debt	135
10.1	Excluding Africans: reports by colonial administrations	144
10.2	*Brown v. Board of Education of Topeka*	146
10.3	Bridge or fence between communities? Prospects for desegregating education in Sri Lanka	155

11.1	The price parents pay for having their daughters schooled	160
11.2	What AIDS prevention message for schoolchildren?	162
11.3	Controversial headscarves	167
12.1	From *hispanicizing* to educating in Latin America	172
12.2	Teachers' rights fare ill in Ethiopia	179
12.3	Is geography about knowledge or power?	183
13.1	Education statistics for Kuwait examined using the human rights yardstick	189
13.2	The purpose of schooling as determined in Saudia Arabia, China and Cuba	191
13.3	Asking politically incorrect questions: how schoolchildren learn about racism	196
13.4	Creating exclusion of migrant workers	197

List of Figures

7.1	G-7 and 0.7: never to meet?	96
9.1	Population Age Pyramids, 2025	132

List of Tables

1.1	Countries in which allocations for defence exceeded education in central government budget, 1992–99	12
2.1	The legally determined minimum age for employment, by country	25
2.2	The legally mandated length of compulsory education, by country	26
2.3	Absent child-rights policy, inconsistent minimum ages	28
3.1	United Nations membership, 1945–2002	37
3.2	Statistics on primary education, 1873	45
6.1	Allocations for education as % of government budgets	86
6.2	Public funding for education in relation to GNP	87
6.3	Declining schooling for 15-year-olds in the former Soviet Union, 1989–97	90
6.4	Development and socio-economic rights at the UN Commission on Human Rights	90
7.1	Basic education in bilateral aid	95
7.2	Gross enrolment in secondary education, 1995–97	103
9.1	Non-registration of children at birth	127
11.1	Countdown to 2005: gender disparities in primary school enrolment	159
11.2	Women aged 20–24 married before 20 by years of schooling	161
11.3	Girls' enrolment in comparison with boys'	164
11.4	Percentage of female primary school teachers	164

List of Credits

Cover picture: South Asian Coalition on Child Servitude, Arvind Yadav and *Hindustan Times*

14   Where has the money for children's education gone? Gary Brookins, *Richmond Times-Despatch*
19   Denied rights: Language, Culture, Identity: Social Services and Child Protection Agency and United Nations Children's Fund, Ankara
40   Berliner Luftbrücke 1948/1949: Landesarchiv Berlin
43   Huckleberry Finn: © 2002, Rector and Visitors of the University of Virginia
49   Cover of *Life*, 23 March 1958: Life Magazine © Times Inc./Timepix
54   Dragged back to school: © Jack Hill/*The Independent*
77   'World Bankenstein' as Santa Claus? World Bank advertisement, *Economist* (most recently 31 August 2002)
113 'Schools are for kids not for sale': © Tess Peni, www.truelove.com.au
116 Tiananmen Square, 4 June 1989: Amnesty International, © Jonathan Annelis
128 The most important piece of paper: © Howard Davies, www.exileimages.co.uk
134 'Haven't we taken enough?': © Martin Argles, *The Guardian*
137 UPE in Uganda: Ministry of Education and Sports, *The New Vision*, Kampala, 29 June 1999
151 Will it come this far? © 2002 Onion, Inc. All rights reserved. Reprinted with permission www.theonion.com
154 Learning is fun! Chicken-and-egg in sign language: © Ine van den Broek, Human Life Photography www.humanphoto.nl
162 What AIDS prevention message to school children?: Uganda School Health Kit on AIDS Control, Kampala, 1987
169 Father serving tea, mother reading newspapers: © Bina Agarwal
182 'Truth in textbooks': National League for Support of the School Textbook Screening Suit, Tokyo, 12 June 1995

Preface and Anti-acknowledgements

'It is a case of chipping away', was how an eleven-year-old schoolboy summed up my work as the Special Rapporteur of the United Nations Commission on Human Rights on the right to education. Happily ignorant about labyrinthine international structures that sprout technical jargon and countless acronyms, schoolchildren have been my favourite audience when explaining what rights-based education means and what difference it makes. They love debating the unfairness of precluding poor children from school and easily understand that law requires children to be at school to protect them from working too early. Dilemmas about inclusive and segregated education raise even more debate, as does asking schoolchildren which decisions about their own education they should be allowed to make, and how they would make them.

Most schoolchildren, as well as their teachers, have never heard of the many international human rights treaties that lay down the right to education, specify how human rights should be protected in education, and define how education should be organized so as to facilitate the enjoyment of all human rights. It is a sobering experience to learn how limited the outreach of internationally generated human rights norms is. However, the correspondence reaching the United Nations whereby people seek an immediate response to what they feel are human rights violations in education shows that outreach is ample. This book aims to facilitate it. It complements the official United Nations documents on the homepage of the High Commissioner for Human Rights (www.unhchr.ch) and the supplementary material created as a public access resource centre (www.right-to-education.org).

The appointment of a Special Rapporteur is the prerogative of the Chairman of the Commission on Human Rights. Financial and institutional independence is secured in two ways. The work is not remunerated, and the appointment is personal – hence the Special Rapporteur is not part of any institution. That the Commission, composed of governments, deals with human rights, by definition abuses of power by governments, summarizes the *mise-en-scène*. Independent outsiders often can accomplish more than would be possible through inter-national institutions or intergovernmental decision-making. My appointment, in 1998, was based on a long track record of working on economic and social rights, the human rights of women and the rights of the child. My work encompasses three tracks: annual reports provide a summarized overview of relevant develop-ments worldwide, country missions are carried out to examine problems *in situ*, and alleged violations are tackled through correspondence with governments and intergovernmental organizations. The right to education was a new mandate and, moreover, the first one in the area of economic, social and cultural rights, which were – still are – marginalized on the global agenda.

Special Rapporteurship is an honorary function, entailing much unpaid work and a great deal of battling to assert and defend the right to education, particularly for children who do not know that such a right exists, least of all that they should be enjoying it. The essential task is to expose and oppose denials and violations. By no stretch of the imagination could one imagine deniers and violators sitting back and applauding.

The essential prerequisites for human rights work are incurable optimism, patience and persistence, willingness to endure endless verbal abuse, and a long attention span. It takes an optimist to argue that education should remain a free public service at a time when trade in education services generates profits that by far exceed international aid for education. Exposing abuses of power by governments, which is the core of human rights work, requires putting up with more verbal abuse than, even after twenty years of experience, I have imagined possible. Acknowledgments would have provided a distorted image of the fate of the right to education. Hence, anti-acknowledgments. If the right to education had support by governments and intergovernmental organizations, there would be no need for a Special Rapporteur. This book identifies a range of unspoken truths and unasked questions that ought to be tackled, worldwide. This will not happen spontaneously or rapidly. It is a case of chipping away – all human rights work is.

Human rights activism started in the 1960s with the slogan that people whose rights were protected should act for those who were less fortunate. The adjective *human* implies everybody's duty to defend rights of all fellow humans. NGOs have led the way, governments have – sometimes – followed. At the core of human rights work is a paradox: the main protector of human rights – the authority one must rely on to enforce human rights – is also the main violator. It requires us to relinquish a belief that the *state* is inherently evil or naturally benevolent; rather, human rights workers need to see it as amenable to moulding.

Knowledge that abuses of power cannot ever be eliminated shapes human rights work into a continuing process. Human rights have been affirmed but are continuously violated by the very governments that solemnly affirmed them. So it is with any abuse of power. Although all criminal codes in the world prohibit killing and hurting people or raping children, such crimes have not been eliminated anywhere in the world nor will they ever be.

Introduction

This book is based on a simple premise. The recurrent theme in global debates about education is the cost of providing it. Hence, there is both reluctance to affirm that education is a human right and silence about the cost of denying education. Leaving seven-year-olds to fend for themselves routinely drives them into child labour, child marriage, or child soldiering. The right to education operates as a multiplier. It enhances all other human rights when guaranteed and forecloses the enjoyment of most, if not all, when denied. Boundaries of belonging are reflected in the willingness of parents to ensure education of *their* children. Governments do the same, but lack of education is attributed to poverty rather than to policy choices. Asking *why are people poor?* reveals denials of human rights; the search for answers reveals abuse of power. Exposing abuse of power, manifested in denials or abuses of education, is the first necessary step towards opposing it. It is the essence of human rights.

International human rights law has defined both the ends and the means of education. It embodies safeguards against its denials and abuses. The world of human rights is small, and dissociated from the worlds of education or economics, however. The building of bridges across disciplinary boundaries is therefore necessary to transcend boundaries amongst sectors. The division of labour amongst various ministries in individual countries is replicated in sectoral international strategies. Education law and funding for education often operate at cross purposes. Both are separated from efforts to combat child labour. Peace-building routinely has no institutional link with gender. Max Weber anticipated this a very long time ago, scoffing, 'I am not a donkey, and I do not have a field,' when accused of writing outside his field. This book weaves threads from many fields and sectors into the dense human rights pattern within which problems need to be located if they are to be solved. Rights-based economic and fiscal policies require the creation of data. A range of professions is needed to mould education so that it can sustain itself and also contribute to self-sustaining livelihoods. Translating the rights of the child from abstract principles into operative guidance for education is a process that has barely begun, worldwide.

Because education is the most heavily populated institutionalized activity, the literature on it is abundant. From the outside looking in, it is possible to single out comparative lessons from deliberate policies that moulded education as public or private, religious or secular, segregated or inclusive. The focus on hardware – funding and schools – stifles the asking of key questions: what should be taught, who should do the teaching, how should this be done; in sum, what is education *for*?

Education is seen as the cause of and panacea for all the diseases of society. This shows what a capacious concept it is and why human rights safeguards are necessary to prevent its abuse.

Development literature adds two key components. First, it documents the reasons for and consequences of governmental reluctance to finance education. In this era of slashing taxes, advocates of the right to education tend to be labelled as tax-and-spend populists. Second, external objectives to assessing education are necessary so that it can respond to maldevelopment. The model of education that anticipates children's progression through the education pyramid towards lifelong employment in the public sector was exported worldwide but did not travel well. If the search for alternative models is at one end of the controversy – denoted by the search for *quality* or *relevance* and the fierce intellectual battles they engender – the need to determine who will pay for education and how funding should be made self-sustaining is at the other. The rule book written in the form of international human rights law provides guidance, and the purpose of this book is to convey it and, more important, to explain why rights-based education makes a difference.

This book is divided into three parts. The first part introduces the essence of the human rights approach to education, and to safeguards against its denial or abuse by governments. The second part addresses the dominant global approach to education which denies that education is a human right and culminates in the progressive liberalization of trade in education services instead of progressive realization of the right to education. The third part focuses on the mobilization for change which aims at reinserting human rights into education, from the global to the local level. As the problem is often denial or abuse of education, the remedy is access to justice.

The first part of the book starts by highlighting the need to ask questions. When the spotlight is directed at minute international aid for education, while aid-seeking governments are prioritizing military over civilian spending, the need for human rights correctives is evident. Getting children to school is deemed to be inherently good although they can be brainwashed or raped there. Again, the need for human rights correctives is evident.

Education as a government-imposed duty is much older than the right to education, and dates back to the eighteenth century. The argument that the state should provide education to all children merged economic and nation-building arguments, adding security. 'The poor, illiterate, indebted and armed' were difficult to govern. The economic argument was strengthened by the International Labour Organization, which linked compulsory education with the minimum age for employment in 1921. Investment in education was defined as a government responsibility, and education as a means to eliminate child labour provided the underpinning for the emergence of the right to education. That component was combined in the Universal Declaration of Human Rights with safeguards against governmental abuses of education. Guarantees of parental freedom to choose education for their children originated from the knowledge that monopoly obliterates choice. Freedom is the essential component of every human right.

Memories of the Great Depression and the retroactive guilt about the Holocaust produced the first global consensus on the right to education. The model of education in the pivotal countries of the time straddled the Cold War fault lines but remained confined to the North. There was full consensus that governments should provide schooling for all children, partial consensus on the right of parental choice of education for their children, and no consensus regarding the fate of non-white people living in colonies and indigenous peoples. The full consensus behind state-provided schooling in the early post-war decades disguised an implicit endorsement of the state monopoly over education.

Translating the political promise of the Universal Declaration of Human Rights into legal obligations for governments took the form of a series of international treaties. Ideological and political battles during the Cold War interfered, and the division of the world into North and South exacerbated obstacles, as did the split between the realms of development and human rights. A selection of watershed moments that undermined the fate of the right to education at the global level in recent decades is presented in Part Two. Although the right to education had been written into the Universal Declaration of Human Rights, it was not used as a template for global development strategies. Rather, education was ultimately converted from a right into a development goal. An increase in school enrolments from 30 per cent to 40 per cent was then recorded as a success. By the human rights yardstick, this increase signifies continued denial of the right to education to 60 per cent of the population.

The model of the 1960s, getting all children to school, resulted in a surge in school enrolments. The imported rather than home-grown model of education led to the subsequent import of reductions of public funding for education in the aftermath of consecutive economic crises in the 1970s. These slanted the definition of government human rights obligations towards the US model of protection *from* the state rather than *by* the state, which was exported by the global creditor community, in which the World Bank has had a prominent role. Its approach was based on a belief that once the economics is right, everything else will fall into place. The World Bank's introduction of school fees in Malawi in 1983 ruptured the previous consensus that at least primary education should be free. The battle to abolish fees is going on. The cost of policy changes is illustrated by retrogression in Africa in the 1980s and Eastern Europe and Central Asia in the 1990s. Changes in Eastern Europe following the end of the Cold War provide a historic lesson, illustrating disadvantages of both models – the state monopoly over education, and free-marketization.

Action to mitigate the symptoms is ultimately futile without tackling the causes. This necessitates changes from the top down, from the global to the local level. Since the Jomtien Conference in 1990, globalized policy-making has replaced the conventional state-centred system, with a new vocabulary reflecting that change. The focus on the grand and fuzzy is exemplified in terms such as *mainstreaming* or *partnership*; defining a common position came down to seeking the lowest common denominator in platitudinous declarations. The Jomtien Conference was followed ten years later by the Dakar Conference. More of what did not work the first time is unlikely to work the second time. The cost of the global policy shift is expressed in guesstimates of the number of children who should be but are not at school. The global discord is exemplified in the subsumption of education under social development while expecting it to eliminate poverty. Basic education for children between the ages of six and eleven does not even bring them to the minimum age for employment. This necessitates asking whether the link between basic education and poverty reduction will work as it is assumed. Moreover, the exclusive focus on basic education is belied by evidence pointing to secondary education as the key to poverty eradication. Demonstrating the adverse impacts of abuses of power has been key to all advances in human rights. The purpose of this book is to highlight adverse impacts in order to inject these insights into decision-making processes.

Rights-based education necessitates two changes: human rights ought to be moved from the margins to the core of the many policies that shape education, and the universality of the right to education ought to be translated into universal human rights obligations. This is a daunting task. Part Three sketches mobilization for change, providing examples of remedies that have proved effective, and highlighting questions that ought to be posed.

The need for human rights originates from the ease with which political commitments are broken or ignored. Education illustrates this well. Political commitments to ensure universal primary education for all children in the world have been made once per decade. None materialized. Each betrayed pledge was followed by a similar pledge, which was also betrayed. The import of human rights can be expressed in one single word – violation. The mobilizing power of calling a betrayed pledge a human rights violation is immense. Moreover, legal enforcement makes violations expensive. Resort to legal enforcement requires pre-existing individual and collective commitment to the right to education. This explains the reluctance to make such a commitment of individual governments, such as the United States, or international agencies, such as the World Bank.

Accepting that education is a human right entails a price. Governmental human rights obligations are based on the premise that education is a public good and institutionalized schooling is a public service. In individual countries, budgetary allocations have to be adjusted to the requirements of international human rights law, that is, converted from discretionary into obligatory allocations. Enforced solidarity functions in individual states in the form of taxation, whereby education is financed through general revenue. There is no counterpart on the global level. Promoting the universality of the right to education through the globalization of corresponding human rights obligations is an unmet challenge.

On the domestic level, human rights law has introduced two innovations. The first one is the affirmation that each individual – including the child – is the subject of rights. The second one is the broad standing for claiming and vindicating human rights. Human rights obligations pertain to all parts of the government, regardless of vertical and horizontal division of powers. The human rights approach is based on regulatory and institutional coherence since human rights are interrelated and interdependent. This requires integration (the currently popular term is *mainstreaming*), a uniform and comprehensive framework encompassing all human rights.

Experiences in putting into practice requirements of international human rights law in different regions and countries reveal a great deal of similarity. The advantage of the rights-based approach is that identical problems are encountered in different countries. As human rights are universal, so are the problems. Problem-defining necessitates asking new and different questions and seeking different types of data to document underlying problems. Rights-based education entails safeguards for the right to education, human rights in education, and the advancing of all human rights through education.

The final chapter of the book consists of a *tour d'horizon*. A look back reveals the learning process whereby human rights have been gradually defined, field-tested, and applied as guidance for education. A look at unsolved problems and, more important, unasked questions demonstrates why human rights work is a permanent process. A look forward identifies the inseparability of global and local, legal and fiscal, social and cultural facets of education. Building bridges between single-issue campaigns is as necessary as are bridges amongst different government institutions or international agencies that deal with different dimensions of education.

Progress is evidenced by looking back just a few decades, when explicitly racist education policies and practices were widespread and legal. Today, legal prohibitions on denying human rights have been put in place in most countries in the world. Denials can be – and are – challenged. Examples of court cases that made a difference are included as they constitute human rights education in the narrowest sense of this term.

The process of combating exclusion and segregation epitomizes the need to turn to the past for lessons. Racial discrimination has been outlawed worldwide but not eliminated. The processes of decentralization and privatization in education threaten to perpetuate it under a different guise, through residential segregation or private schooling. Hence the need to use human rights as the yardstick for assessing the myriad of exogenous determinants of education.

Dilemmas generated by segregated education, even when addressed as human rights issues, yield answers that differ in time and place. Increased international involvement in conflict resolution and conflict prevention has not, as yet, addressed the impact of educational segregation on conflict generation. Education of children with disabilities fails by the yardstick of financial return on investment, highlighting the values that underpin human rights. Disability has triggered the most creative and far-reaching interpretations of the right to education, furnishing powerful arguments for all-inclusive education.

Much has been accomplished in exposing and opposing gender discrimination in access to school, and in revision of curricula and textbooks. Broadening the rights of girls and women through education is, nevertheless, a daunting challenge because much more is expected from education than it can possibly deliver. As with poverty reduction, the evidence shows that secondary, rather than primary education makes a difference in women's ability to exercise their rights.

The term 'human rights education' is commonly defined as a specialized branch of education that is an add-on, especially in higher education. It is much more demanding. It requires all education to support – rather than denying – equal rights for all. A simple review of the language of instruction, the status of teachers, and the contents of school textbooks points out why human rights safeguards are needed in education and what happens when they are absent. Perhaps the most serious indictment of education is evidenced in self-professed racism and xenophobia amongst school-going young people in countries with richly endowed, all-encompassing public education. This epitomizes the abyss between education and rights-based education. An immense amount of research has been generated to tackle this racism and a vast array of specialized education programmes is in place. This book ends with a message that answers may be much easier and simpler. It is not new knowledge that ought to be created. Rather, the key is recognizing denials and abuses of education and responding to them.

WHY THE RIGHT TO EDUCATION?

Why Do We Need Safeguards Against Denials and Abuses of Education by Governments?

Chapter 1

If you do not know where you are going, an old saying goes, any road is good enough. A visiting Martian could easily conclude that this observation aptly describes how education is tackled on our planet. Some commentators point to poverty and urge increased funding for education to governments of poor countries, others point to human rights violations by these governments and urge a halt to funding. Within the international community, one part advocates submitting education to free-market discipline, another argues that education should be a taxpayer-funded government monopoly. In one country girls are excluded from school if they wear a headscarf, in another they are not allowed to go to school unless they wear a headscarf. Teachers form the largest segment of government employees in some countries, in others they are imprisoned for conducting human rights education. Some pupils have access to the internet, others finish school without having seen a single book in a language they could understand. Some pupils are forced to regurgitate the official dogma and are physically punished for failure to do so, and this, adding insult to injury, is called their enjoyment of the right to education. An explanatory narrative that would enable a visiting Martian to understand the complexity and diversity of education in today's world has yet to be found. This book offers one possibility, embodied in the human rights approach. Its starting point is that luck determines which children have access to school, and which are subjected to indoctrination in the name of education. The rights-based approach posits that this should not be so.

Human rights focus on vertical relations, between the people and the state, through a series of entitlements and prohibitions. These specify what governments, individually and collectively, ought to do (such as ensuring that free and compulsory education encompasses all school-age children) and what they ought not to do (such as subjecting schoolchildren to indoctrination). Like Janus, governments have two faces: they are the principal protectors as well as the principal violators of human rights. Hence, human rights safeguards address both roles of the government.

'We only need to increase aid to governments of poor countries'

The most frequently cited reason for children's lack of schooling is the inability of their governments to afford the cost. Hence, demands for increased aid are made by these governments on children's behalf, if not always at their behest. A cynical definition of aid says that poor people in rich countries are thereby helping rich people in poor countries. The continuous decrease of aid threatens its demise. The roots of the problem can be traced to misrule. There is too little aid in part because enforced solidarity (that is, taxation) has not been extended to the global level, but also because too little of the aid that is provided reaches its intended beneficiaries. A consistency test between formally declared priorities and budgetary allocations frequently shows that military expenditure exceeds the allocation for education, that debt repayments exceed investments in development, that educational funding tends to prioritize university students over primary schoolchildren, or that the educational bureaucracy soaks up most of the funds intended for teaching and learning.

Box 1.1 shows why aid to governments of poor countries may not benefit education. It provides a glimpse into the scope of corruption during the military reign in Nigeria and its devastating effects on education. Children have paid the

Box 1.1 • The educational cost of corruption in Nigeria

'In November 1998, the Federal Government announced that it had recovered over 63 billion naira (nearly US$750 million) from the family of the late Head of State, General Sani Abacha, allegedly stolen within one year. Added to the money and other property recovered from the Security Adviser to the late Head of State, the recovered sums amount to about 125 billion naira (US$1.4 billion). This amount surpasses the total federal budget for education, health, social welfare, transportation and power generation in two consecutive years (1997 and 1998).

Unaccounted federal revenue of about US$12.4 billion is still uninvestigated. It is documented as having been received from surplus oil sales in 1991 and was reportedly misappropriated by General Ibrahim Babangida, Nigeria's erstwhile military ruler. Up till now, no charges have been brought against the former Head of State or those who collaborated with him. Also, the Abubakar administration has not investigated widespread allegations of corruption levelled at former and serving State military administrators. By not taking action against these people, the Abubakar administration condones the crime of corruption and the systematic violations of economic and social rights.

As a consequence of the massive misappropriation of national resources, critical service sectors of the nation are in acute dysfunction. ... Many schools, including primary and post-primary institutions, have resorted to imposing various fees and levies on students as a direct result of grossly inadequate funding; this has led to massive withdrawals of pupils from schools.'

Source: Report submitted by the Special Rapporteur of the Commission on Human Rights, Mr Soli Jehangir Sorabjee, United Nations (UN) Doc. E/CN.4/1999/36 of 14 January 1999, paras. 60–62.

cost of corruption twice. First, they were deprived of education as money destined for their schooling was stolen. Second, they have to pay back the loans which successive military governments took out. In April 2002, the government of Nigeria reached a settlement with the family of Sani Abacha, a former military ruler, whereby $1 billion was returned to the government.[1] How much more should have been but never will be returned remains an open question; how the complicity of international creditors and donors should be tackled is a question that is rarely asked, while whether any new aid or revenue will be protected from a similar fate is a question posed much too often. Pini Jason has commented on the political class who 'made their money under the military, or were financially empowered by the military to succeed them and watch their rear' and are now 'boasting about matching their opponents naira for naira and dollar for dollar'.[2]

The prominence of corruption on the agenda of international financial agencies and the donor community seems to promise a change. But this will require a great deal of courage and determination, which are in short supply. The postulate of international human rights law, that governments should use the available resources to their utmost to secure all human rights for all, provides ready-made guidance. However, officials of international creditors 'get promoted for making loans, not getting into pitched battles with underpaid government officials about the way aid is being disbursed'.[3] The vocabulary of international development cooperation, translated from rhetoric, explains why corruption remains widespread:

> Donor agencies have the function to spend money, recipient governments have, amongst others, the function to raise money. If donors don't disburse, they fail their mandate, and lose their budget. If recipients don't raise the necessary funds, they can't do what they are supposed to do, they also fail their mandate. Thus, the interdependence is complete.
>
> Remember, donor agencies have no interest in holding on to their money. The pressure on them to spend is even greater than the pressure on recipients to raise that money. Spending money is their *raison d'être*. It is much easier to justify a failed project than an unspent budget. If the funds don't flow your way, then they flow somewhere else, usually in the direction of someone who knows how to play the partnership game better than you do.[4]

Although international cooperation is defined as the principal means for facilitating the realization of the right to education, it is hampered by a vicious circle. The volume of aid is at its lowest in history, a mere $53 billion in 2001 for the entire developing world, half of what the former East Germany continues receiving more than a decade after reunification with its population of 14 million.[5] Diminished development aid is justified by assertions that much of it is misappropriated or squandered.

Alongside corruption, military expenditure is a frequent target of criticism. Weapons kill even before they are used, by starving budgets of funds that could be used for life-sustaining essentials or for education (see Table 1.1).

Table 1.1 • Countries in which military spending exceeded allocations for education in the central government budget, 1992–99

Country	Defence (% of total budget)	Education (% of total budget)
Albania	4	2
Angola	34	15
Azerbaijan	11	3
Bahrain	17	13
Bangladesh	11	10
Belarus	5	4
Bulgaria	8	4
Burundi	26	14
Canada	6	3
China	14	2
Congo	18	0
Croatia	11	6
Georgia	9	5
Guinea	29	11
Guinea-Bissau	4	3
Israel	18	13
Jordan	18	15
Kuwait	20	12
Mongolia	9	8
Mozambique	35	10
Myanmar	31	9
Nigeria	4	3
Oman	32	16
Pakistan	31	1
Russia	12	2
Saudi Arabia	36	14
Singapore	29	19
Sri Lanka	17	11
Switzerland	5	2
Syria	24	9
Tanzania	16	8
Uganda	26	15
United Arab Emirates	31	18
United Kingdom	7	4
United States	15	2

Source: UNICEF, *The State of the World's Children 2001*, New York, 2002.

Box 1.2 • Why Pakistan cannot afford schools for girls

In February 2002, American columnist Jim Hoagland quoted General Musharraf, who said that 'he would not increase the miserly amounts now spent to educate girls in rural areas because that would be culturally controversial'.* General Musharraf did not deny that statement at the time, or later, when he became President of Pakistan. Joining the USA's war-against-terrorism secured for Pakistan the support of its international creditors and donors, despite its frequent breaches of the conditions for continued funding. Most of the aid was, probably still is, spent on the military and on servicing previous debts. Funding to educate girls has not increased.

Pakistan's tax-to-GDP ratio is 13 per cent (about one-third of the OECD countries' average). Raising revenue was the government's key priority, declared General Musharraf when he took power. He said that taxation would 'make or break' Pakistan, and that just 1 per cent of the population of 140 million paying income tax was 'shameful'.† Six nuclear tests, whose cost has never been revealed, led in May 1998 to economic sanctions, which further aggravated Pakistan's inability to service its foreign debt. Sanctions were quietly lifted.

In 1997, Sartaj Aziz, the finance minister at the time, announced that 'annual government revenue was insufficient even to pay for debt servicing and defence'.‡ Both items have subsequently been provided for, especially at this time of war-against-terrorism, but funding for education remains minuscule. One consequence is an estimated 16 per cent literacy rate amongst rural women; another is that education for girls is not free: parents have to pay fees.§ Widespread avoidance of taxation is reflected in a dual economy and creative accounting. What is officially recorded and what is unofficially charged for girls' education varies a great deal.

> Girls in rural Sindh usually say 'yes' when asked if they like primary school. They belong to the literate minority in Pakistan. But their eyes darken as they start to talk about daily charges for invisible things in exchange for an education. They pay for teacher attendance, fees for fake school committees, and for textbooks and tuition that are supposed to be free. Some girls have to do domestic chores in the homes of their teachers if they cannot make cash payments.**

* J. Hoagland, 'In Pakistan they pretend to govern', *International Herald Tribune*, 25 February 2002.
† F. Bokhari, 'Musharraf firm on Pakistan tax reforms', *Financial Times*, 26 May 2000.
‡ F. Bokhari, 'Plan to widen tax base in Pakistan', *Financial Times*, 14–15 June 1997.
§ J. Kim, et al. *Evaluation of the Balochistan Rural Girls' Fellowship Program: Will Rural Families Pay to Send Girls to School?*, World Bank, Washington, DC, November 1999.
** C. Carlsson, 'Invisible burdens', *Guardian Weekly*, 8–14 June 2000.

The pattern of government expenditure prioritizing military expenditure over investment in education is epitomized in India and Pakistan. They, statistically speaking, have the majority of out-of-school children in the whole world. Both are recipients of aid for education. If the countries are poor, the same cannot be said for their governments. Both governments have entered the nuclear club, at huge but undisclosed expense. Asked where the government of India would find the money to educate all its children, Amartya Sen has replied, 'to say that India does not have the money is absolute, utter, unmitigated nonsense'.[6] This also applies to India's neighbour, Pakistan, as Box 1.2 illustrates.

Box 1.3 • Where has the money for children's education gone?

Funds allocated to education may be soaked up by its bureaucracy. Thus, tax revenue or aid is passed by the government to its own employees. The high level of political control over the civil service exercised by many governments often encompasses teachers, who may be part of the civil service, or access to teaching posts may be restricted to those loyal to the government.

Education bureacracies tend to be large. In Indonesia, the number of employees of the Ministry for National Education is 1.8 million. In New York there is one employee for each ten pupils, and Emanuel Tobier has found that only 55 per cent of money for education goes for teaching and learning.* Emanual Ablo and Ritva Reinikka studied the fate of budgetary allocations on their way from Uganda's central government to individual schools and concluded that only 30 per cent actually reached schools.†

* E. Tobier, 'New York City's public schools: The facts about spending and performance', *Civil Bulletin* No. 26, The Manhattan Institute, May 2001, p. 2.
† E. Ablo and R. Reinikka, *Do Budgets Really Matter? Evidence from Public Spending on Education and Health in Uganda*, Policy Research Working Paper No. 1926, World Bank, Washington, DC, 1996, p. 31.

From the recipients' perspective, the glaring discrepancy between vast aid needs and minuscule aid flows does not give the donors moral credibility to demand accountability. At its extreme, such an attitude is expressed as 'Give us the money and go away'. Children who cannot go to school because the dialogue between donors and recipients has worked itself into a blind alley have no voice. Getting the children, their parents and teachers, involved in ensuring that funds for education reach their destination is not an impossible task. It would rupture the vicious circle of enriching intermediaries and impoverishing beneficiaries which aid often sustains. It would also reveal what safeguards need to be in place to ensure that funds earmarked for education reach their intended beneficiaries. These safeguards need to be in place in all countries, not only countries receiving aid, as Box 1.3 shows.

'Education is a taxpayer-funded government monopoly'

International human rights law obliges individual states to ensure that each child has access to education, but it also prohibits them from monopolizing education, let alone transforming it into institutionalized indoctrination. The language of law is normative rather than empirical, and there are few states that have secured access to education for all their children and have ensured human rights safeguards in education while also respecting people's freedom to establish schools alternative to those offered by the state.

What happens in schools, public or private, is seldom examined through the human rights lens. Because the number of children not having access to school is large, they are a priority. Examining what happens to children at school requires questioning of the state's prerogative of compulsory education. The US Supreme Court has explained that 'the State exerts great authority and coercive power through mandatory attendance requirements'.[7]

Education constitutes the largest item in the government budgets of many countries, and teachers often form the majority of government employees. Moreover, education is widely – albeit wrongly – perceived as inherently good. Getting all children to school is thus mistaken for their right to education. Brian Hill has singled out education and law enforcement as the main agencies of social control.[8] Questions about what children are taught are asked much too rarely, and abuses of education are detected retrospectively, if at all. When children are exposed to advocacy of racism or incitement to genocide, remedying the harm done by such abuse is difficult, often impossible.

The assumption that any education is better than none is as unfounded as it is prevalent. Box 1.4 provides an example from China. Another has been un-earthed by Victoria Brittain in Angola: 'When a *soba* (chief) explains that people do not want to send their children to school because they see that those who go become politicians or businessmen and are thieves and liars, you know you have got a really fundamental need for a change'.[9] Yet another comes from Johnson Kingayo, a Masai herder: 'We pick out the brightest children, those with the most

Box 1.4 • Re-education in China

Resort to re-education aimed at curing ideological or political dissidents of their subversive ideas by forcing them to regurgitate the official dogma has been defined as a human rights violation by the International Labour Organization (ILO). It has dealt with re-education through labour under the Abolition of Forced Labour Convention. During the Cold War the cases brought to the attention of the ILO as apparent human rights violations included measures applied against people categorized as 'unproductive and/or anti-social' in countries such as Mozambique or Romania. The cases brought before the ILO also included the 're-education and production centres' established in Rwanda in 1975 to tackle vagrancy,* and 'security measure of re-education' applied to people who were defined as a risk to society because of their 'anti-social, immoral or prejudicial activities' in El Salvador.[†]

The ILO has found China's education-through-labour practice to be 'a clear infringement of basic human rights'. It has focused on a widespread 'form of forced labour and administrative detention of people who have not been convicted by the courts and who, in some cases, are not even liable to sanctions imposed by the judicial authorities. This form of detention and forced labour has been declared to violate basic ILO standards.'[‡]

Education-through-labour has been described by China as follows:

> Under the State's relevant administrative regulations, the education-through-labour programme is aimed at persons over 16 years of age who live in large and medium-sized cities, who are not subject to criminal sanctions or who are spared these sanctions, but disturb the peace and refuse to mend their ways in spite of repeated warnings, or who commit petty crimes (mainly theft, fraud, indecent behaviour, fighting, etc.). The objective of education-through-labour is to educate, to bring about a change in and to redeem persons who have committed such crimes. This education plays a role in the maintenance of social order and prevents crimes by educating those who are about to commit offences, in an effort to discourage the pursuit of illegal activities and crime. Education-through-labour is an effective measure, suited to the situation in China, pertinent to its social needs and beneficial in maintaining social stability.[§]

* Joint ILO/UNESCO Committee of Experts on the Application of the Recommendation on the Status of Teachers: Individual direct request of February 1995 concerning Convention No. 105, Abolition of Forced Labour (1957).
† Ibid.
‡ The Freedom of Association Committee has repeatedly had to deal with resort to re-education. The first complaint by the International Confederation of Free Trade Unions (ICFTU) against China was dealt with in November 1989 (268th Report, paras. 668–701) and then again in February 1990 (270th Report, paras. 287–334). In May 1990 the Committee urged China to furnish the requested information so that it could continue examining the case in November 1990 (275th Report, paras. 323–63) and adopt its findings and recommendations (279th and 281st Reports, paras. 637 and 81).
§ Freedom of Association Committee, Report No. 279, Case No. 1500 (China), para. 605.

potential, and then send them off with goats. It takes brains to identify each animal, find water, and ward off cattle rustlers. School is for those who are less quick'.[10]

Freedom from abuse of education was written into the Universal Declaration of Human Rights at the time that the right to education was first affirmed. Any subject which is taught can be abused. Anti-human-rights messages can be found in textbooks for young children including even mathematics textbooks.

- In Hitler's Germany, a mathematics textbook nudged learners to calculate the financial savings that would ensue from eliminating mentally ill people. 'The construction of a lunatic asylum costs 6 million DM. How many houses at 15,000 DM each could have been built for that amount?'[11]

- One maths book printed in the US during the USSR's Afghanistan war for use amongst Afghani refugees offered the following mathematical problem: 'If you have two dead Communists, and kill three more, how many dead Communists do you have?'[12]

- A school textbook in Tanzania in the 1970s included the following mathematical problem: 'A freedom fighter fires a bullet into an enemy group consisting of 12 soldiers and 3 civilians all equally exposed to the bullet. Assuming one person is hit by the bullet, find the probability that the person is (a) a soldier, (b) a civilian'.[13]

Box 1.5 • Why was compulsory education in Turkey prolonged in 1997?

Much as in many other countries, education in today's Turkey was initially religious. Secular education was introduced during the Ottoman Empire, in 1839. The predecessor of today's Ministry of Education was established in 1847, the first training centre for civil servants in 1859, and the first university in 1863. The 1876 Constitution mandated compulsory primary education for all, but this was translated into practice much later. However, the seeds of an all-encompassing, free secular education and a matching administrative infrastructure had been sown. Schools with French as the language of instruction, or those where Muslim and Christian pupils were educated together, demonstrated innovative features of the time.

The establishment of the Turkish Republic was followed by the unification of education, making all schools subordinate to the Ministry of National Education.* Education was made compulsory for both sexes. Nation-building was translated into unilingualism, patriotism and nationalism in education. Forging a new identity was hastened by the 1927 language law, with the shift to

▷   Turkish as the language of instruction. The introduction of the Latin alphabet represented a break from the Ottoman-Islamic heritage and the Arabic and Persian languages. Cherishing 'the esteem of the glorious Turkish history' and honouring 'the great Turks whose services have made the great Turkish nation' became part of the curriculum.[†] A textbook for human rights education ends its first chapter by giving the pupils as homework the task of studying the love that Turkey's army has for the country by going to the nearest military unit to inquire into the army's enthusiasm.[‡]

The extension of compulsory education in 1997 from five to eight years was hailed, although its aim was to undermine religious education. TV journalist Ferhat Boratav noted that the decision originated from the National Security Council 'as a basic precaution against the Islamists'.[§] Heinz Kramer commented that 'the introduction of an uninterrupted eight-year compulsory education [aimed to] dissolve the religious junior high schools'.[**] The World Bank joined the chorus (although it did not diminish loans to Turkey's education), also attributing the prolongation of compulsory education to the influence of Turkey's armed forces: 'The push for implementation appears to have originated with the National Security Council which may have been motivated more by concerns over security and maintaining a secular ideology than by economic or EU accession arguments for the expansion of education offered in the plan'.[††]

[*] The law No. 430 of 3 March 1924 whereby education was unified and placed under the control of the Ministry of National Education was cited in Turkey's reservation to Article 2 of the First Protocol to the European Convention on Human Rights.
[†] A.M. Kazamias, *Education and the Quest for Modernity in Turkey*, University of Chicago Press, 1966, p. 148.
[‡] E. Yamanlar, *Vatandaslik ve insan haklari egitimi* (Education in Citizenship and Human Rights), Ders Kitaplari Anonim Sirketi, Istanbul, 2000, p. 62.
[§] W. Kristianasen, 'Between the generals and the Islamists: Secular Turks in search of reform', *Le Monde Diplomatique*, February 1999.
[**] H. Kramer, *A Changing Turkey: The Challenge to Europe and the United States*, Brookings Institution Press, Washington, DC, 2000, p. 30.
[††] World Bank, *Turkey: Public Expenditure and Institutional Review*, Report No. 22530-TU, 20 August 2001, p. 96.

The widespread belief that getting children into school and prolonging compulsory education is good is belied by government policies that rely on this captive audience to instruct the new generation in what to think. Box 1.5 portrays the key actors and factors behind the prolongation of compulsory education in Turkey in 1997. In addition, a segment of the blueprint for assessing Turkey's education by child-rights criteria is reproduced in Box 1.6, as developed by UNICEF in 2000. That segment notes that the right to the child's own language is 'not applicable'; nor, it says, is the right to the child's own identity and culture.[14] The outcome is an endorsement of government refusal to accept that human rights are indeed *human* and cannot be taken away by government fiat.

Box 1.6 • Denied rights: language, culture, identity

NO	INDICATOR	YES	YES BUT	NO
14.	Have measures been adopted to encourage school attendance and prevent school drop-out?	✔		
15.	Do these measures take into account			
	• the child's home circumstances (such as a need to secure an income, to do domestic chores or to work at harvest time)?	✔		
	• the appropriate geographical location of schools and their hours and times of opening?	✔		
	• the relevance of the curriculum to the child's life and the provision of vocational education?	✔		
	• the appropriateness of the curriculum to the child's intellectual development?	✔		
	• the child's first language?		not applicable	
	• any special needs of the child (such as disability, sickness or pregnancy)?		✔	
	• respect for cultural or religious traditions and gender difference?	✔		
	• respect for the child's views?	✔		
	• respect for the child's dignity?	✔		
	• identification of learning difficulties and help provided to avoid exam failure or forced repetition of grade years or classes?	✔		
	• the need to involve the local community in the delivery of education and the need to involve schools in the life of the community?	✔		
	• the effectiveness of teacher recruitment and training in preventing school disaffection?	✔		
16.	Have all appropriate measures been taken to ensure that all forms of school discipline are consistent with the child's human dignity?		✔	
17.	Is corporal punishment prohibited by law in all schools?	✔		
18.	Have all appropriate measures been taken to ensure that corporal punishment is never used?	✔		
19.	Do all forms of school discipline conform with the Convention, including the child's right			
	• not to be discriminated against?	✔		
	• to be treated in a manner consistent with his or her evolving capacities?	✔		
	• to maintain direct contact with both parents on a regular basis (save where contrary to best interests)?	✔		
	• to freedom of expression, thought, conscience and religion?	✔		
	• to freedom of association (save where it is necessary to protect others)?		✔	
	• to privacy?			✔
	• to protection from all forms of physical or mental violence, injury or abuse, neglect or negligent treatment, maltreatment or exploitation?	✔		
	• to his or her identity, culture and language?		not applicable	
	• to rest and leisure?	✔		
	• to social inclusion and reintegration?	✔		
20.	Is an appropriate level of development aid sought for, or directed at, educational programmes?	✔		
21.	Do programmes of international technical cooperation include			
	• teacher training methods?	✔		
	• access to scientific and technical knowledge?	✔		
	• the effective delivery of primary and secondary education?	✔		

Throughout history, education has been particularly effective in the militarization of boys. Participation in warfare has been part of traditional initiation rituals through which boys become men. Glorification of war continues by means of history textbooks which are dotted with wars and war heroes. A judgement about the contribution that education made to the genocide in Rwanda is pending. The UN Special Rapporteur on Rwanda described in 1997 how successive governments not only conditioned the population to ethnic discrimination but also instrumentalized education in the preparation of genocide:

The schools took it upon themselves to develop actual theories of ethnic differences, based on a number of allegedly scientific data which were essentially morphological and historiographical. In the first case, the two main groups can be differentiated by appearance, as the Tutsi are 'long' whereas the Hutu are 'short'; the Tutsi are handsome, genuine 'black-skinned Europeans' while the Hutu are 'ugly', genuine 'Negroes'.

Box 1.7 • Killing schoolchildren: Emperor Bokassa's shameful legacy

In Africa, the priority for self-determination and the struggle against apartheid cloaked abuses in education in silence, even when they were gross. The brutal suppression of school children's protests in the Central African Empire in 1979 was saved from oblivion in the records of Amnesty International:

On 16 August 1979 a report was published in Dakar (Senegal) by the International Commission of Inquiry (La mission de constatation des événements de Bangui), which was established to investigate reports that children had been massacred in Bangui, the capital of the Central African Empire, in April 1979.... The main purpose of the Commission was to investigate reports first publicised by Amnesty International in a news release on 14 May 1979 (AI Index: AFR 19/01/79) according to which between 50 and 100 young people had been killed at Ngaragba prison in Bangui between 18 and 20 April 1979. In addition, the Commission also collected information about events in Bangui in January 1979 when an order that all school children should wear uniforms led to demonstrations which were suppressed with considerable violence.... The Report of the Commission of Inquiry is clear in its conclusions. It states that in April 1979 there were between 50 and 200 deaths at Ngaragba prison and suggests a figure of 100 dead as being the most accurate estimate. It also concludes that although the Central African Empire government claimed that only 13 people were killed in January 1979, the real number of deaths was about 150. Finally, the Report states: 'In conclusion, the Commission of Inquiry believes that during January 1979, riots in Bangui were suppressed with great cruelty by the security forces and that in April 1979 about 100 children were massacred at the order of Emperor Bokassa, who almost certainly participated personally in the killings.' ('En conclusion, la Mission de Constatation estime qu'au mois de janvier 1979, à Bangui, des émeutes ont été atrocement reprimées par les forces de l'ordre et qu'au mois d'avril 1979, des massacres d'une centaine d'enfants ont été perpétrés sous les ordres de l'Empereur Bokassa et avec sa participation quasi-certaine.')*

The schoolchildren's protest was triggered by the requirement that they buy school uniforms which carried the picture of Emperor Bokassa, uniforms which had reportedly been produced by his own factory to generate profits for him. The expressions of public outrage included the throwing of stones at the presidential car. That led to arrests, detentions and killings.

* Amnesty International News Release AFR 19/04/79 of 28 August 1979.

The fact that the Hutu occupied the country before the Tutsi makes them indigenous, whereas the Tutsi, as descendants of Europeans, are invaders. These purportedly scientific data inevitably created a psychosis of fear and mistrust which gradually became a veritable culture of mutual fear and led to another theory, that of pre-emptive self-defence based on the 'kill or be killed principle'. This theory was a major factor in the 1994 genocide.[15]

Resort to human rights safeguards to constrain the power inherent in writing history books is rare. The issue is deemed 'technical' although it is a veritable political minefield. Dubravko Lovrenovic, a professor of history at the University of Sarajevo, has recalled a voice which euphorically told him by phone on the eve of the 1992–5 war, 'It is now our turn to write history'.[16] Writing history to describe to both Tutsi and Hutu children what happened in Rwanda, and how and why, writing history to describe to all children in Bosnia what happened, and how and why, will be as difficult as it is important. The emergence of truth commissions has played a pioneering role in quite a few countries in rewriting recent history, negotiating a version of history that could be – at least temporarily – accepted by both the victims and their victimizers, by both the oppressed and their oppressors.

Notes

1. 'Dirty laundry', *Financial Times*, 19 April 2002.
2. P. Jason, 'Poor Nigeria', *New African*, October 2001.
3. D. Dapice, 'What would doubling aid do?', *Far Eastern Economic Review*, 28 February 2002.
4. J. Decosas, 'The behaviour of donors', Canadian International Development Agency (CIDA), Regional Meeting on Behavioural Interventions for STD and HIV Prevention, Kingston, Jamaica, December 1990, mimeograph.
5. S. Collignon, 'Germany: Which way to turn?', *World Today*, August/September 2002.
6. N. Chanda, 'Ethics pays: Interview with Amartya Sen', *Far Eastern Economic Review*, 18 March 1999, p. 30.
7. US Supreme Court, *Edwards v. Aguillard*, 482 US 578, 19 June 1987.
8. B. V. Hill, 'Values education: The Australian experience', *Prospects*, Vol. 28, No. 2, June 1998, p. 177.
9. V. Brittain, 'Building tomorrow from today's rubble', *Guardian Weekly*, 27 April–3 May 2000.
10. 'Kenya: No swots, please, we are Masai', *The Economist*, 23 March 2002.
11. M. Mazower, *Dark Continent: Europe's Twentieth Century*, Penguin, 1999, p. 176.
12. T. McGirk, 'Afghan warrior joins the Great Game', *Independent*, 30 September 1993.
13. P. McCormick, 'Political education as moral education in Tanzania', *Journal of Moral Education*, Vol. 9, No. 3, 1980, p. 171.
14. Social Services & Child Protection Agency & UNICEF, *Convention on the Rights of the Child [CRC]: Implementation Checklist of the Republic of Turkey*, Ankara, June 2000, p. 36.
15. Commission on Human Rights, Report on the Situation of Human Rights in Rwanda, submitted by Mr. René Degni-Ségui, Special Rapporteur, UN Doc. E/CN.4/1997/61 of 20 January 1997, para. 25.
16. B. Magas, *Question of Survival: A Common Education System for Bosnia and Herzegovina*. Proceedings of a seminar organized by the Bosnian Institute, London, and held at St Anthony's Monastery, Sarajevo, April 1998; The Bosnian Institute, London, 1999, p. 43.

The Economics of
the Right to Education

Investment in education was historically assigned to the state because such investment yields economic returns after much delay and only in combination with other assets. The history of compulsory education did not revolve around economic arguments alone, but these carried considerable weight. The need for a large pool of literate and skilled people was a driving force behind compulsory education during the early period of industrialization, as was the need to keep children out of the labour market so as to enable adult workers to negotiate fair wages with employers. Part of the economic rationale behind compulsory education was an attempt to ensure that people could support themselves after leaving school rather than becoming a financial burden on public authorities. The argument underlying this economic rationale is a definition of development as the attainment of human rights through a process that respects human rights. This argument was turned on its head with a shift to calling people *human capital* and treating them accordingly. People became seen as an object of investment if the rate of return was satisfactory, and thus were turned into means rather than the end. Moreover, the objectives of markets and states were confused: 'Markets are efficient in allocating scarce resources in the short-run. By contrast, the state is the conduit for investing in the future'.[1]

A consequence of the belief that the free market can supplant, if not replace, the state is that education rarely attains the priority in budgetary allocation which international human rights law requires. South Korea is hailed as a good example of the sound economic rationale for investing first in primary and then in secondary education. Two-thirds of public funds were allocated to primary education in 1960–1975, followed by one-third of the total to secondary education in 1975–1990.[2] This rationale is summarized in Box 2.1, which reproduces an extract from a 1996 retrospective overview by Korea's ministry of education. The importance given to secondary education differs from the current global emphasis on primary education as the passageway out of poverty; this issue is revisited in Chapter 7.

Box 2.1 • The economic rationale for education in South Korea

'With scarce natural resources, Korea has relied heavily on human resources to develop its economy. Education being a major source for trained manpower, educational policies have changed in accordance with the types of human ➡

resources demanded by a changed economy. In the 1950s, when low-level skilled workers were needed in manual industries, efforts were geared to undertake a massive-scale literacy campaign to produce a manual workforce. In the 1960s, skilled workers were in great demand for light industries, and the focus was shifted to expand vocational education at the secondary school level. As the importance of heavy industries grew in the 1970s, technicians who could deal with complex modern manufacturing processes were in demand. The government responded by expanding junior technical colleges. The number of junior colleges nearly doubled in this period. In the 1980s, economic competitiveness based on high-level technology and information industries became fierce and this challenge urged the Korean government to strengthen research and education in basic science and technology.

Though there have been some mismatches, it is generally agreed that secondary school enrollment and investment in education have a positive and crucial relationship with economic growth in Korea. Expansion of secondary enrollment and public investment in secondary education were very important in offsetting diminishing returns to investment in physical capital, and thus made significant contributions to achieving sustained per capita income growth. It is often pointed out that the positive effect from public investment in secondary education was made possible because Korea had a universal elementary education and had, as well, comparable rates of investment in physical capital along with export-oriented growth strategies. In other words, Korea expanded and universalized elementary education followed by secondary education, and only after achieving this, shifted its emphasis to the expansion of higher education.

What Korea did right in the 1970s was that it spent four-fifths of its education budget on basic education, while countries with a similar level of economic development focussed on higher education. One significant effect of this improvement in basic education was that due to the increased number of women with a basic education, the number of school age children remained stable. Thus a growing amount of resources could be devoted to a stable number of children, allowing for improvements in the quality of education. In contrast, other countries which neglected the importance of basic education observed a growing number of school age children, and had to direct their educational resources to build more schools, with less resources left to improve the quality of education. Amongst the other ingredients of the relatively successful story of Korea's educational development, a right choice of policies, and an undisrupted implementation of these policies are deemed to have been crucial.'*

* *The Development of Education: National Report of the Republic of Korea*, Ministry of Education, Seoul, September 1996, pp. 1–2.

Why primary education was made free and compulsory

Nobody today publicly advocates that primary-school children should work as was done in 1723:

> Going to School in comparison to Working is Idleness, and the longer boys continue in this easy sort of life, the more unfit they will be when grown up for downright Labour.[3]

The change in the past two centuries has been profound. Although children are often forced to work, nobody openly demands that they should do so. Verbally, at least, there is agreement that children should be at school until they reach the minimum age for employment, usually set at 15. There often is no financial commitment to make this happen, even though poverty is routinely cited as the major cause of child labour. Conventional wisdom relates the lack of education to poverty and sees the solution in throwing money at the problem. It may do no good. Suffice it to mention that only 60 per cent of educational budgets in Benin, Burkina Faso and Mali were spent in the late 1990s,[4] although the need for additional funding was — and is — constantly emphasized. Increasing a central government budget does not automatically translate into funding for teachers, schools, textbooks, and everything else that children need. Most children do not live in national capitals — hence their schooling necessitates a functioning, country-wide educational system. Problems are inversely related to proximity to the national capital — the more distant children are, the less likely problems are to be addressed.

The human rights rationale for compulsory education provides useful guidance as it merges otherwise dissociated strategies and sectors. There is rarely a ministry dealing with children. Education and child labour are thus separated between at least two ministries; gender might be within the remit of a separate ministry. Separate laws and policies address interrelated issues. The law on education may substantively differ from labour law, while the development or poverty eradication strategy may follow an approach different from both, as may also the ministry of finance. It is useful to recall the economic rationale behind the linkage between education and child labour. It constitutes one of the oldest parts of international human rights law and emerged therein because of its sound economic rationale.

The International Labour Organization linked the age for completion of compulsory education and the minimum age for employment in 1921. The ILO Convention No. 10 prohibited employment which prejudices children's school attendance and set the minimum age for employment at 14. It posited in 1945 that 'school attendance should be compulsory up to an age not lower than 16 years'.[5] The ILO Convention on Minimum Age for Employment obliges all states that become party to set such a minimum age officially. As Table 2.1 shows, few have established 16 as the minimum age; even fewer are likely scrupulously to enforce children's freedom from work before they turn 16. Table 2.2 lists

Table 2.1 • The legally determined minimum age for employment, by country

Age	Country
14	Angola, Argentina, Bahamas, Belize, Benin, Bolivia, Botswana, Cambodia, Cameroon, Central African Republic, Colombia, Congo/Brazzaville, Congo/Kinshasa, Dominican Republic, Ecuador, Egypt, El Salvador, Equatorial Guinea, Eritrea, Ethiopia, Macedonia, Gambia, Guatemala, Honduras, Malawi, Mauritania, Namibia, Nepal, Nicaragua, Niger, Panama, Rwanda, Sri Lanka, Tanzania, Togo, Venezuela, Yemen, Zimbabwe
15	Austria, Barbados, Belgium, Bosnia, Burkina Faso, Chile, Costa Rica, Croatia, Cuba, Cyprus, Denmark, Dominica, Finland, Georgia, Germany, Greece, Guyana, Iceland, Indonesia, Iraq, Ireland, Israel, Italy, Japan, Korea, Kuwait, Lesotho, Libya, Luxembourg, Madagascar, Malaysia, Mauritius, Morocco, Netherlands, Norway, Philippines, Poland, Senegal, Seychelles, Slovakia, Slovenia, South Africa, Sweden, Switzerland, Syria, Turkey, United Arab Emirates, Uruguay, Yugoslavia, Zambia
16	Albania, Algeria, Antigua and Barbuda, Azerbaijan, Belarus, Brazil, Bulgaria, Burundi, China, France, Hungary, Jordan, Kazakhstan, Kenya, Kyrgyzstan, Lithuania, Malta, Moldova, Papua New Guinea, Portugal, Romania, Russia, San Marino, Spain, Tajikistan, Tunisia, Ukraine, United Kingdom

Source: The 116 countries that have become party to the ILO Minimum Age Convention by May 2002 (information is available at www.ilo.org) have had formally to declare the minimum age for employment and the ratifications have been used as the source for these figures.

countries by their legally mandated lengths of compulsory education, ranging from 13 years in the Netherlands to 4 years in São Tomé and Principe. This difference illustrates both the willingness and the ability of individual states to secure schooling, highlighting the intrinsic link between desire and performance.

The idea that free education and compulsory education are linked, that education should be made free so that it could be compulsory, has fallen into oblivion. Even if the direct costs of education are borne by the state, the indirect costs (such as transport or school meals) may be beyond the capacity of the family, while the opportunity cost may be impossible to bear. The obligation of the state to compensate parents who otherwise cannot afford to send children to school has not changed from 1952:

> Where [poverty] prevails, legal measures for the raising of the minimum age for admission to work or for compulsory school attendance will remain ineffective and may be argued as even harmful, unless accompanied by other measures of social assistance to the families and the children. Where possible, the institution of family allowances and other privileges (tax concessions, loans, etc.) should be contemplated.[6]

Table 2.2 • The legally mandated length of compulsory education, by country

No. of years	Country
13	Netherlands
12	Belgium, Brunei Darussalam, Germany, St Kitts and Nevis
11	Antigua and Barbuda, Armenia, Azerbaijan, Barbados, British Virgin Islands, Dominica, Grenada, Israel, Kazakhstan, Malta, Moldova, United Kingdom
10	Argentina, Australia, Belize, Canada, Congo, Costa Rica, Dominican Republic, DPR Korea, Ecuador, France, Gabon, Hungary, Iceland, Kyrgyzstan, Liberia, Monaco, Namibia, New Zealand, Seychelles, Spain, St Lucia, St Vincent and the Grenadines, Venezuela, USA
9	Algeria, Austria, Bahamas, Bahrain, Belarus, Cambodia, China, Comoros, Cook Islands, Cuba, Cyprus, Czech Republic, Denmark, El Salvador, Estonia, Finland, Georgia, Greece, Hong Kong, Indonesia, Ireland, Japan, Jordan, Korea, Kiribati, Lebanon, Libya, Lithuania, Luxembourg, Mali, Netherlands Antilles, Norway, Portugal, Russia, Sierra Leone, Slovakia, South Africa, Sri Lanka, Sweden, Switzerland, Tajikistan, Tunisia, Ukraine, Yemen
8	Albania, Angola, Bolivia, Brazil, Bulgaria, Chile, Croatia, Egypt, Fiji, Ghana, Guyana, India, Italy, Kenya, Kuwait, Latvia, Macedonia, Malawi, Mongolia, Niger, Poland, Romania, Samoa, San Marino, Slovenia, Somalia, Sudan, Tonga, Turkey, Yugoslavia, Zimbabwe
7	Burkina Faso, Eritrea, Lesotho, Mauritius, Mozambique, Swaziland, Tanzania, Trinidad and Tobago, Tuvalu, Zambia
6	Afghanistan, Benin, Burundi, Cameroon, Cape Verde, Central African Republic, Chad, Côte d'Ivoire, Djibouti, Ethiopia, Guatemala, Guinea, Guinea-Bissau, Haiti, Honduras, Iraq, Jamaica, Madagascar, Mauritania, Mexico, Morocco, Nicaragua, Nigeria, Panama, Paraguay, Peru, Philippines, Rwanda, Senegal, Suriname, Syria, Thailand, Togo, United Arab Emirates, Uruguay, Vanuatu
5	Bangladesh, Colombia, Equatorial Guinea, Iran, Laos, Macao, Myanmar, Nepal, Vietnam
4	São Tomé and Principe

Sources: Information from UNESCO's *World Education Report 2000* (pp. 140–3) has been supplemented by government reports under human rights treaties for Cambodia (HRI/CORE/1/Add.94 para 9), Latvia (CRC/C/11/Add.22 para.197), and Sierra Leone (CRC/C/3/Add.43 para.77). Education is not compulsory in Botswana, Bhutan, Pakistan, Uganda.

In many countries, the period of compulsory schooling has been lengthened beyond primary schooling. This trend follows a twofold rationale:

- Raising the school leaving age through prolonged compulsory education prevents children from venturing into adulthood too early, which is particularly important in combating child labour and child marriage;

- Prolonged compulsory education provides all children with a common core of learning and skills, which is especially important for knowledge-based societies and economies; inclusive education socializes all children in the same schools and classrooms and provides foundations for inclusive societies.

Differences in the length of compulsory education shown in Table 2.2 reflect to some extent the economic capacity of individual countries and their demographic structures. Countries in which compulsory schooling is short (such as Bangladesh, Laos, Nepal or Vietnam) share financial obstacles to the lengthening of education, while the tendency in Western Europe to extend compulsory education beyond ten years reflects a merging of the willingness and the ability to do so. At the turn of the millennium, the unintended consequence of this merging has been a sin of omission: the self-indulgence of a tiny fraction of humanity involved in 'the new economy' has relegated to oblivion problems of child labour that have hardly changed in the past two centuries.

Blaming poverty rather than policy choices

The prohibition of exploitative child labour has been reinforced by obligatory provision of schooling to children rescued from exploitation. ILO Convention 182 (Convention concerning the prohibition and immediate action for the elimination of the worst forms of child labour of 17 June 1999) broadened safeguards against intolerable forms of child labour to all children up to eighteen years old. It also re-emphasized government obligations to ensure access to free education for all children, and mandated vocational training for children removed from labouring. The challenges are many. Although all blame is usually attributed to poverty, it is often inconsistent government policies towards children that hamper progress.

Table 2.3 shows the legally determined ages at which children should leave school, start work, marry, or be deemed criminally responsible, in selected countries. The figures provide food for thought because the ages do not match. Even without knowing the law, one would intuitively expect that the minimum age for employment or marriage should not be lower than the school leaving age, and yet this is often not the case. Moreover, what message emanates from a law that holds children criminally responsible at an age when they are merely starting school? As Table 2.3 shows, children can be employed at an age when they are required to go to school, revealing the lack of coherence in national laws, and leading the ILO to state that 'the link between those campaigning for the abolition of child labour and those calling for education for all tends to be weak at all levels'.[7]

Table 2.3 • Absent child-rights policy, inconsistent minimum ages

Country	School-leaving age (girls/boys)	Minimum age for employment	Minimum age for marriage (girls/boys)	Minimum age of criminal responsibility
Burundi	12	12	—	13
Cambodia	15	16	18/20	—
Cent. African R.	21/14	14	18	13
Chad	15	—	—	13
China	15	13	20/22	14
Denmark	16	13	15	15
France	16	14	15/18	13
Honduras	13	14	16	12
Iran	11	12	—	—
Jordan	17	16	15/16	7
Laos	11	15	15	15
Niger	16	14	—	13
Sierra Leone	15	—	—	10
South Africa	15	—	12/14	7
Switzerland	15	13	18	7
Tunisia	16	13	17	13
United Kingdom	16	13	16	8

The figures in this table have been reported by governments under the Convention on the Rights of the Child and they reflect the laws of the respective countries at the time of reporting. Differences in the legally determined ages mean that, in Laos, for example, children finish school at the age of 11 and have to wait until they become 15 to be able to work. The obvious question is what they are supposed to do during these four years. In Central African Republic the school-leaving age for girls has been set at 21, which begs the question of whether there are enough schools and teachers for all girls to be able to comply with this requirement, and what happens if this is not the case.

Prevention of child labour necessitates a conceptual shift in the orientation of education towards the acknowledgment of one simple fact: 'the unavoidable labour reality is very much local'.[8] Global or foreign models require adaptation to the local reality. The dominant trend of conceiving work as access to employment in the formal sector rather than self-employment in the informal sector does not provide a promising background for responding to this challenge; nor does the heritage of designing primary education so as to lead pupils to secondary and higher education. Adaptability is often hampered by school curricula 'developed centrally by groups of "experts" who design them to prepare children for the next level of education to which many children will be unable to proceed'.[9]

Box 2.2 • When is education relevant?

There are endless calls to make education relevant. These are routinely inter-preted as instrumentalizing schooling to make it useful to children, and this, in turn, is construed as enabling children to do better the work for which they are destined by their family and community. However, both parents and children often see education as the key to rupturing the intergenerational transmission of that pattern as well as the stepping stone for children's occupational and geographical mobility. The donors may prioritize their definition of relevance (keeping children where they are), the beneficiaries their own (the pass key for mobility). The result may be failure:

Sixteen years of good work in vain. This is the most brutal interpretation of an evaluation report on one of FINNIDA's [Finland's International Development Agency's] longest standing programmes in Africa.

The project, which cost FINNIDA more than FIM 30 million during 1974-1990, aimed at establishing practical subjects such as carpentry, woodwork and leatherwork in all upper primary schools in Zambia. It was launched following the Zambian education authorities' drive to provide practical education to all pupils to balance the theoretical subjects. Since most Zambian students are unable to continue their education beyond primary school, the plan didn't sound far-fetched as the mastering of practical subjects would have offered them at least a basis for employment.

Perhaps the saddest thing about the project is that it failed despite good and pro-fessional input from the FINNIDA project staff because the whole concept was based on totally wrong assumptions.

The weakness in the project concept stemmed from the fact that FINNIDA and the Government of Zambia worked on the assumption that the parents would welcome the opportunity for their children to learn such useful skills, whereas in fact their priority aim was for their children to pass examinations in academic subjects and to progress to relatively well paid office jobs. They saw practical subjects as either irrelevant or an obstacle.*

* 'Harsh criticism of FINNIDA education programme in Zambia', *Development Today*, vol. 5, No. 2, 8 February 1995.

Box 2.3 • The costs of ill-chosen models of education in Sierra Leone

Sierra Leone has provided a blatant example of everything that can go wrong with education. Ill-suited to the country, the model of education helped to spawn warfare. At its end, the government reported that most of the country's education infrastructure had been destroyed and 70 per cent of school-age children were out of school. Funding was available for three years of primary schooling only.* The demobilization of child soldiers required much more funding than was available. In the meantime, foreign-funded projects on peace education included messages that actually legitimized polygamy and thus worsened the position of women.

The education system was based on the premise that children would complete primary school and continue in education, ultimately obtaining jobs. With the benefit of hindsight, this proved to have been wrong:

> Arguably, the most negative aspect of Sierra Leone's elitist system of education has to do with a complete failure to cater for those who do not make it within the system. School drop-outs are simply not provided for in any serious or meaningful way. Thus, those who do not survive and rise to the top of this narrow and competitive system simply become the 'forgotten aspirants' in a very elitist educational process.
>
> In situations where only a tiny minority can get a complete and reasonable quality education, the price of ignorance weighs more heavily on those who have some schooling than those who never had access to school. This creates considerable frustration in the semi-schooled population of 'forgotten aspirants', which is turn could serve as a time-bomb waiting to explode. It is not surprising therefore to find 'forgotten aspirants' playing a role as combatants on both sides of the rebel war in Sierra Leone.
>
> Because of the demonstrated impact of education in promoting social mobility in newly independent Sierra Leone, wrong signals have been sent to the subsequent generations. This has given rise to unrealistic expectations about what can be achieved by virtue of mere school attendance and certification. At independence in 1961, the drive for indigenisation meant that nationals with little more than secondary level qualifications were catapulted to top positions. Later, the new and expanding population of university graduates were guaranteed high-level jobs regardless of specialisation. Most secondary school graduates could also be certain of reasonable jobs within the public sector.
>
> When economic growth and job creation began to lag behind output of universities and schools, reality dictated that educational qualifications per se could no longer be a guarantee of any job, much less top level jobs. Unfortunately, expectations continued to fly in the face of this new reality. The belief that schooling leads to good jobs could not be questioned. Hence a strong sense of delusion persisted amongst learners that society owes them something once they have gone through the education system.†

➡️

Frustrated expectations of early school leavers – especially boys – were shown to lead to criminality, violence and warfare. Their abandonment to their own fate was accompanied by the paucity of lawful methods for securing livelihood and the attraction of pursuing unlawful ones with impunity. The abundance of bad models to imitate made the choice of many adolescents a foregone conclusion. The neglect of adolescents – and of gender analysis – has been an unintended consequence of the priority for primary education in global education strategies and will hamper efforts at peace-making unless and until it is reversed.

Where education is aimed at peace-making, it is likely to omit those human rights components which are seen as unrelated, such as the rights of women. A training package developed by the Norwegian Red Cross and UNICEF, used in Sierra Leone in 2000, included a module on peace and human rights education which included a story depicted as a 'cultural way of managing conflict'. The story went like this:

> There was a man who had two wives. These wives had four children each and they were all living in the same compound though they had separate huts. One of the wives was very quarrelsome. As a result the husband was always out of the home to have peace of mind. The wife who did not like *palava* became fed up. She went to a traditional healer to tell him the problem. The healer told her that the problem was simple. The woman could not believe it. The traditional healer told her to put water into her mouth as soon as her mate started abusing her. He further told her that she must not swallow the water nor allow it to drop from her mouth. If she did, evil spirits will haunt her. The woman obeyed and there was peace in the compound.[‡]

This story illustrates two facets of the process learners are likely to go through. First, they will not associate polygamy with human rights. This link may be included in a training manual on gender, which is likely to be used separately from the one on peace-making and, probably, for a different audience. The story treats polygamy as part of Sierra Leone's landscape and there is nothing nudging the learners – or their teachers – to question it. Second, there is a casual reference to abuse as a possible reason for one of the co-wives having become labelled as quarrelsome; it is possible that the husband was beating her. Again, there is no indication that whatever abuse might have taken place has anything to do with human rights or gender. The happy end of this story is the silencing of a woman. It is likely that the message learners will internalize is that women should keep their mouths shut, whatever may be happening to them.

* Committee on the Rights of the Child, Initial report of Sierra Leone and the concluding observations of the Committee, UN Docs. CRC/C/3/Add. 43 and CRC/C/15/Add. 116 (2000).

† C. Wright, 'Reflections on Sierra Leone', in: S. Tawil (ed.), *Final Report and Case Studies of the Workshop on Educational Destruction and Reconstruction in Disrupted Societies, 15–16 May 1997, Geneva, organized jointly by the International Bureau of Education and the University of Geneva*, Geneva, 1977, pp. 21–2.

‡ 'Rapid Response Education Programme – Peace and Human Rights Education' (mimeograph), UNICEF, Ministry of Youth, Education and Sports, and the Norwegian Refugee Council, Freetown, March 2000, p. 45.

Opportunities for working children to 'learn and earn'[10] have been grounded in the necessity for poor people – including children – to work so as to be able to survive. In those circumstances full-time education appears to be a luxury rather than a basic right of the child, and changing that cruel reality requires a great deal of political and financial commitment. The Supreme Court of India has accepted this 'learn and earn' approach for non-hazardous employment of children below fourteen, mandating a reduction of their daily working hours to six and at least two hours of education at the expense of the employer. For hazardous work, the court has recognized that child labour cannot be eliminated without tackling underlying poverty and suggested ensuring work for an adult member of the family in lieu of the child. If this proves impossible, a minimum income to the family should be paid as long as children are attending school.[11]

The adaptation of education to local circumstances requires protection against the institutionalization of disadvantage which can result in 'educational ghettos.'[12] A shift away from denigrating vocational as inferior to academic education is also necessary. The increasing shortage of public sector jobs worldwide is likely to alter the inherited hierarchy of education, which prioritized general at the expense of vocational education. Endless international declarations emphasize that education should be 'relevant', a slogan which urges its linkage to children's lives but does not clarify what the role of education should be. Should it be a pathway to mobility or a solidifier of the status quo? The aim of education may be to improve children's working skills so as to keep them where they are but in, perhaps, reduced poverty, while they and their parents may expect education to be the children's passport to higher status. Such conflicting expectations are illustrated in Box 2.2, p. 29.

Studies into the cause of wars seldom single out the role of ill-chosen models of education in spawning frustration and providing fertile grounds for violence and warfare. Sierra Leone provides a tragic example, summarized in Box 2.3 (pp. 30–1). It provides an unlearned lesson – international post-war strategies exhibit myopic approaches, with poverty eradication separated from education, education separated from human rights, and human rights separated from gender.

Making policy choices: why people are not human capital

Without education, people are impeded from gaining access to employment. Lower educational accomplishment prejudices their career advancement. Lower salaries negatively affect their security in old age. Denial of the right to education triggers exclusion from the labour market and marginalization into some form of informal sector, accompanied by exclusion from social security schemes because of the prior exclusion from the labour market. Redressing imbalances in life chances without full recognition of the right to education is impossible. Moreover, illiterate people in quite a few countries are precluded from political representation. Thus, a large number of problems cannot be solved unless the right to education is addressed as the key to unlock other human rights.

From the human rights viewpoint, education is an end in itself rather than merely a means for achieving other ends. Education should prepare learners for parenthood and political participation, it should enhance social cohesion and, more than anything, it should teach the young that all human beings – themselves included – have rights. Economists define education as efficient production of human capital and its purpose is then, in Alain Mingat's words, to structure 'the supply of qualified people over a long period of time to make it more in line with economic demands'.[13]

The contrast between the human-rights and human-capital approaches is best illustrated by taking children with physical and learning disabilities as an example. To refuse to educate children with disabilities on the grounds that there is no evidence that such an investment would help eliminate poverty or enhance the rate of economic growth would be cruel. Thus, no state admits to doing it. Nevertheless, children with disabilities may be excluded from school because providing wheelchair access might not be commercially viable, or because their learning is deemed not to yield a sufficient marginal return on investment. This type of reasoning challenges the very assumption of human rights, namely that there should be equal human rights for all. Furthermore, the obsession with enhancing economic growth depletes education of most of the purposes it is designed to serve. The criterion of profitability is generally not used as a yardstick for fire departments or public security. When profitability does become the criterion, as came to light in the aftermath of September 11th when the detrimental consequences of the privatization of airport security became apparent,[14] public outrage leads to a swift change back to public funding of public institutions in the public interest.

Human capital is commonly defined as the sum of economically relevant attributes (knowledge, skills, competences) held by the working-age population. Accepting the underlying market value of human capital risks turning upside-down the idea that the economy should serve the people rather than the other way around. Amartya Sen has added his voice to the opposition to labelling humans as *capital* or as a *resource*:

> Is the recognition of the role of 'human capital' adequate for understanding the importance of what has been called 'human development', to wit, the development of the capability of people to do the things they have reason to value and choose? There is a crucial difference here between means and ends. Seeing human qualities in terms of their importance in promoting and sustaining economic growth, significant as it is, tells us nothing about why economic growth is sought in the first place, nor much about the role of enhanced human qualities in making it directly possible for us to lead freer and more fulfilling lives. If an expansion of educational facility or health care increases labour productivity and thus the income level, the perspective of 'human capital' would give it immediate recognition. But if that expansion adds directly to the length of our lives, reduces our ailments, and makes us happier and more fulfilled *without* changing labour productivity or increasing commodity production, then that achievement would simply not get the recognition it deserves.
>
> There is, thus, something of substance that is missed in the much-used perspective

of 'human capital'. The same applies, I am afraid, to the concept of 'human resource development', if it is narrowly interpreted as the improvement of human beings seen as a resource for further development. Being educated, being more healthy, and so on, expand our lives *directly* as well as *through* their effects on making us better resources for further production, thereby expanding our productivities and incomes. To correct what is missed in the narrower perspective of 'human capital' and 'human resource development,' we need a broader conception of development that concentrates on the enhancement of human lives and freedoms, no matter whether that enhancement is – or is not – intermediated through an expansion of commodity production. Human beings are not only the most important *means* of social achievement, they are also its profoundest *end*. Being a fine piece of capital is not the most exalted state that can happen to a human being.[15]

In 1962 Theodore Schultz examined the imbalance between non-human capital, such as land and physical capital, and human capital, defined as a healthy and educated population. He advocated investing in people so as to raise their capabilities.[16] The literature on human capital has evolved in the decades since then, from the relationship between education and income, focusing on the economic value of schooling and/or the rate of return on schooling, especially private, to affirming 'the productive utility of human knowledge'.[17] This is only one out of many purposes of education. Such reductionism frustrates the very foundations for human rights education which require sharing knowledge rather than trading it and co-operating rather than competing.

Notes

1. R. Boyer and D. Drache (eds), *States against Markets: The Limits of Globalization*, Routledge, London, 1996, p. 3.
2. V. Thomas et al., *The Quality of Growth*, World Bank and Oxford University Press, Washington, DC/New York, September 2000, p. 68.
3. I. Fägerlind and L. Saha, *Education and National Development: A Comparative Perspective*, Pergamon Press, Oxford, 1983, p. 36.
4. B. Conhye and M. Coulibaly, *Policies, Procedures and Strategies for the Allocation of Resources for Education in Sub-Saharan Africa: A Review of the Literature*, Association for the Development of Education in Africa (ADEA) and Council for the Development of Social Science Research in Africa (CODESRIA), Paris/Dakar, May 1999, p. 19.
5. Resolution concerning the protection of children and young workers of 1945, in 'Child labour in relation to compulsory education', *Studies on Compulsory Education*, No. 5, ILO/UNESCO, Geneva/Paris, 1952, Section IIIA-9(2).
6. UNESCO/ILO, *Child Labour in Relation to Compulsory Education*, Geneva, 1952, p. 26.
7. International Labour Office, *A Future without Child Labour: Global Report under the Follow-up to the ILO Declaration on Fundamental Principles and Rights at Work 2002*, International Labour Conference, 90th session, Report I (B), Geneva, May 2002, para. 192.
8. D. Atchoarena and S. Hite, *Training Poorly Educated People in Africa*. Document prepared for the International Labour Office (ILO) by the International Institute for Educational Planning, Paris, April 1999, p. 65.
9. N. Haspels et al, 'Action against child labour: Strategies in education. Country

experiences in the mobilization of teachers, educators and their organizations in combatting child labour', ILO-IPEC, Geneva, May 1999, p. 41.

10. ILO-IPEC, 'Action against child labour: The role of education'. Briefing paper produced for Consortium Meeting on Secondary Education, Paris, 10–11 June 1999, p. 10.

11. Supreme Court of India, *Mehta v. State of Tamil Nadu*, judgement of 10 December 1996, (1996) 6 SCC 756; AIR 1997 SC 699; (1997) 2 BHRC 258.

12. IWGE, *Disadvantage, Dialogue and Development Co-operation in Education*. Meeting of the International Working Group on Education (IWGE), Feldafing, Munich, 23–26 June 1998, International Institute for Educational Planning, Paris, 1999, p. 56.

13. A. Mingat, 'The strategy used by high-performing Asian economies in education: Some lessons for developing countries', *World Development*, Vol. 26, No. 4, 1998, pp. 697 and 700.

14. Commission on Human Rights, Report submitted by Katarina Tomasevski, Special Rapporteur on the right to education: Mission to the United States of America, 24 September–10 October 2002, UN Doc. E/CN.4/2002/60/Add. 1, para. 5.

15. A. Sen, 'Human development and financial conservativism', *World Development*, Vol. 26, No. 4, 1998, p. 734.

16. G.M. Meier, *Leading Issues in Economic Development*, Oxford University Press, New York, 1995.

17. OECD, *Measuring What People Know: Human Capital Accounting for the Knowledge Economy*, Paris, 1996, p. 22.

Chapter 3

The Promise of the 1948 Universal Declaration of Human Rights

Human rights are safeguards against abuse of power by government. They are created after mobilization of shame and peer pressure has compelled governments to act. Peer pressure is crucial in translating political promises into legal obligations because international law is horizontal. There is no supra-structure to impose human rights obligations upon governments.

Protection of human rights depends on institutions and procedures for challenging their denials and violations. Unless these institutions and procedures are both willing and able to oppose abuses effectively, substantive human rights guarantees remain paper promises. The number of such promises is immense. The United Nations (UN) is notorious for generating them, and academics thrive on describing and analysing the wording of each and every resolution or declaration.

The UN uses the term *standard-setting* to denote the process of generating normative statements, both legal and extra-legal. Documents embodying these standards are referred to as *instruments*. This choice of words is purposeful: the instruments are merely tools that have no intrinsic value – they are useful only when used. The difference between legal obligations and political promises is evidenced by the small number of the former and the immense number of the latter.

The first task of the UN was to lay down substantive human rights standards in order to develop a globally applicable yardstick, to define *what* before proceeding to *how*. This was normatively accomplished with the very establishment of the UN, but it took two decades to empower the UN to respond to gross and systematic violations. A system designed by governments to restrain their own abuses of power has its inherent limitations.

Whose rights? Which rights?
The initial intergovernmental blueprint

The UN's work on defining human rights started with a surge of goodwill after the Second World War but was immediately paralysed by the Cold War.

The UN started small. Table 3.1 traces the size and composition of the UN from 1946 to 2002, showing that just over one-quarter of today's states were members at the time when the Universal Declaration of Human Rights was adopted. There could have been little African influence because only Ethiopia and Liberia were original members, as well as South Africa, which became

Table 3.1 • United Nations membership, 1945–2002

1945	Argentina, Australia, Belarus, Belgium, Bolivia, Brazil, Canada, Chile, China, Colombia, Costa Rica, Cuba, [Czechoslovakia], Denmark, Dominican Republic, Ecuador, Egypt, El Salvador, Ethiopia, France, Greece, Guatemala, Haiti, Honduras, India, Iran, Iraq, Lebanon, Liberia, Luxembourg, Mexico, Netherlands, New Zealand, Nicaragua, Norway, Panama, Paraguay, Peru, Philippines, Poland, Russia, Saudi Arabia, South Africa, Syria, Turkey, Ukraine, United Kingdom, USA, Uruguay, Venezuela, [Yugoslavia]
1946	Afghanistan, Iceland, Sweden, Thailand
1947	Pakistan, Yemen
1948	Burma
1949	Israel
1950	Indonesia
1955	Albania, Austria, Bulgaria, Cambodia, Finland, Hungary, Ireland, Italy, Jordan, Laos, Libya, Nepal, Portugal, Romania, Spain, Sri Lanka
1956	Japan, Morocco, Sudan, Tunisia
1957	Ghana, Malaysia
1958	Guinea
1960	Benin, Burkina Faso, Cameroon, Central African Republic, Chad, Congo, Côte d'Ivoire, Cyprus, Gabon, Madagascar, Mali, Niger, Nigeria, Senegal, Somalia, Togo, Zaire
1961	Mauritania, Mongolia, Sierra Leone, Tanzania
1962	Algeria, Burundi, Jamaica, Rwanda, Trinidad and Tobago, Uganda
1963	Kenya, Kuwait
1964	Malawi, Malta, Zambia
1965	Gambia, Maldives, Singapore
1966	Barbados, Botswana, Guyana, Lesotho
1968	Equatorial Guinea, Mauritius, Swaziland
1970	Fiji
1971	Bahrain, Bhutan, Oman, Qatar, United Arab Emirates
1973	Bahamas, Germany
1974	Bangladesh, Grenada, Guinea Bissau
1975	Cape Verde, Comoros, Mozambique, Papua New Guinea, São Tomé and Principe, Suriname
1976	Angola, Samoa, Seychelles
1977	Djibouti, Vietnam
1978	Dominica, Solomon Islands
1979	St Lucia
1980	St Vincent and Grenadines, Zimbabwe
1981	Antigua and Barbuda, Belize, Vanuatu
1983	St Kitts and Nevis
1984	Brunei Darussalam

Table 3.1 • cont.

1990	Liechtenstein, Namibia
1991	DPR Korea, Estonia, Korea, Micronesia, Latvia, Lithuania, Marshall Islands
1992	Armenia, Azerbaijan, Bosnia and Herzegovina, Croatia, Georgia, Kazakhstan, Kyrgyzstan, Moldova, San Marino, Slovenia, Tajikistan, Turkmenistan, Uzbekistan
1993	Andorra, Czech Republic, Eritrea, The Former Yugoslav Republic of Macedonia, Monaco, Slovak Republic
1994	Palau
1999	Kiribati, Nauru, Tonga
2000	Tuvalu
2002	Switzerland, East Timor

targeted for its institutionalized racial discrimination at the very first session of the General Assembly (the first big wave of African countries only joined in 1960). The Middle East did not and does not now constitute a region, hence its influence is still subdued. The Western group had the dominant influence, and the inspiration for human rights guarantees was derived from written constitutions – Western and chief negotiators were either Western or Western-educated.

The small size of the UN was mirrored in its modest beginnings. The initial decades of the UN's human rights work were marked by ideological and political disagreements about the meaning and implications of individual rights. In the past, governments had been free to treat their populations as they pleased, shielded by the prohibition of interference in other countries' internal affairs and by the notion of the sovereign equality of states. A break with the past took place on the normative level with the adoption of the UN Charter and the Universal Declaration of Human Rights. But twenty years was to elapse before their human rights provisions were translated into UN's powers of naming-and-shaming.

In 1945 the UN Charter affirmed human rights in its preamble and proclaimed human rights to constitute one of the main purposes of the United Nations. By the Charter all members of the United Nations were legally bound to strive towards full realization of all human rights and fundamental freedoms. Human rights were thereby elevated from a noble aim to an obligation of all governments. It is important to add here that the United Nations never did – or could – oblige itself to ensure governments' compliance with their human rights obligations. Rather, words like 'encourage' and 'promote' are self-descriptors. This caution reflected the absence of a collective political will of governments. However, the mission statement of the first UN High Commissioner for Human Rights committed him 'to ensure the universal enjoyment of all human rights by giving practical effect to the will and resolve of the world community'.[1] A promise to *ensure* human rights went much too far, and, like the first UN High Commissioner for Human Rights, was soon forgotten.

A general plan, forged in 1947, was to adopt a human rights declaration, and to follow that with a treaty to translate political promises into legal obligations; thereafter implementation measures would be specified. Only the first step materialized, with the adoption of the Universal Declaration of Human Rights in 1948. Because the Cold War was already being fought in earnest, the UN vote in favour of the Universal Declaration was not unanimous: eight members abstained (all the Eastern European members at the time, namely Byelorussia, Czechoslovakia, Poland, Ukraine, Soviet Union and Yugoslavia, joined by Saudi Arabia and South Africa). The Cold War prevented translation of the Universal Declaration into a universal human rights treaty. Two Covenants were adopted instead in 1966 and came into force ten years later. The division of human rights into civil and political rights on one hand, and economic, social and cultural rights on the other was transposed from the two dominant ideologies of the time into law and formalized in the names of the two Covenants. The third planned step, implementation, was silently dropped.

The Commission on Human Rights was the main forum for negotiating human rights commitments. Of the initial eighteen seats on the Commission the Western Group had the largest number, six, while Eastern Europe had three. The rest of the world had nine seats altogether (Latin America had four as did Asia, and Africa had one). Evan Luard has described the first decade of the Commission on Human Rights as the years of Western domination.[2] The West's voice was not confined to its seats and votes. All drafts of the future Universal Declaration of Human Rights were in English except two in French.[3] Howard Tolley has pointed out that non-Western members of the Commission were American-educated diplomats. Thus, the 'influential diplomat P. C. Chang of China [Taiwan] held a Columbia University PhD, but challenged the Western orientation of the Harvard-educated Malik [Lebanon]', and the profile of the first two decades of the Commission looked like this:

A United States delegate served as Chair for six consecutive sessions, and no Eastern block member ever held that office. The Soviets were excluded from the initial three-member drafting committee for the Universal Declaration, and two anti-American NGOs were stripped of their consultative status. The People's Republic of China was blocked from membership, the Asian region was generally underrepresented, and there was no black African representative before 1964.[4]

Whether human rights should apply to people in colonies (*non-self-governing territories*, in the official UN jargon), was debated during the adoption of the Universal Declaration of Human Rights. An amendment favouring full application of human rights was tabled by the Soviet Union but it was rejected in favour of a counterproposal by the UK; the vote was close: 29 in favour of the counterproposal, and 17 against, with 10 abstentions.[5] The eagerness of the newly independent countries to extend human rights to those who had yet to attain independence was supported by the East and opposed by the West. The changed balance between the North (divided between the West and East) and the growing South led to profound changes.

Box 3.1 • Negotiating the Universal Declaration, fighting the Cold War

An image of the world according to which some governments favour and others oppose human rights belies the divisions that exist within each government. At the time when the Universal Declaration of Human Rights was being negotiated, the Berlin Airlift by the three Western permanent members of the Security Council – the US, the UK and France – impeded an attempt by the fourth, the Soviet Union, to starve Berlin into submission. The risk of war was evaluated daily, at some points receding, at others seeming certain, and everybody was on full wartime footing. Berlin was in the midst of the Soviet zone, manned by 18,000 troops and surrounded by a further 300,000. The 6,500 Western troops estimated that they had two hours to live if war did break out. That it did not was no credit to the promise of no war contained in the United Nations Charter or to the pledges of the newly negotiated Universal Declaration of Human Rights. Making such pledges was a separate activity. One part of each government was negotiating promises of all human rights for all, another was fighting rearguard diplomatic battles, a third was involved in public diplomacy, a fourth was debating the currency regulations for the divided Germany that had been used by the Soviet Union as the pretext for imposing the blockade, a fifth was combating the Soviet blockade. It ended on 12 May 1949, after 327 days, in 'a strange mixture of hilarity and anti-climax', as the *International Herald Tribune* commented that day.

➡️ Beforehand, Western military aircraft had been adapted to ferry everything from flour, yeast and salt, to coffee and fuel, one landing every four minutes. Military pilots, trained to obliterate cities rather than keep them alive, chalked up makeshift signs: 'Coal-and-feed company, round-the-clock-service, delivery guaranteed'. The waving children in the photograph may have been those who were supplied with additional mini-parachute-loads of candy through a self-organized pilots' initiative that had been a secret between the pilots and the children until a candy bar landed on a journalist.

The process of decolonization ruptured that Cold War paralysis that had dogged the UN's work on human rights. Two parallel processes took place in the 1950s: human rights standard-setting was pursued by bodies having 'human rights' in their title with the exclusive focus on individual rights in independent states, while the General Assembly of the UN dealt with decolonization without reference to human rights. The two tracks were merged in the 1960s, when self-determination was added to the human rights agenda and affirmed as *the* collective human right. Broadened UN membership, with an increasing majority of developing countries, rescued the UN human rights agenda from dominance by the Cold War. Treaties against racial and gender discrimination reintegrated human rights that had been split into civil/political and economic/social rights. The concept of economic and social rights was, however, dominated by the distortions of the Cold War.

Enter the right to education

Much as subsequent international instruments, the Universal Declaration of Human Rights could not say simply 'everybody has the right to education' and stop there. The meaning and import of education had to be defined, which necessitated a lengthy formulation. The ultimately adopted provision of the Universal Declaration of Human Rights reads as follows:

1. Everyone has the right to education. Education shall be free, at least in the elementary and fundamental stages. Elementary education shall be compulsory. Technical and professional education shall be made generally available and higher education shall be equally accessible to all on the basis of merit.
2. Education shall be directed to the full development of the human personality and to the strengthening of respect for human rights and fundamental freedoms. It shall promote understanding, tolerance and friendship among all nations, racial or religious groups, and shall further the activities of the United Nations for the maintenance of peace.
3. Parents have a prior right to choose the kind of education that shall be given to their children.

All international human rights instruments are products of intergovernmental negotiations. The Universal Declaration of Human Rights, although drafted and adopted with unparalleled speed (in less than two years), was the outcome of a process that is recorded in hundreds of pages of the official documents in which proposals and counterproposals, discussions, objections and changes in wording were carefully recorded.

The right to education had a great deal of support amongst the negotiating delegations and the UN secretariat. One reason was that most of the negotiators came from countries where education was a public responsibility and primary education was compulsory. Another reason was that the West and the East both accepted the right to education, albeit defined differently.

Safeguards against the denial of education

Two of the three initial proposals for the listing of rights that a future declaration should encompass (one generated by the secretariat, another by the USA) included the right to education.[6] The secretariat's draft affirmed the right to education and stipulated that governments should ensure that all children receive primary education. The second draft was produced by René Cassin, bringing the first part of the draft closer to the finally adopted text. It said:

> Everyone has the right to education. Primary education shall be free and compulsory. There shall be equal access for all to such facilities for technical, cultural and higher education as can be provided by the State or community on the basis of merit and without distinction as to race, sex, language, religion, social standing, political affiliation or financial means.[7]

Nothing was said at the beginning of this process about the purpose and contents of education, a section on which was added in December 1947. The initial draft amounted to an implicit acceptance of abuses of education since its purpose and contents were not specified.[8] The World Jewish Congress reminded delegates that the initial draft 'provided a technical framework of education but contained nothing about the spirit governing education which was an essential element. Neglect of this principle in Germany had been the main cause of two catastrophic wars'.[9] Nothing had been said in 1947 about parental choice, a statement on which was added in May 1948.

Terms such as 'elementary', 'primary', 'fundamental' or 'basic' were used, often interchangeably, and translated between different official languages with much difficulty ('fundamental' in English translated in French as 'élémentaire'). These difficulties were resolved without controversy. A huge controversy was triggered by suggestions that education should be both a right and a duty. Two delegations (Lebanon and India) argued that it was contradictory to posit that education was a right and add that it was compulsory; the UK argued that 'it was dangerous to include the word "compulsory" in the Draft Declaration because it could be interpreted as acceptance of the concept of State education'. An early vote taken to delete the word 'compulsory' saved it by just one vote.[10]

The controversy was repeated before the Third Committee of the General Assembly during the final stages of negotiations. If the notion of education as a duty was accepted, the argument went, then it could be used against adults, not only children, to force them into school. The final compromise was to retain compulsory education only for children and only at primary school level.[11]

Box 3.2 • Huckleberry Finn, the most famous truant in history

Law allows schools to exclude children but children have no right to exclude themselves from school. Truancy is called 'the kindergarten of crime'.

Nobody who has read Mark Twain's *Adventures of Huckleberry Finn* could fail to sympathize with the boy's predicament and admire his ingenuity. That this book was censored when originally published reinforces the message that safeguards against government's coercive powers are necessary. In March 1885, *Adventures of Huckleberry Finn* was removed from Concord Public Library. The cited reasons were 'a very low grade of morality' and 'a systematic use of bad grammar'. The book was deemed to be 'flippant and irreverent' and assessed as 'trash of the veriest sort'.*

Coercing children into attending school – where they may be bullied or bored – seldom makes them learn, which is what schooling is supposed to be for. Moreover, law tends not to anticipate a situation where a child could have a perfectly legitimate reason for rejecting school attendance; there is no way for guilty children to prove themselves innocent. Enforcement of school attendance can lead recalcitrant children to prison; prisons are not even in law slanted towards learning.

* *Censorship: 500 Year of Conflict*, New York Public Library, Oxford University Press, 1984, p. 9.

Preventing abuse of education

As a counterweight to compulsory education, parental choice was added to the definition of the right to education during the last stage of negotiations. The idea that education should be left to governments' discretion, and without safeguards against abuse of their power, conflicted with the spirit of the Universal Declaration of Human Rights. No notion of the rights of the child existed at the time: hence the debate revolved around a balance between the powers of the state and the rights of parents. The chairman of the UN Commission on Human Rights, Eleanor Roosevelt, had the final word on the issue:

> The chairman said that, in her understanding, it was the general view of the Commission that acceptance of the word 'compulsory' in no way put in doubt the right of the family to choose the school which its children should attend.
>
> Speaking as the United States representative, she said that she considered the amendment [adding the right of the family to determine the education of its children] unwise. The obligation of the State to provide free and compulsory education meant that children had to attend school, but not necessarily the school provided by the State. While the latter was distinctly obligated to provide schools for all children without distinction, the choice of the school was left to the parents. [12]

The apparent conflict between education being compulsory and also a right was left, and UNESCO reported in 1951 that 'the principle of universal compulsory education is no longer questioned'.[13]

Sources of inspiration

Defining the right to education was limited in 1948 by the small number of countries where it was recognized, however imperfectly. Its corollary, government responsibility to provide or finance education, was used as a proxy. The first law positing that all children should be educated in state schools originated from the Prussian state in 1717. Schooling was subsequently institutionalized as a government responsibility in large parts of Europe.[14]

The notion of rights was unknown in 1717. Had it been discussed, it would have been confined to states as the sole subjects of rights. Their right to impose education and the corollary duty of individuals to be educated were reflected in compulsory education. Schooling was instrumental to a range of goals, economic and political, social and cultural. Justifications for free and compulsory public schooling were encapsulated in two goals – the virtue of being industrious, and piety – as Hannah More, a British missionary who established schools in the Gold Coast (today's Ghana) wrote in 1801.[15]

The first justification, to inculcate industriousness, defined schooling as a means to prevent pauperism. Schools for poor children were designed to ensure employability and prevent the poor from being a long-term financial burden on the state. A large pool of literate workers was needed in industrializing economies. A related purpose was to prevent riots and revolutions. Schooling was intended to create a place and a stake in society for those who might other-wise have rebelled.

The second justification, to instil piety, derived from the heritage of religious education and focused on values. The beginnings of this approach are often attributed to Martin Luther, who in 1530 defined the purpose of education thus:

> I hold that it is the duty of the government to compel its subjects to keep their children in school ... so that preachers, jurists, pastors, writers, physicians, schoolmasters and the like may continue, for we cannot do without them. If it can compel its subjects who are fitted for the work to carry the pike and musket, man the walls, and do other kinds of work when war is necessary, how much more can it and ought it compel its subjects to keep their children in school, because there is a worse war on, a war with the very devil, who goes about to suck out secretly the strength of cities and empty them of able persons, until he has bored out the pith, and left an empty shell of useless folk, with whom he can play and juggle as he will.[16]

Table 3.2 • Statistics on primary education, 1873

Country	Number of schools	Number of pupils enrolled in primary school	Estimated coverage of school-aged children %
Austria	15,200	1,829,000	9
Bavaria	8,200	631,000	13
Belgium	5,641	593,000	12
Brazil	4,202	125,000	1
Denmark	2,600	257,000	15
France	70,179	4,792,000	13
Greece	1,194	79,000	5
Hungary	14,550	1,233,000	7
Italy	42,178	1,798,000	6
Netherlands	3,734	484,000	14
Norway	6,500	215,000	13
Peru	790	34,000	2
Prussia	34,000	3,650,000	15
Russia	44,033	1,525,000	2
Saxony	2,267	438,000	18
Spain	28,382	1,425,000	9
Sweden	7,528	577,000	14
Switzerland	7,000	420,000	16
Turkey	13,146	464,000	1
United Kingdom	58,975	3,000,000	12
United States	141,000	7,209,000	18
Uruguay	245	16,000	4

Source: 'La statistique de l'enseignement primaire: Deuxième rapport par M. E. Levasseur', *Bulletin de l'Institut International de Statistique*, Vol. IV, 1889.

The 1873 statistics on education, presented in Table 3.2, demonstrate the scope of inspiration that the drafters of the Universal Declaration of Human Rights could have had. Africa and Asia did not exist on the education map generated by early comparative research. South America ranked low with only a small fraction of school-aged children enrolled, as did Turkey. In Western Europe, Saxony ranked the highest. The USA and the UK also exhibited high enrolment ratios although their model of public schooling differed substantively from those followed in continental Europe.

Continental European models

The earliest comparative studies and statistics on primary education appeared in the volumes of the *Bulletin de l'Institut International de Statistique* at the end of the nineteenth century.[17] They revealed an array of early government approaches to making education compulsory:

Prussia The earliest development of public schools started in today's Germany. In Saxony, the ecclesiastical decree of 1540 mandated the establishment of schools and this was copied by Protestant states. From 1533, Wittenberg had a school for girls. The Thirty Years' War halted that process. ... On 30 July 1736, *Principia regulativa* set forth rules for all schools in Prussia. ... Compulsory education had been introduced by a decree of 1717. ... 'The man and citizen is formed through instruction and education, and these two tasks pertain to school', wrote the monarch on 3 July 1798 to his minister. Three ministries were established in 1817, for religious affairs, education and medicine. Altenstein, the first minister for education, a post he held until his death in 1840, was a vigorous promoter of primary education. He published an ordinance in 1819 which specified rules for compulsory education, and, with his advisors Süvern and Beckendorf and under the influence of Pestalozzi, he started seminars to prepare teachers for the establishment of a large number of primary schools. ... Primary education was made compulsory for children aged six to fourteen. This was implemented without difficulty. Only between 0.05 and 0.06 per cent of children were out of school – vagabonds, and Protestant children who left school after confirmation.

France The 1791 Constitution posited public education as a fundamental pillar of the new French society: 'A system of public education shared by all citizens will be created and organized, it will be free of charge for that part of education that is indispensable for all people, and education establishments will be gradually distributed throughout the Kingdom.' ... As part of the restoration of the monarchy, administrative ordinances of 1816, 1820 and 1830 allocated the powers to educate children to all local communities but without the corresponding power to impose financial obligations upon citizens. The first law that effectively introduced education in France was adopted on 28 June 1833. It established two phases: elementary and secondary education. It obliged all local communities to have at least one elementary primary school; those with more than 6,000 residents had also to have a secondary school.

The Netherlands   The first laws on education were adopted on 15 June 1801 and 15 February 1806. The 1806 law, which primarily regulated school inspection, giving inspectors a great deal of power, remained in force until 1857, even through the time when Dutch provinces were annexed to the French Empire. As the 1806 law mandated, and the 1848 Constitution stipulated even more explicitly, education in the strict sense of that word had to be completely separate from religious instruction. The law of 13 August 1857 maintained the principle of religious neutrality and left the power of regulating the cost of education to communities, leaving open both the possibility of financial contribution by those pupils who were able to contribute and the possibility of making education completely free of charge. ... Local communities were empowered to offer primary education free of charge and the state contributed 30 per cent of its cost. The law did not make education compulsory, but it authorized communities to provide incentives for school attendance and to refuse to provide assistance to families whose children were not attending school.

Belgium   In the aftermath of the 1830 revolution, free education was proclaimed in Article 17 of the Constitution of the Kingdom of Belgium: 'Education is free. ... Public education, paid by the state, is regulated by law.' This regime resulted in a multi-plication of private religious schools while the numbers of pupils in public schools stagnated. ... Liberals complained constantly about this situation, and the law of 23 September 1842 was a compromise between the parties in dispute over primary education. That law recognized three types of school: communal, 'adopted' and completely free, and obliged each local community to have at least one primary school, which it could do by adopting a private school. Religious instruction was provided under the direction of ecclesiastical authorities.

The Anglo-American model

The long history of education in England, and its export to different corners of the world, especially the United States of America, provide a fascinating back-ground for studying education today.

Primary schooling in England draws its beginnings from the Society for Promoting Christian Knowledge in 1699, even if the schooling it provided consisted of learning catechism by heart. The expansion of what was subse-quently termed 'popular education' through Sunday schools reinforced the religious grounding of education. The 1802 Health and Morals of Apprentices Act institutionalized this practice, obliging all apprentices to attend religious education each Sunday and adding that they should receive some education in reading, writing and 'rithmetic (the three Rs) during their working hours.

A legislative proposal before the House of Commons in 1807 to provide two years of free primary education in parochial schools was rejected on two grounds: unwillingness to bear the anticipated costs, and fear that education might make 'the lower orders' discontented. Decades of disagreement about religion post-poned the first Education Act to 1870. It introduced education for children aged five to twelve in two types of schools, non-denominational schools governed by school boards (with the parental right to withdraw their children from religious education) and denominational voluntary schools.

Secondary schools reach much further back in history, to Winchester College (founded in 1382) and Eton (founded in 1440). Such schools were either called a 'grammar school' (*libera schola grammaticalis*, originating from the teaching of classical languages) or a 'college' (stemming from its establishment as a collegiate foundation). These earlier, academic secondary schools (based on the values of elitism and excellence) and the later religious, popular schools, bifurcated access to education. Schools were segregated by religion and by class. All-encompassing compulsory education introduced in 1944 did not go as far as equalizing the orientation and quality of education. Stratified schools have continued ever since. Today's vocabulary retains unique features of Englishness: an English 'public school' would be defined as private in all other countries; what is called a 'public school' elsewhere corresponds to a state school in England.

The 1944 Education Act introduced universal access to primary education for all, free of charge, four years before such a right was affirmed in the Universal Declaration of Human Rights. On this basis, the post-war education strategy initially prioritized equality of opportunity. Making education compulsory has meant that it is parents' duty to ensure that their children receive education; this understanding has continued ever since.[18] The corollary emphasis on parental duties and rights has hampered the notion of the right of the child to education and the child's rights in education.

In the United States, nineteenth-century initiatives aimed at institutionalizing education were driven by the 'common school' ideal, aimed at forging a nation out of a variety of immigrants. The popular image of the United States as a melting pot vividly illustrates what the common school was expected to accomplish. It was to be all-inclusive and combine two distinct purposes: economic self-sufficiency and religious instruction.

It was deemed cheaper to educate and train people for economic self-support than to guard them in perpetual pauperism. In 1643 the state of Virginia introduced compulsory apprenticeship for 'orphans, poor children, illegitimate children, and mulattoes born of white mothers'.[19] Its rationale was summed up in 1676 by Virginia's Governor, who lamented the difficulties of governing a population which was 'poore, endebted, discontented and armed'.[20] The state of Massachusetts enacted the first law mandating compulsory education in 1647, slanting it towards religious instruction so as to counter 'one chiefe project of that ould deluder, Satan, to keepe men from the knowledge of the Scriptures'.[21] Public schools were financed by local taxes, and education was provided free of charge to all school-age children. These two features – local financing and local control of education – have continued ever since.

Much like international economic competitiveness today, in the 1950s the Cold War was a driving force for improving education. Domestic changes heralded in 1954 by the Supreme Court ruling that racial segregation in public schools was unconstitutional (see Chapter 9), were overshadowed by the Soviet launch of *Sputnik* in 1957. Education was seen as key to catching up with the technological superiority of the Soviet Union.

Education as the key to technological superiority: *Life* magazine, 24 March 1958

Notes

1. The mission statement of the High Commissioner at the time was reproduced on the front page of each issue of *HCHR News*, the monthly bulletin issued by the Office of the High Commissioner from November 1995 till his departure.

2. E. Luard, *A History of the United Nations: The Years of Western Domination*, 1945–55, Vol. 1, Macmillan, London, 1982.

3. J.P. Humphrey, *Human Rights and the United Nations: A Great Adventure*, Dobbs Ferry, New York, 1984, pp. 31–2; J. Robinson, *Human Rights and Fundamental Freedoms in the Charter of the United Nations: A Commentary*, Institute of Jewish Affairs, New York, 1946, pp. 98–9.

4. H. Tolley, *The UN Commission on Human Rights*, Westview Special Studies in International Relations, Westview Press, Boulder, 1987, pp. 11 and 187.

5. United Nations, *Yearbook of the United Nations. Special Edition: UN Fiftieth Anniversary 1945-1995*, Martinus Nijhoff Publishers, The Hague, 1995, p. 303.

6. G. M. Johnson, 'Writing the Universal Declaration of Human Rights', *Universal Declaration of Human Rights: A History of Its Creation and Implementation*, UNESCO, Paris, 1998, pp. 11–75.

7. UN Doc. E/CN.4/21 (1947).

8. UN Doc. E/CN.4/AC/SR. 14 (1947).

9. UN Doc. E/CN.4/AC.2/SR.8 (1947).

10. UN Doc. E/CN.4/SR. 68 (1948).

11. UN General Assembly, Third Session, *Summary records of meetings of the Third Committee, 21 September – 8 December 1948*, Lake Success, New York, p. 583.

12. UN Doc. E/CN.4/SR. 68 (1948).

13. UNESCO/IBE, *Compulsory Education and Its Prolongation*, Geneva, 1951, p. 24.

14. UNESCO's 1971 survey of education shows that only sixteen countries had introduced compulsory education before 1815; fourteen did so during 1815–1850, and four before the turn of the century (UNESCO/IBE, *World Survey of Education Handbook, 1955–1971*, Geneva, 1971).

15. F.H. Hilliard, *A Short History of Education in British West Africa*, 1957, p. 12.

16. Martin Luther's sermon on keeping children in school is quoted in R. Ulich, *The Education of Nations: A Comparison in Historical Perspective*, 1967, p. 201.

17. M.E. Levasseur, 'Rapport sur la statistique de l'enseignement primaire', *Bulletin de l'Institut International de Statistique*, Rome, Vols I–VI, Rome, 1873–92.

18. The 1944 Act stated: 'It shall be the duty of the parent of every child of compulsory school age to cause him to receive efficient full time education suitable to his age, ability and aptitude', while the 1996 Act only slightly altered that formulation: 'The parent of every child of compulsory school age shall cause him to receive efficient full-time education suitable (a) to his age, ability and aptitude, and (b) to any special educational needs he may have, either by regular attendance at school or otherwise'.

19. Acts 34 and 27, *Laws of Virginia, 1642–43 and 1646*.

20. E.S. Morgan, 'Slavery and freedom: The American paradox', in J. Schreiber and R.C. Elliott (eds), *In Search of the American Dream*, 1974, p. 179.

21. The Massachusetts Compulsory School Act of 1647, *Records of the Governor and Company of Massachusetts, 1647*.

The Core Contents of the Right to Education

No right could exist without corresponding government obligations. International human rights law is best visualized as a network of different treaties whereby governments explicitly accept specific human rights obligations. The realm of the acceptable is delineated by minimum standards which should be in place worldwide; optimal standards vary in time and place. The obligations relate to human rights as a whole, involving the need to act and react, pursue specific conduct and achieve a particular result. The basic framework of government obligations is outlined through the explicit guarantees of the right to education which are detailed below. The core contents of the right to education which emerges from them can be structured into a 4-As scheme.[1] Governments are obliged to make education available, accessible, acceptable and adaptable:

- *Availability* embodies two different government obligations: the right to education as a civil and political right requires the government to permit the establishment of schools, while the right to education as a social, economic and cultural right requires the government to ensure that free and compulsory education is available to all school-age children.

- *Access* is defined differently for different levels of education. The government is obliged to secure access to education for all children in the compulsory education age range, but not for secondary and higher education (see next section). Moreover, compulsory education ought to be free of charge while post-compulsory education may entail the payment of tuition and other charges, assessed by the criterion of affordability. The right to education should be realized progressively, facilitating access to post-compulsory education as circumstances permit.

- *Acceptability* requires a guaranteed quality of education, minimum standards of health and safety, or professional requirements for teachers which have to be set, monitored and enforced by the government. Acceptability has been considerably broadened through the development of international human rights law: indigenous and minority rights have prioritized the language of instruction; the prohibition of corporal punishment has transformed school discipline. The emergence of children as subjects of the right to education and rights in education has further extended the boundaries of ensuring acceptability of education.

- *Adaptability* requires schools to adapt to children, following the yardstick of the best interests of each child in the Convention on the Rights of the Child. This change reversed the heritage of forcing children to adapt to whatever schools may have been made available to them. As human rights are indivisible, adaptability requires safeguards for all human rights within education as well as enhancing human rights through education.

International legal obligations which defined the nature and scope of the right to education were first set in the 1960s. As mentioned in Chapter 3, the two core human rights treaties that, together with the Universal Declaration of Human Rights, have been proclaimed by the United Nations to constitute the International Bill of Human Rights, were adopted in 1966 and came into force in 1976. Their names – the International Covenant on Civil and Political Rights and the International Covenant on Economic, Social and Cultural Rights – epitomized the Cold War split.

Two human rights treaties preceded the Covenants. The UNESCO Convention against Discrimination in Education was adopted in 1960 and came into force in 1962, and the Convention on the Elimination of Racial Discrimination was adopted in 1965 and came into force in 1969. They resulted from the changed composition of the United Nations and, thereby, its changed agenda. Racial discrimination was prioritized by the new members, especially the African states.

Box 4.1 • Key treaty provisions on free and compulsory education

Universal Declaration of Human Rights (1948)
'Education shall be free, at least in the elementary and fundamental stages. Elementary education shall be compulsory.'

UNESCO Convention against Discrimination in Education (1960)
'The States Parties to this Convention undertake to formulate, develop and apply a national policy which ... will tend to promote equality of opportunity and of treatment ... and in particular: (a) To make primary education free and compulsory.'

International Covenant on Economic, Social and Cultural Rights (1966)
'Primary education shall be compulsory and available free for all.'

Convention on the Rights of the Child (1989)
'States Parties recognize the right of the child to education, and with a view to achieving this right progressively and on the basis of equal opportunity, they shall, in particular: (a) Make primary education compulsory and available free for all.'

The Cold War ideological split was, fortunately, ignored and the Convention against Racial Discrimination addressed all human rights in turn. This was repeated in the 1979 Convention on the Elimination of All Forms of Discrimination against Women as well as the 1989 Convention on the Rights of the Child.

These treaties define the core contents of the right to education: to ensure that primary education is all-encompassing, free and compulsory; to guarantee parental choice in the education of their children; to apply non-discrimination to the right to education and human rights in education; and, most important, to prevent abuse of education by defining what education is for. A summarized overview follows. The tables include key provisions of global human rights treaties only so as to lay down the framework that applies worldwide.

Free and compulsory education

The first government obligation relates to ensuring that primary schools are available for all children, which necessitates a considerable investment. While the government is not necessarily the only investor in education, international human rights law obliges it to be the investor of last resort. If the intake capacity of primary schools is below the number of children, the right to education cannot be translated into practice. Investment in education yields benefits after a long time. Therefore, as explained in Chapter 2, public education was made a public responsibility.

Education as a universal human right requires universality of government human rights obligations because inequalities accumulate in time and space. Those with the least access to education leave this heritage to the next generation. Making individual families and local communities responsible for funding education broadens the gap between haves and have-nots. Breaking this vicious circle requires governments, individually and collectively, to prioritize and equalize funding for education, from the local to the global level.

'Progressive realization' was the key phrase used for the right to education in international human rights treaties. Thus, governments were obliged to ensure free and compulsory primary education for all children immediately, or elaborate a plan and seek international assistance so as to comply with this obligation as fast as possible. Post-compulsory education was to be made progressively available and accessible. Contrary to what human rights treaties anticipated, post-compulsory education is being progressively traded rather than made accessible as a matter of right, as Chapter 8 describes.

Pre-school education was not defined as a government responsibility, and for good reasons. The tension between parental and government prerogatives regarding children's education was a constant bone of contention in drafting international human rights treaties. Their early slant towards affirmation of the right of the government to impose and enforce uniform schooling in the name of the right to education was a product of Cold War political compromises. This was resisted, and the right to education was categorized as a civil and political right as well as an economic and social right. The aim was a balance between two different roles of the government, as protector and as violator of human rights.

Box 4.2 • Dragged back to school

A small boy dragged back to school by a policeman and a welfare officer, in May 2002 in London, illustrates how compulsory education can be. Indeed, Western European heritage includes the right of the state to deprive a child of liberty for the purpose of educational supervision, which is affirmed in the European Convention on Human Rights. Education as the child's duty can lead to the imprisonment of a truant. The European Court of Human Rights, in interpreting that provision of the Convention, identified a human rights violation in a case where a child was ostensibly deprived of liberty for the purpose of educational supervision while detained 'in conditions of virtual isolation and without the assistance of staff with educational training'. This, the Court held, could not further any educational purpose.* It has, however, accepted that compulsory education could entail the detention of a child in an institution over a considerable period of time.[†] The European Convention on Human Rights is fifty years old and it does not reflect either the right to education or the even more recent concept of the rights of the child.

* European Court of Human Rights, *Bouamar v. Belgium*, Judgement of 29 February 1988, A- 129.
[†] European Court of Human Rights, *Nielsen v. Denmark*, Judgement of 28 November 1988, A-144.

Parental freedom of choice

The right to education involves four key actors: the government as the provider and/or funder of public schooling, the child as the bearer of the right to education and of the duty to comply with compulsory-education requirements, the child's parents who are the first educators, and professional educators, namely teachers.

Although the child is today deemed to be the principal subject of the right to education, the child is not party to decision-making on the realization of the right to education. The rights of the child entered international law late, with the Convention on the Rights of the Child in 1989. Previously, international human rights law divided decision-making between the parents and the state. Each of these actors claims to represent the best interests of the child. As often as not, adults disagree among themselves as to what the best interests of the child may be.

The guaranteed freedom and the corollary responsibility of parents to choose education for their children protects educational pluralism and prevents a state monopoly over education.[2] The rationale behind the right to parental choice is not to legitimize denial of their children's right to education. In a conflict between parental choice and the best interests of the child, the rights of the child prevail and the government has to ensure that children are protected. Canada's Supreme Court rejected a claim by a parent to be able to 'educate his children as he pleases' which he had justified by 'his authority over his children and his duty to attend to their education' coming from God. Canadian law allows parents to exempt their children from school if they are 'under efficient instruction at home or elsewhere', but they have to apply for approval. The Supreme Court has found that 'accommodation of defendants' religious beliefs would entail a complete exemption from state regulation ... [and thus] severely impede the achievement of important state goals'.[3]

Box 4.3 • Guarantees for parental freedom of choice

Universal Declaration (1948)
'Parents have a prior right to choose the kind of education that shall be given to their children.'

UNESCO Convention against Discrimination in Education (1960)
'The States Parties to this Convention agree that: ...
(b) It is essential to respect the liberty of parents, ... firstly to choose for their children institutions other than those maintained by the public authorities but conforming to ... minimum educational standards, and secondly, to ensure ... the religious and moral education of the children in conformity with their own convictions.'

International Covenant on Economic, Social and Cultural Rights (1966)
'The States Parties to the present Covenant undertake to have respect for the liberty of parents ... to choose for their children schools, other than those established by the public authorities, which conform to such minimum educational standards as may be laid down or approved by the State and to ensure the religious and moral education of their children in conformity with their own convictions.

'No part of this article shall be construed so as to interfere with the liberty of individuals and bodies to establish and direct educational institutions ...'

International Covenant on Civil and Political Rights (1966)
'The States Parties to the present Covenant undertake to have respect for the liberty of parents ... to ensure the religious and moral education of their children in conformity with their own convictions.'

Convention on the Rights of the Child (1989)
'No part of [articles 28 and 29] shall be construed so as to interfere with the liberty of individuals and bodies to establish and direct educational institutions ...'

As Box 4.3 shows, respect for parental freedom to have their children educated in conformity with their religious, moral or philosophical convictions has been affirmed in all general human rights treaties. The obligation to make primary education all-encompassing is in practice frequently, albeit erroneously, associated with state-provided schooling. Government can secure education by funding diverse schools but not operating any. Parental freedom to opt out of state schools is a frequent subject of litigation.

The right to education 'by its very nature calls for regulation by the state'[4] because it is responsible for ensuring that all education complies with prescribed standards.[5] Allowing anybody to set up an institution, call it a 'school', carry out a programme called 'education', and issue pieces of papers called 'diplomas' constitutes dereliction of government responsibility. In India, the Supreme Court was faced with this problem in 1992. Students from an unrecognized school sought permission to take an exam. Out of 129, only one passed. The court described government obligations thus:

> This Court judicially noted mushroom growth of ill-equipped and under-staffed unrecognized educational institutions in Andhra Pradesh, Bihar, Tamil Nadu and Maharashtra States and other States too are no exceptions. Obviously the field of education is found to be fertile, perennial and profitable business venture with least capital outlay. This case is one such case from the State of Maharashtra.

It would appear that individuals or societies, without complying with the statutory requirements, establish educational or training institutions ill equipped to impart education and have students admitted, in some instances despite warnings by the State Government and in some instances without knowledge of the State Government concerned, but with connivance at lower levels.

The ill-equipped and ill-housed institutions and sub-standard staff therein are counter-productive and detrimental to inculcating spirit of inquiry and excellence in the students. The disregard of statutory compliance would amount to letting loose of innocent and unwary children.[6]

Non-discrimination

In the course of the history of education, children have been excluded from education by means of all the forms of discrimination that are nowadays prohibited. Education strategies are not based on international human rights law and there are no internationally comparable statistics on access to education by race, ethnicity or religion. Consequently, it is impossible to monitor progress and retrogression using internationally prohibited grounds of discrimination as the yardstick. With the exception of sex, discrimination remains unrecorded, which creates a vicious circle. Because discrimination is officially unrecorded, it can be ignored. Because there is no quantitative data, anybody trying to prove discrimination is doomed to fail for lack of data. It is impossible effectively to oppose discrimination without exposing it first.

The essential prohibitions of discrimination are reproduced in Box 4.4. Centuries of experience with legalized and institutionalized discrimination have led to a listing of prohibitions which single out those grounds of discrimination that were prevalent in history, whereby girls or black or indigenous children should not be admitted to school because they are female, black or indigenous. Once in school, however, children are not necessarily taught that females, black or indigenous people have been excluded from education for centuries and now compete with the categories that were privileged from a position of disadvantage. Thus, mere admission of previously excluded categories to school is only one of governmental human rights obligations.

Identifying those features which typically entail the denial of the right to education and listing them as prohibited grounds of discrimination was the first step. In 1988, the International Labour Organization highlighted the way ahead:

[A]ttempts to define race and colour are of little value in the application of legislation that is intended to combat discrimination in so far as it is not the race, colour or ethnic origin of the person who is discriminated against that is really the point at issue, but rather the negative aspects that the author of the discrimination imputes to the person who is the victim of discrimination.[7]

The initially simple prohibitions of discriminations have therefore become complex, trying to capture the changing pattern of discrimination out of school, in

Box 4.4 • Key treaty provisions on non-discrimination in education

UNESCO Convention against Discrimination in Education (1960)
'The States Parties to this Convention undertake to formulate, develop and apply a national policy which … will tend to promote equality of opportunity and of treatment …

'… the term 'discrimination' includes any distinction, exclusion, limitation or preference which, being based on race, colour, sex, language, religion, political or other opinion, national or social origin, economic condition or birth, has the purpose or effect of nullifying or impairing equality of treatment in education and in particular:

(a) Of depriving any person or group of persons of access to education of any type or at any level;

(b) Of limiting any person or group of persons to education of an inferior standard;

(c) Of establishing or maintaining separate educational systems or institutions … [such systems are permitted for pupils of the two sexes, for religious or linguistic reasons, and private education is also permitted if its object is not to secure the exclusion of any group].'

International Convention on the Elimination of All Forms of Racial Discrimination (1965):
'… States Parties undertake to prohibit and to eliminate racial discrimination in all its forms and to guarantee the right of everyone, without distinction as to race, colour, or national or ethnic origin, to equality before the law, notably in the enjoyment of the following rights: … The right to education and training.

'States Parties undertake to adopt immediate and effective measures, particularly in the field of teaching, education, culture and information, with a view to combating prejudices which lead to racial discrimination …'

Convention on the Elimination of All Forms of Discrimination against Women (1979)
'States Parties shall take all appropriate measures to eliminate discrimination against women in order to ensure to them equal rights with men in the field of education and in particular to ensure, on a basis of equality of men and women:

(b) Access to the same curricula, the same examinations, teaching staff with qualifications of the same standard and school premises and equipment of the same quality;

(c)	The elimination of any stereotyped concept of the roles of men and women at all levels and in all forms of education by encouraging coeducation ...

(f)	The reduction of female student drop-out rates and the organization of programmes for girls and women who have left school prematurely ...

(h)	Access to specific educational information to help to ensure the health and well-being of families, including information and advice on family planning.'

ILO Convention Concerning Indigenous and Tribal Peoples (1989)

'Measures shall be taken to ensure that members of the [indigenous] peoples have the opportunity to acquire education at all levels on at least an equal footing with the rest of the national community.

'Education programmes and services for the [indigenous] peoples shall be developed and implemented in co-operation with them to address their special needs and shall incorporate their histories, their knowledge and technologies, their value systems and their further social, economic and cultural aspirations.

'The imparting of general knowledge and skills that will help children belonging to the [indigenous] peoples to participate fully and on an equal footing in their own community and in the national community shall be the aim of education for these peoples.

'Educational measures shall be taken among all sections of the national community, and particularly amongst those that are in most direct contact with the [indigenous] peoples, with the object of eliminating prejudices that they may harbour in respect of these peoples. To this end, efforts shall be made to ensure that history textbooks and other educational materials provide a fair, accurate and informative portrayal of the societies and cultures of these peoples.'

Convention on the Rights of the Child (1989)

'Recognizing the special needs of a disabled child, assistance ... shall be designated to ensure that the disabled child has effective access to and receives education ...

'In those States in which ethnic, religious or linguistic minorities or persons of indigenous origin exist, a child belonging to such a minority or who is indigenous shall not be denied the right, in community with other members of his or her group, to enjoy his or her own culture, to profess and practise his or her own religion, or to use his or her own language.'

school, and in the interaction between school and society, and to forge rights-based responses. The end is nowhere in sight because discriminatory practices often merge a host of prohibited grounds of discrimination with additional exclusionary criteria that have not yet been outlawed. Moreover, fear may prevent children from going to school because they are female, improperly dressed, or have been victims of harassment. Girls are targeted more than boys; the cause of bullying can be their dress code, and the consequence their dropping out of school.[8] The UN special representative on the internally displaced has emphasized 'fear of the identification of children for what they are and repression or reprisals that may target the family if children are sent to school'.[9]

Aims and purposes of education

In 1947, the first United Nations report on discrimination emphasized that 'the whole field of action to prevent discrimination requires a vast programme of education'. It was the knowledge that law would not be effective, and might be counterproductive, unless it enjoyed support from those whom it addressed, and general support in the population, that led to an emphasis on education:

> Forcing a prejudiced person to read or hear exhortations on tolerance may only increase his prejudice. Overenthusiastic appraisals of the contributions of a minority may create a reaction of distaste for members of that minority; and programmes improperly presented, even with the best intentions, may create an awareness of group difference that did not previously exist. [10]

Schools reflect their surroundings and tend to reinforce prejudicial portrayals of victims of discrimination. Education is embedded in the existing values but also helps create new values and attitudes. Hence, human rights law mandates its deliberate employment to eliminate discrimination, which requires a permanent process so that education can be adjusted to change and foster further change. Our knowledge is, however, inversely correlated with the importance of the object of our interest. We know a great deal about the wording of education policies and laws since these are available in a codified form and translated into English. We know less about the process of teaching, and least of all about learning. Children learn the value of their education after they finish school:

> It's hard to know if school is doing a good job of getting you ready for life. You can't know until you've left school.[11]

Because education can prepare children for life well or badly, and they can be abused in the name of being educated, international human rights law specifies the objectives and purposes of education. The main provisions are distilled in Box 4.5.

Much as other human rights instruments, these are intended to be tools for challenge and change. An implicit agenda of schooling may be to keep children conformist and deferential, to kneel when addressing adults, to recite the official

Box 4.5 • Key treaty provisions on the orientation and purpose of education

UNESCO Convention against Discrimination in Education (1960)

'The States Parties to this Convention agree that: (a) Education shall be directed to the full development of the human personality and to the strengthening of respect for human rights and fundamental freedoms; it shall promote understanding, tolerance and friendship among all nations, racial and religious groups, and shall further the activities of the United Nations for the maintenance of peace.'

International Convention on the Elimination of All Forms of Racial Discrimination (1965)

'States Parties undertake to adopt immediate and effective measures, particularly in the fields of teaching, education, culture and information, with a view to combating prejudices which lead to racial discrimination and to promoting understanding, tolerance and friendship among nations and racial or ethnical groups, as well as to propagating the purposes and principles of the Charter of the United Nations, the Universal Declaration of Human Rights, the United Nations Declaration on the Elimination of All Forms of Racial Discrimination, and this Convention.'

International Covenant on Economic, Social and Cultural Rights (1966)

'The States Parties to the present Covenant ... agree that education shall be directed to the full development of the human personality and the sense of its dignity, and shall strengthen the respect for human rights and fundamental freedoms. They further agree that education shall enable all persons to participate effectively in a free society, promote understanding, tolerance and friendship among all nations and all racial, ethnic or religious groups, and further the activities of the United Nations for the maintenance of peace ...'

Convention on the Elimination of All Forms of Discrimination against Women (1979)

'States Parties shall take all appropriate measures to eliminate discrimination against women in order to ensure to them equal rights with men in the field of education and in particular to ensure, on the basis of equality of men and women ... (c) The elimination of any stereotyped concept of the roles of men and women at all levels and in all forms of education by encouraging coeducation and other types of education which will help to achieve this aim and, in particular, by the

☞ revision of textbooks and school programmes and the adaptation of teaching methods ...'

Convention on the Rights of the Child (1989)
'States Parties agree that the education of the child shall be directed to: (a) The development of the child's personality, talents and mental and physical abilities to their fullest potential; (b) The development of respect for human rights and fundamental freedoms, and for the principles enshrined in the Charter of the United Nations; (c) The development of respect for the child's parents, his or her own cultural identity, language and values, for the national values of the country in which the child is living, the country from which he or she may originate and for civilizations different from his or her own; (d) The preparation of the child for responsible life in a free society, in the spirit of understanding, peace, tolerance, equality of sexes, and friendship among all peoples, ethnic, national and religious groups and persons of indigenous origin; (e) The development of respect for the natural environment.'

dogma, to become used to physical punishment for faults which they cannot understand. An excerpt from a textbook on children's accounts of their childhood from the 1970s, describes the fearful, uncomprehending obedience which was inculcated through school:

Children were trained from their earliest years to be respectful, obedient and mannerly, these being the standards by which adults became acceptable in society. All parents, and fathers in particular were very stern with their children who in any way departed from such standards. Furthermore the punishment for children who misbehaved, however harsh, had to be accepted without question or complaint. Thus the children, respectfully submissive, learned to fear their fathers as harsh and severe. Strong feelings of dislike though dutifully suppressed were very frequently mixed with this fear.[12]

Inculcating obedience leads to children following orders without questioning them, especially when punishment accompanies failure to do so. Corporal punishment socializes children into accepting violence, and the combination of obedience and violence makes them into ideal child soldiers. Nevertheless, abuses of education have been placed on the United Nations human rights agenda only very recently, and on the global education agenda not at all. Strong domestic and international constituencies were necessary to start this process in the 1970s.[13] In the meantime, only one segment of the right to education was addressed, government provision of schooling. That fitted the global priority for universalizing schooling as well as the dominance of the Soviet Union and its allies in defining economic and social rights.

Box 4.6 • The United Nations: splitting the right to education to fit the divided world

Less developed countries

'Economic and social development in the less developed countries is not yet suf-ficient to allow the provision of free education for all at all school levels. Many countries have been able to legislate for free elementary education. None the less, owing to many factors, including the unavailability of facilities and teachers in remote areas and the partial absorption of the school-age population by the labour market, the enrolment ratios at the primary school level of almost all the less developed countries are quite low. ... Primary schools in the less developed countries, in general, operate on a very inferior standard with regard to equip-ment, school premises, pupil–teacher ratio, size of classes and quality of teachers. This is particularly true in the poorest countries, the poorest regions of a country and the poorest sections of the urban and rural areas. ...

'Firstly, there has not been adequate provision of equal opportunity for women, for different ethnic groups, for rural areas, for backward regions and for lower income groups. ... Secondly, the content of education does not, in most cases, conform to the manpower requirements of the less developed countries.'

The socialist countries of Eastern Europe

'Compulsory free education goes well beyond the primary stage in all the social-ist countries of Eastern Europe. ... In general, it may be said that all the socialist countries of Eastern Europe have now achieved universal, compulsory and free education at the primary level. Shortfalls below 100 per cent attendance, where they do occur, are of negligible proportions and largely attributable to nomadic or incompletely settled minorities, whose children the Government is making every effort to enrol in the normal school programme.'

The developed market-economy countries

'At the time of the present study, every country with a developed market econo-my has compulsory free education of at least six years duration, and most of them considerably longer. ... Educational inequality is particularly pronounced with respect to two factors which can only be touched upon: these are sex and race. The number of girls and boys in primary schools is now roughly the same, but there are many more young men than young women who receive higher education. In the United States of America, negroes are still under-represented in institutions of higher learning ...'

Source: Commission on Human Rights, The Realization of Economic, Social and Cultural Rights: Problems, Policies, Progress, by Manouchehr Ganji, Special Rapporteur, UN Doc. E/CN.4/1108/rev. 1 and E/CN.4/1131/Rev. 1 (1973), paras. 170, 178, 483–84, and 65–8.

Divided world: West/East, North/South

During the Cold War, there was much praise by the UN of the accomplishments of the socialist countries of Eastern Europe in providing free schooling, and no critique of the denial of human rights in education. The classification of the right to education as an economic and social right made Eastern Europe its chief proponent in intergovernmental fora. Since the US and the whole Western Group championed civil and political rights, there was no challenge. The UN divided the world in three, as Box 4.6 illustrates. Universality of the right to education was undermined by the very organization that proclaimed it.

The 1990s were a time of fiftieth anniversaries, and interest in the developments of the previous five decades surged. The fiftieth anniversary of the Universal Declaration of Human Rights in 1998 was preceded by the fiftieth anniversary of the Marshall Plan in 1997. Although they were treated as separate events, the Cold War linked the two immediately and inextricably, as described in Chapter 2. At the time of the programme's inception, George Kennan, the intellectual father of 'containment of communism', predicted that the European Recovery Program (nicknamed the Marshall Plan after the US Secretary of State, General George Marshall) would be 'the last major effort of this nature which our people could, or should, make'.[14] General Marshall's definition of aid was instructive:

> Europe's requirements for the next three or four years of foreign food and other essential products – principally from America – are so much greater than her present ability to pay that she must have substantial additional help or face economic, social and political deterioration of a very grave character.
>
> It is logical that the United States should do whatever it is able to do to assist in the return of normal economic health in the world, without which there can be no political stability and no assured peace. Our policy is directed not against any country or doctrine but against hunger, poverty, desperation and chaos. Its purpose should be the revival of a working economy in the world so as to permit the emergence of political and social conditions in which free institutions can exist. [15]

The rationale whereby hunger, poverty, desperation and chaos have to be eliminated before free political institutions can be established gradually disappeared from US foreign policy. At the global level, the assumption embodied in the United Nations Charter, that international cooperation would be a key method for promoting human rights, proved erroneous.

Notes

1. Commission on Human Rights, Annual report of the Special Rapporteur on the right to education, Katarina Tomasevski, UN Doc. E/CN.4/1999/49, paras. 51–74; E/CN.4/2000/6, paras. 32-65; E/CN.4/2001/52, paras. 64–77, and E/CN.4/2002/60, paras. 22–45.
2. Supreme Court of Spain, Ruling of 24 January 1985.

3. Supreme Court of Canada, *R. v. Jones*, [1986] 2 S.C.R, 284.
4. European Court of Human Rights, *Belgian Linguistic Case*, Judgement of 23 July 1968, Series A, No. 6, para. 5.
5. European Commission on Human Rights, *40 Mothers v. Sweden*, Application No. 6857/74, Decision of 9 March 1977, *Decisions and Reports*, Vol. 9, p. 27; *Ingrid Jordebo Foundation of Christian Schools and Ingrid Jordebo v. Sweden*, Application No. 11533/85, Decision of 6 March 1987, in *Decisions and Reports*, Vol. 51, p. 125.
6. Supreme Court of India, *State of Maharashtra v. Vikas Sahebrao Roundale and Others*, Judgement of 11 August 1992, paras. 2-3 and 12 (1992), 4 *Supreme Court Cases* 435.
7. International Labour Organization, *Equality in Employment and Occupation: General Survey by the Committee of Experts on the Application of Conventions and Recommendations*, 75th Session, 1988, Report III (Part 4 B), para. 33.
8. T. Ohsako (ed.), *Violence at School: Global Issues and Interventions*, International Bureau of Education, UNESCO, Paris, 1997, pp. 40 and 48.
9. Commission on Human Rights, Analytical report of the Secretary-General on internally displaced persons, UN Doc. E/CN.4/1992/23 of 14 February 1992, paras. 70–1.
10. Sub-Commission on the Prevention of Discrimination and the Protection of Minorities, Report on the prevention of discrimination (Prepared by the Secretary-General), UN Doc. E/CN.4/Sub.2/40 of 7 June 1949, paras. 17 (c) and 177.
11. Educable, *No Choice, No Chance*, Save the Children & Disability Action, Belfast, n.d., p. 14.
12. R. Dagenais and C. Mackay, *Christians and the Holy Spirit. Pupil's Book, Primary 7*, Uganda Joint Christian Council, Kampala, 1976, p. 32.
13. K. Tomasevski, *Responding to Human Rights Violations 1946–1999*, Martinus Nijhoff/Kluwer, 2000, pp. 26–33.
14. Quoted from J.L. Gaddis, 'Containment: A reassessment', *Foreign Affairs*, Vol. 55, No. 4, July 1977, p. 876.
15. Address by General George C. Marshall, Secretary of State of the United States, at Harvard University, 5 June 1947, text available on http://www.oecd.org/about/ms-eng2.htm.

RUPTURING THE GLOBAL CONSENSUS

E xpansion of public education was rapid during the first decades after the
Second World War. Enrolments skyrocketed as newly independent states
gave a high priority to educating their populations. Between 1960 and
1975, there was a fourfold increase in primary enrolments, a ninefold increase in
secondary enrolments, and a tenfold increase in tertiary enrolments; expenditure
on education per capita quadrupled.[1] New states of the 1960s introduced
constitutional guarantees of free and compulsory primary education within the
first two years after attaining independence, while this had taken fifty years in the
nineteenth century.[2] The right to education was written into the independence
constitutions of countries such as Chad (1960), Mali (1960), Mauritania (1961),
or Togo (1960). Ten years later, education statistics revealed that promise to have
been a mirage. Primary school enrolments for Chad were 25 per cent, for Mali
15 per cent, for Mauritania 12 per cent, and 53 per cent for Togo.[3] In countries
with higher enrolments, children began but did not complete primary school:

> In Africa, of 100 pupils enrolled in 1960 in the People's Republic of Congo, Dahomey,
> Gabon and Libya, 50 had dropped out of school before the end of primary cycle. In
> Algeria, Burundi and Upper Volta, drop-outs numbered 60 out of 100, in Botswana, the
> Central African Republic and Madagascar over 70, and in Rwanda and Chad over 80. [4]

The will to provide education for all children may have been there, but the
ability to translate it into reality was lacking. International cooperation was
written into the UN Charter to nurture that ability. Global education strategies
anticipated the full realization of the right to education, mandating provision of
free education at the primary level and up the education pyramid to the
university. What was in the 1990s dubbed *education for all* (EFA) had been planned
to be attained by the year 1980 as *universal primary education* (UPE). The right to
education was premised on the ability and willingness of individual states to
generate revenue through taxation to finance education. Those unable to do so
were to be assisted. Full global consensus underpinned attainment of – at least –
free and compulsory primary education throughout the world.

In its own words:
the World Bank's approach to education

The consequence of defining education as a right is the corresponding government responsibility. Law is symmetrical and one cannot exist without the other.

Economists tend to have in-built blinkers that steer them from people to figures. Gunnar Myrdal described the impact of these blinkers thus:

> Place an economist in the capital city of any underdeveloped country and give him the necessary assistance and he will in no time make a plan. ... No sociologist, psychologist or anthropologist would ever think of doing such a thing.[5]

The underlying rationale is epitomized in the much-quoted statement by Paul Samuelson that he did not care what national constitutions said as long as he could write economics textbooks. The World Bank's self-exemption from the rule of law reinforces the argument that economic incentives and disincentives should override law. Rather, a rule book for child labour would have no laws prohibiting it and mandating education instead; it would look like this:

> If politicians were to consider child labor as the result of a rational economic decision rather than just a violation of human rights, they would be cautious about abolishing child labor through prohibition or compulsory schooling laws. Such laws would force households to choose sub-optimal behavior. For instance, if laws forced a poor household, which is living close to the subsistence level, to send their children to school instead of work, an exogenous shock (for example, poor harvest) would have an unnecessarily harsh impact on their welfare. If they were allowed to use child labor, they could take a child out of school if the harvest failed, or they could decide to let one child work permanently, and use the income to smooth consumption. ... From an economist's point of view, policies that do not distort economic incentives, such as subsidies, taxes, or even a consumer boycott, would be preferred over legislation.[6]

The World Bank was not established to deal with child labour or poverty eradication or education. It was set up before the founding of the United Nations, together with the International Monetary Fund, to deal with the industrialized countries. All, except the United States, had been ruined by the Second World War. The World Bank's original aim was to provide loans to facilitate post-war reconstruction. Its early years have been described thus:

> The Bank began its life lending primarily to finance postwar reconstruction in industrial countries and infrastructure projects in developing ones. The Fund began its life as a central part of the fixed exchange rate regime established at Bretton Woods, supporting countries with temporary balance of payments difficulties to forestall damaging trade restrictions. The Bank's lending was long-term and structural; the Fund's short-term and macro-economic.
>
> Their roles began to converge in the mid-1970s, when competition from commercial banks and the abandonment of fixed exchange rate meant industrialized countries no longer needed to borrow from the Fund. Within a few years both institutions found themselves lending to developing countries caught up in the international debt crisis.[7]

The World Bank started lending for education in 1962, eighteen years after it was established. The reasons why not before and why then were explained by two World Bank education staff at the time, George Psacharoupoulos and Maureen Woodhall:

> Education, like other forms of investment in human capital, can contribute to economic development and raise the incomes of the poor just as much as investment in physical capital …
>
> When the Bank was first established in 1944, however, education was not counted among the productive purposes for which it was authorized to provide investment capital. This attitude prevailed right through the 1950s, when official statements of Bank policy took the view that the Bank should concentrate its lending on projects designed to make a direct contribution to the productive capacity of its members …
>
> One of the principal reasons for the shift in thinking was the growing interest during the 1960s in the economic value of education … Before long, economists were trying to measure the contribution of education to economic growth, and many were examining the concept of investment in human capital. … Eventually World Bank policy reflected this recognition that education is a productive investment in human capital. … Education was seen as one of the most important ways of contributing to social progress, and in 1962 the first education project was initiated. The justification for this investment was that education is not only a basic human right, but also a basic component of social and economic development, and that properly planned investments in education pay great economic dividends, especially in the poorest countries.[8]

As this quotation illustrates, education was referred to as a human right in early World Bank thinking. The term disappeared because education was transferred from the public to the private sector with the following explanation:

> Few of the traditional criteria used to determine whether public provision is appropriate apply to education. There are economies of scale in teaching, but not of the kind that justify public involvement. There are also externalities to elementary education: for example, ignoring health and hygiene practices can have deadly consequences; further, society finds it easier to deal with people who can read and sign their names. But these externalities also apply in the case of the production of books and newspapers, and it would be difficult to make a convincing case for public provision of them. Moreover, there is no technical difficulty in charging for education or in excluding from classes those who do not pay. …
>
> However, two aspects of education lead some to believe that it should be a public sector activity. Firstly, many of the beneficiaries – the children – are considered to be too young to make choices for themselves. Second, it is said that government should make the choice for them and should provide the service because parents may not recognize their children's educational needs or have the means to pay for meeting them.
>
> This argument is weak for two reasons. First, it relates not specifically to education, but to all services provided for people who are not able to look after their own affairs. These include not only the very young and the very old, but also those incapacitated by disease. The fact that some people, such as the very young, are unable to look after themselves implies that society has a responsibility to ensure that their interests are not

neglected. But it by no means implies that education should be provided by a public agency.

Second, there is no obvious indication that state provision is the best solution for poor families who cannot afford to pay for their children's education. The needs of these families can be met by systems of student loans, or by scholarships (grants). ... [P]ublic authorities can provide money for the service without providing the service itself. And there are strong arguments for having private institutions serve these people: private institutions are more likely to tailor their curricula to the needs of their clients; they are more likely to be economical in the use of their teachers and of other scarce resources and have greater incentives than government agencies to avoid waste; and private schools are better adapted than state institutions to change their methods to meet new requirements. [9]

This rationale transferred education from the public sector into the free-market mechanism of fee-for-service. The long term effect was that education as a right and corresponding public responsibility disappeared from World Bank documents. The theory was first applied, with disastrous consequences, to Malawi.

School fees: trial-and-error in Malawi

In the contemporary history of introducing fees in primary school, Mateen Thobani's study of Malawi for the World Bank has an important place; the story is summarized in Box 5.1. His argument that to increase school fees would not decrease enrolments and that the poorest would not drop out of school was proved wrong. The government of the time, led by president-for-life Banda, followed his recommendations on school fees, which resulted in plummeting enrolments.[10] The government of president-for-life Banda became a target of an aid suspension by the donor community in 1992,[11] which hastened the change of regime. After the change of government, the elimination of school fees in 1994 led to the immediate doubling of enrolments.[12]

The World Bank's rationale for school fees in Malawi in 1982–83 became known as *the Thobani rule*. It posits that families and individuals ought to pay fees in order to access nominally available public services, otherwise these services would not be available or their quality would become unacceptably low.[13] The importance of education for parents was assessed through their willingness to pay for the education of their children. Thus determined, that willingness translated into the demand for education which was to be matched by an adequate supply. Education was subjected to the free market. However, no matter how willing the parents, their lack of purchasing power could not create a demand. That *excess demand*, stemming from those who might have been willing but were unable to pay, could not be met. Education was thereby converted from an entitlement into a commodity, and the rule of law was replaced by the power of the purse.

The World Bank's self-exemption from the rule of law makes challenging its approach to education difficult, as described in an excerpt from my 2001 annual report to the United Nations Commission on Human Rights in Box 5.2.

Box 5.1 • The World Bank's recipe for curbing demand for primary education in Banda's Malawi

' Thobani suggests as a rule of thumb that whenever there is excess demand for a service, the price should be raised and additional revenues used to expand the service, up to the point where further investment is no longer socially profitable. Provided that the social rate of return can be accurately measured, this method would lead to a more efficient use of resources than rationing, since it would maximize social benefits. Thobani also suggests that it would be more equitable than rationing since the poorest pupils, or regions, are the ones likely to be denied access to schools or to suffer from low-quality schooling. This is the situation in Malawi, where an open-door admissions policy combined with low fees has led to a steady deterioration of quality, as is reflected in the high student–teacher ratio.

Fees for primary education remained unchanged in Malawi between 1975 and 1982, when they covered approximately 20% of total primary school recurrent expenditure. They were originally intended to cover all costs apart from teacher salaries (they were to include textbooks and other materials, for example) but beginning in 1978 the government received a credit from the International Development Association to finance textbooks. When that expired, it had the choice of increasing school fees, providing an additional K3.8 million in subsidy (which represents nearly a third of the total primary education budget), or allowing the supply of textbooks to fail.

Malawi's open-door policy for primary education meant that anyone who could pay fees [of] between K2 and K7.5 could enroll (1K was approximately equal to 1US$ in 1982). At first sight, therefore, it seems meaningless to talk of excess demand for primary school education. Thobani shows, however, that because total expenditure is limited by budgetary constraints, the result is over-crowding and low-quality schooling. The average class size at present is sixty-six; the government's aim is to reduce this to fifty. But at present levels of subsidy the government cannot afford to satisfy the demand for primary education and also raise quality. Thobani therefore argues that for the sake of efficiency primary school fees should be raised and the additional funds used to reduce the average class size and provide more books and supplies. An increase in fees could also be justified on grounds of equity since the poorest pupils are likely to suffer most from a deterioration in quality.

This was the argument of a World Bank report on Malawi in 1981, as a result of which the government of Malawi decided in April 1982 to increase fees in both primary and secondary schools. '

Source: G. Psacharoupoulos and M. Woodhall, *Education for Development: An Analysis of Investment Choices*, World Bank and Oxford University Press, Washington/New York, 1985, pp. 149–50.

Box 5.2 • Dialogue between the Special Rapporteur on the right to education and the World Bank*

* The Special Rapporteur has continued her dialogue with the World Bank as the Commission on Human Rights has requested, and ... visited Washington DC on 27–29 November 2000 in order to discuss key issues with Bank's officials.

The extent to which a single institution can combine different, sometimes mutually conflicting roles (to be a leader in capital markets and to dream about a world free of poverty), is the object of much discussion, within and around the Bank. The Special Rapporteur has encountered this dilemma within the World Bank, with some advocating the abolition of school fees in primary education in order to combat poverty and another tolerating, if not encouraging them, so as to diminish governmental budgetary allocations through cost-sharing. One example is Zambia, where 'reducing cost barriers for the ultra-poor' through bursaries has been emphasized as a method for coping with school fees in primary education.[†] The administrative costs of collecting school fees (necessarily minuscule in poor rural Zambia) and administrating the bursaries demonstrate why primary education was designed to be free.

During her visit, the Special Rapporteur [discussed] how best to overcome the gap between Bank's policies and the international human rights obligations of borrowers regarding the right to education, especially the requirement that primary education be made free of charge. ... She talked to the Inspection Panel, which was set up in 1993 and has been hailed for the explicit acknowledgment that the Bank can violate individual rights.[‡] The Inspection Panel is a non-judicial body, limited to determining whether the Bank has followed its own operational policies and procedures. ... The Panel has noted that Bank's Management 'has used every possible defense to avoid an investigation' and 'has consistently denied violation of policies.'[§] It has mainly dealt with environmental protection and forced displacement because Bank's binding rules have been created for these issues. ... The Panel's remit was revised twice, in 1996 and 1999. The second change has introduced a requirement for complainants to prove deterioration compared to a without-project situation.[**] In education, proof would be required that Bank's lending diminished access to education as was the case in Malawi in the 1980s. At the time, the Bank was endorsing 'judicious use of modest fees' to increase accountability.[††] In 1990, it noted that cost-sharing was more appropriate in post-primary education but hailed significant sums raised by school fees in primary education.[‡‡] Its 1992 commitment to social expenditure, including primary education (OD 8.60),[§§] marked a change, but on-going lending operations may include the charging of fees. Adjustment lending operations should be compatible with, at least, OD 8.60, while it is uncertain what binding rules there are for investment lending, if any. All lending should probably be consistent with the overarching objective of poverty reduction. The Special Rapporteur cannot see the rationale of advocating education as a key to poverty reduction while school fees prevent poor children from access to education, thus closing off their path out of poverty. There is, as yet, no in-house mechanism to ensure that fees have been eliminated from Bank's lending and the Special Rapporteur recommends that this be made a priority.

The Special Rapporteur's meetings with the Inspection Panel as well as Bank's General Counsel, Ko-Yung Tung, included an examination of the sources of operative rules which inform Bank's lending. The former General Counsel, Ibrahim Shihata, has limited the remit of the Inspection Panel to 'the Bank's failure to meet its standards, which are only required by itself and not by any binding rule of law'.*** This has affirmed exemption of the World Bank from any judicial oversight because it enjoys legal immunity before domestic courts and no international litigation has ever been attempted. A unique situation thus persists whereby the World Bank is apparently bound only by those rules which it has created for itself ...'

* Commission on Human Rights, Annual report of the Special Rapporteur on the right to education, Katarina Tomasevski, UN Doc. E/CN.4/2001/52, paras. 31–41.
† World Bank, Program appraisal document on a proposed credit in the amount of SDR 28.5 million to the Republic of Zambia in support of the first phase of the Basic Education Subsector Investment Program (BESSIP), Report No. 19008 ZA, 5 March 1999.
‡ K. Tomaševski, 'The influence of the World Bank and IMF on economic and social rights', *Nordic Journal of International Law*, Vol. 64, 1995, pp. 385–95.
§ E. Umanna (ed.), *The World Bank Inspection Panel. The First Four Years (1994–1998)*, The World Bank, Washington, DC, November 1998, p. 324.
** World Bank, Conclusions of the Board's second review of the Inspection Panel, 20 April 1999, text available at www.worldbank.org/html/extdr/ipwg/secondreview.htm.
†† World Bank, *Education in Sub-Saharan Africa: Policies for Adjustment, Revitalization and Expansion*, Washington, DC, 1988, p. 53.
‡‡ World Bank, *Primary Education*, Washington, DC, 1990, pp. 44–5.
§§ The World Bank's adjustment lending policy, Operational Directive 8.60 of 21 December 1992, specifies that explicit conditionality may be appropriate to enhance the poverty orientation of social expenditures and to sustain their levels.
*** I.F.I. Shihata, 'The World Bank Inspection Panel – A background paper on its historical, legal and operational aspects'. Paper submitted to the Expert Meeting on the Inspection Panel, Lund, Sweden, 23–25 October 1997, mimeograph, p. 28.

Where fees are charged in primary school, those who are too poor to afford the cost nevertheless have to pay them. If they cannot afford them, their children will be penalized by being denied education. Where exemptions are nominally provided, they may be too cumbersome to comply with or too expensive to administer. Thereby, school fees epitomize the key question in development, how to balance benefits and burdens. Even though this is an inherently political issue, it tends to be addressed as 'technical'. This is perhaps why the World Bank's shift into addressing poverty at the turn of the millennium may prove as unsuccessful as it did in the 1970s.

The World Bank launched itself into poverty eradication in the early 1970s, at a time when the words 'basic human needs' were popular in international development jargon. This change emerged from disappointment with the first post-war decades and gained ground with the elevation of the status of the developing countries on the global political agenda, as unresolved controversies about remoulding the international economic order proliferated. The World Bank rapidly adjusted to that change:

> For many, Mr McNamara was the model president. ... Nobody will ever better him as a salesman for the Bank. He launched a compelling moral crusade for a development strategy aimed specifically at alleviating poverty. He backed up his exhortations with a shift in the Bank's own lending priorities to favour the poorest countries and towards projects that would bring the biggest direct benefits to the poor. How much the latter was simply a change of presentation rather than of substance is an issue that is still debated.[14]

Repeating that earlier experiment, the World Bank's mission statement in 1999 pledged 'fighting poverty with passion and professionalism'. Passion may be easy or difficult to assess, but professionalism was made difficult. The World Bank's remit broadened in the 1990s to the political dimensions of development and broadened likewise the professional landscape for in-house economists. The much-quoted 1989 World Bank study on Africa introduced the notion of governance, defined as 'the exercise of political power to manage a nation's affairs'.[15] The Development Assistance Committee (DAC/OECD) followed suit to enquire into 'the nature of relationship between the ruler and the ruled'.[16]

No mention of human rights as safeguards against abuse of power has followed. The World Bank has defined access to the prerequisites of economic growth (including education) as the key to poverty reduction, emphasizing that ethnic, religious and racial minorities are particularly frequent victims of exclusion.[17] In the first series of poverty assessments, ethnic and gender discrimination was identified as an obstacle to poverty reduction in Bolivia, for example, with a call that 'at the very least, legal and regulatory codes should be revised to remove institutionalized discrimination'. Similarly, minorities were found to constitute 'a highly disproportionate share of the rural poor' in China.[18] That institutionalized and/or legalized discrimination was identified in some countries while not in others was left unexplained. Perhaps the question of *why* people are poor could not be subsumed under 'technical' issues, especially as it would have led to denials and violations of human rights. The choice of including or excluding mention of abuses of power must have been left to the discretion of individual teams.

Pressures for a change in 'the international financial infrastructure' intensified in the aftermath of the Mexican, East Asian, Brazilian, Russian, and then Argentinian financial crises. One lesson has been that a deep economic crisis in a country with a history of ethnic or religious strife easily sparks turmoil, and the World Bank has added conflict to its portfolio. Another lesson is that austerity and corruption make an explosive cocktail. Coping with consecutive financial crises focused attention on global financial instability and revealed how little public institutions can do since their role is 'to support rather than supplant private finance'.[19] Public–private partnership was alternatively defined as a panacea for all ills and challenged as crony capitalism. Another challenge originated from widespread protests against the abdication of governmental responsibility – individual and collective – for economic security.

The message of street protests

On 16 April 2000, demonstrators encircled the World Bank and IMF premises where the annual meeting of the two agencies was to be held. Boys and young men naked to their waists demonstrated against 'World Bankenstein' having taken off their 'last shirt', girls with banners inscribed 'Spank the Bank!' gleefully advocated its dismantling. The protest combined a jamboree of students, trade unionists, anti-globalizationists, environmentalists, human rightists and leftists, and attracted a great deal of publicity. That demonstration (with a convenient website address www.a16.org[20]) followed the demonstration of 30 November 1999 (www.n30.org), the 'Battle of Seattle'. Using positive aspects of globalization such as computerization and travel, protesters raised their voices in support of people excluded from the exercise of these privileges. Street protests reiterated Marcuse's 'philosophy of the no',[21] rejecting a model of governance that defined people as human capital. As in the 1960s, the loud and clear 'no' prompted sympathy for the protesters, especially as the policing of street demonstrations toughened.

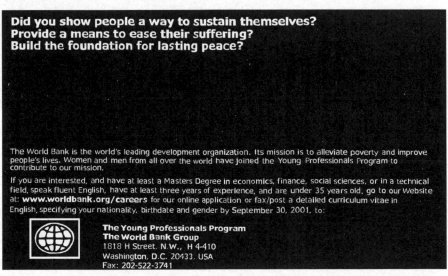

Did you show people a way to sustain themselves?
Provide a means to ease their suffering?
Build the foundation for lasting peace?

The World Bank is the world's leading development organization. Its mission is to alleviate poverty and improve people's lives. Women and men from all over the world have joined the Young Professionals Program to contribute to our mission.

If you are interested, and have at least a Masters Degree in economics, finance, social sciences, or in a technical field, speak fluent English, have at least three years of experience, and are under 35 years old, go to our Website at: **www.worldbank.org/careers** for our online application or fax/post a detailed curriculum vitae in English, specifying your nationality, birthdate and gender by September 30, 2001, to:

The Young Professionals Program
The World Bank Group
1818 H Street, N.W., H 4-410
Washington, D.C. 20433, USA
Fax: 202-522-3741

Fig 5.1. 'World Bankenstein' as Santa Claus? Job advertisement, *Economist*, 25 August 2001

A softer rhetoric emerged from the main targets of the protest. (This was not new, since the protests against structural adjustment had converted the World Bank into a household word and forced it to start talking to actors beyond its usual constituencies, a tactic depicted as the 'three-Is': inviting NGOs, informing them, and ignoring them.)[22] A new strategy was now adopted to alter the image of the Bank, as illustrated in the advertisement for the Bank's Young Professionals Program, conveying an image of easing people's suffering and building foundations for peace.[23]

Two high-level resignations kept the spotlight on the World Bank in 2000. The first was of Joseph Stiglitz, the chief economist, and the second was of Ravi Kanbur, who was in charge of preparing the 2000/2001 World Development Report entitled *Attacking Poverty*. Kanbur did not speak publicly about his resignation, but, in the usual journalistic jargon, 'it was understood' that disagreements had centred on his advocacy of redistribution (taxation and social spending) against the World Bank's preference for 'opportunity'.[24] One code word that typified the underlying conflict was *empowerment* (entailing redistribution), but the winning term was *opportunity*, (entailing reliance on economic growth alone).[25] Translated into education, *opportunity* was defined as follows:

> [E]quitable distribution of opportunities is preferable to a redistribution of existing assets or incomes. This is because education creates new assets and improves social welfare by its spill-over effect, without making anyone worse off. Ensuring access to the opportunity of education by distributing education services more equally, is a win–win policy.[26]

It is easy to understand the ease with which a win–win approach could be advocated, against the battle that would have ensued from defining education as a way to attack (to use World Bank's own term) poverty. A convenient back-up has been to define poverty in absolute terms, and a whole cottage industry emerged estimating how many people in the world live on less than $1 per day. Relative poverty, especially inequality, has been carefully avoided.

Whether a win–win approach could be designed so as to equalize access to education was no longer a pertinent question because the chosen term was not *equality* but *equity*. Pareto efficiency was the point of departure, 'the condition in which no one can be made better off without making someone else worse off',[27] and such efficiency was to be counterbalanced by the notion of equity. What equity means has yet to be determined. Evidence on the intergenerational transmission of inequality is ample. Research carried out in 1998–99 for the UK's ministry of finance (Treasury) has shown that the educational development of 22-month-old infants from the highest class is 14 per cent superior to that of those in the lowest class.[28] This gap expands with time into an abyss unless there is a comprehensive, sustained and well-resourced strategy to equalize opportunities. This vicious circle was described by the United Nations in 1975:

> Inequality in education is the most important means by which occupational selection takes place, and hence the most important means by which advantages and disadvantages are transmitted from generation to generation.[29]

Box 5.3 • Why is the World Bank popular with G-7?

1986

‘ The IBRD's power to lend depends on negotiations between the rich countries – but not quite in the way that is often supposed. … The source of [one of the prevailing myths] is the rule that the Bank can lend out only as much as the sum of its subscribed capital and retained earnings: the so-called one-for-one rule. This implies that the Bank is not leveraged, i.e., that it lends out only what it has been given by governments. But, it is the biggest non-sovereign borrower in the world. The answer to the puzzle is simple. The Bank has two kinds of subscribed capital: paid-in capital and callable capital. As the name suggests, paid-in capital is money that governments have actually handed over to the Bank; more to the point, it is the only money that governments have ever handed over to the Bank. The United States, for example, paid in $635m in 1947, and not another cent for 25 years. … The members have been more generous with the money they never have to hand over. Callable capital consists of funds that the members promise to provide if the Bank ever needs it to service its debts; in other words it cannot be used to meet loan commitments, only to protect the Bank's creditors. Callable capital has risen from $6.4 billion in 1947 to $70.8 billion in 1986. For member governments it is contingent liability that they believe will never fall due. The Bank has never had to call its callable capital. And if it ever happened, the Bank would, in effect, be in receivership.

So, especially since 1960, the Bank has leveraged its paid-in capital as successfully as any bank could wish. These [developments] point to two important facts.

First, although the Bank will soon need an increase in its total capital if it is to expand its lending, it does not necessarily need an increase in paid-in capital … the Bank will be asking not for new cash but, in effect, merely for permission to borrow more in order to lend more. Second, the Bank must continue to be successful as a bank. … As throughout its history, the Bank will stand or fall by its ability to raise money cheaply and lend it to creditworthy borrowers. The two sides of its business – raising money cheaply and lending it prudently – are closely linked. The Bank can borrow its money on competitive terms partly because the international markets understand that the Bank is a safe place for their money.’

1998

‘ In practice the amount of money paid into the World Bank from the budgets of the rich member countries is now nearly zero. The World Bank's large reserves, together with the negligible default rate amongst its borrowers, mean that the liabilities of rich countries are also, in practice, almost zero. Yet power, as expressed in voting rights, continues to be heavily skewed towards rich countries. The Group of Seven large industrial countries have a combined share of 43 per cent, and their influence costs them practically nothing. They can demand more and more environmental and social assessments, push for more special projects in places of geopolitical concern to them without facing the slightest risk of having to pay more. The borrowers have to pay.'

Sources: 'Taking up the running: A survey of the World Bank', *Economist*, 27 September 1986; D. Kapur and R. Wade, 'Paying for privilege', *Financial Times*, 29 September 1998.

The classic technique of appropriating the language of one's critics may have been behind the World Bank's softer rhetoric. The term *equity* has remained undefined but it sounds similar to *equality*. The critique of conditionality has led to insistence on *country ownership*, with the borrower-country government in the driving seat. *Participation* has been emphasized, including through countrywide consultations in the forging of PRSPs (Poverty Reduction Strategy Papers). Country-wide consultations are not cheap and it is likely that the participants did not know that the next generation will be repaying loans thus incurred:

Spending $1.8m (Kshs 140m) to organize workshops about poverty just doesn't make sense to many Kenyans. ... Consultations will take place in 25 of Kenya's 69 districts, followed by the preparation of the Poverty Reduction Strategy Paper by April 2001. 'The talks will enable the affected people to come together and outline their priorities as opposed to the past where decisions were made in boardrooms by government techno-crats,' says Harold Wackman, the World Bank director in Kenya. According to him, the strategy paper is worth more than the amount it will cost. But Beth Mugo, an MP, strongly disagrees: 'The economists in the government must be joking,' he said. 'It is high time they advised the government on how to kick-start the economy. If they are spending the money to build a hospital, one will understand, but seminars and work-shops make no sense.' ... The business analyst Mutahi Mureithi says, 'Let me put it plainly: I think this is good money being flushed down the drain, pure and simple ... I don't think one needs 140 million shillings to hear people say how they want to come out of poverty. What is the point of going all over the country in expensive four-wheel vehicles soliciting views from villagers? Even if the money is coming from the donors, it is still too much of a useless exercise.'[30]

Mutahi Mureithi's optimistic view that it was the donors who were wasting their money on what he deemed to be a useless exercise stems from the blurring of the difference between donors and creditors. The perception that the World Bank is a donor is, unfortunately, widespread. 'Moving the money' in Bank's jargon means providing loans so that they will be repaid, and the cost of countrywide consultations in Kenya will be repaid, as all World Bank loans are. Thus, unlike donors, the World Bank is popular amongst its own potential donors because it is self-financing, as Box 5.3 illustrates.

Outside the rich countries, the World Bank's financing methods are judged differently. While studying the real-life economics that prompted him to set up the Grameen Bank, Muhammad Yunus learned from a destitute woman making bamboo stools that 'people who start with money-lenders only get poorer'.[31] There is no evidence that governments fare any better.

Notes

1. P.H. Coombs, *The World Crisis in Education: The View from the Eighties*, 1985, Oxford University Press, New York/Oxford, p. 267.
2. F.O. Ramirez and J. Boli-Bennett, 'Global patterns of educational institutionalization', in Altbach, P.G. et al. (eds.), *Comparative Education*, 1982, p. 29.
3. UNESCO/IBE, *World Survey of Education Handbook 1955–1971*, UNESCO/IBE, Geneva, 1971.
4. G.C. Breis, 'Stark profile of wastage in education', *UNESCO Courier*, Vol. 25, June 1972, p. 20.
5. G. Myrdal, *The Challenge of World Poverty: A World Anti-Poverty Programme in Outline*, Penguin Press and Pantheon Books, New York, 1970, p. 17.
6. S. Canagarajah and H. Skyt Nielsen, *Child Labour and Schooling in Africa: A Comparative Study*, World Bank, Social Protection Discussion Paper No. 9916, Washington DC, July 1999, p. 22.
7. R. Chote, 'A gruesome twosome', *Financial Times*, 30 September 1998.
8. G. Psacharoupoulos and M. Woodhall, *Education for Development. An Analysis of Investment Choices*, World Bank/Oxford University Press, 1985, pp. 3–4.
9. G. Roth, *The Private Provision of Public Services in Developing Countries*, EDI Series in Economic Development, World Bank/Oxford University Press, Washington, DC, 1987, pp. 29–31.
10. B. Fuller, 'Eroding economy, declining school quality: The case of Malawi', *IDS Bulletin*, Vol. 20, 1989.
11. K. Tomasevski, *Between Sanctions and Elections. Aid Donors and Their Human Rights Performance*, Pinter Publishers/Cassell, London, 1997, pp. 189–90.
12. S. Reddy and J. Vandemoortele, *User Financing of Basic Social Services: A Review of Theoretical Arguments and Empirical Evidence*, UNICEF Staff Working Paper, New York, 1996.
13. P. Penrose, *Planning and Financing Sustainable Education Systems in Sub-Saharan Africa*, Department for International Development, Education Research, Serial No. 7, London, 1998.
14. 'Taking up the running: A survey of the World Bank', *Economist*, 27 September 1986.
15. World Bank, *Sub-Saharan Africa: From Crisis to Sustainable Growth, A Long-Term Perspective Study*, Washington, DC, 1989.
16. DAC/OECD, *Participatory Development and Good Governance*, Development Cooperation Guidelines Series, Paris, 1995, Part III, para. 31.
17. World Bank, *Development and Human Rights: The Role of the World Bank*, Washington, DC, 1998, pp. 14 and 7.
18. World Bank, *Implementing the World Bank's Strategy to Reduce Poverty: Progress and Challenges*, Washington, DC, April 1993, p. 60, 63 and 77.
19. L. Summers, 'The troubling aspects of IMF reform', *Financial Times*, 23 March 2000.
20. 'Mobilization for Social Justice' was the logo of the movement and it described itself

as 'a powerful US movement for economic and human rights and fair trade [which] had its coming-out party at the WTO meetings in Seattle. A range of forces who value human and ecological dignity over corporate profits and trickle-down economics'. A. Beattie, 'Protester wars of "Seattle East" in Washington', *Financial Times*, 10 April 2000.

21. H. Marcuse, *One-dimensional Man: Studies in the Ideology of Advanced Industrial Society*, Beacon Press, Boston, 1964.
22. S. Fidler, 'Opening up to criticism', *Financial Times*, 22 September 2000.
23. *Economist*, 2 September 2000.
24. 'World Bank alters tactic for war on poverty', *Financial Times*, 13 September 2000; 'World Bank report on poverty censored, say aid agencies', *Guardian Weekly*, 21–27 September 2000.
25. 'World Bank report author quits in protest', and 'Kanbur's resignation shows deep strains in World Bank model', *Financial Times*, 15 and 16 June 2000.
26. V. Thomas et al., 'Measuring education inequality: Gini coefficients of education', Working Paper No. 2525, World Bank, Washington DC, 15 December 2000, p.3.
27. J.E. Stiglitz, *Economics of the Public Sector*, W.W. Norton & Company, New York, 3rd edn, 2000, p. 93.
28. HM Treasury, *Persistent Poverty and Lifetime Inequality: The Evidence*, London, March 1999, para 3.06, p. 29.
29. United Nations, *The Realization of Economic, Social and Cultural Rights: Problems, Policies, Progress* by Manouchehr Ganji, Special Rapporteur of the Commission on Human Rights, Publication E.75.XIV.2, New York, 1975, para. 68.
30. J. Kamau, 'IMF and World Bank's "useless exercise"', *New African*, January 2001.
31. M. Yunus, *Banker to the Poor*, Aurum Press, London, 1998, p. 8.

The Impoverishment of Public Education and Its Cost

Chapter 6

When global human rights treaties mandating free primary education were adopted, there was global consensus behind them. Economic growth was high in the first decades after the Second World War, and primary school enrolments rapidly expanded, only to halt later as a result of the economic crises of the 1970s and 1980s and diminished public funding. The deep economic recession that was triggered by the Arab oil embargo in 1973 led to decreased fiscal allocations for education in the North. Primary school enrolments decreased in consequence. The percentage of children aged six to eleven in primary school declined between 1970 and 1984 in Belgium, France, Greece, Ireland, Italy, the United Kingdom, and the United States.[1]

Box 6.1 • From economic optimism to consecutive economic crises

For a large proportion of humanity, economic and social rights mean self-provisioning; only for a much smaller proportion of humanity, does it mean reliance on public services. Human rights treaties followed the latter approach, envisaging heavy reliance on the government as the provider of free public services. There were two reasons for that approach in the 1960s. First, the (subsequently defeated) socialist bloc, led by the Soviet Union, favoured governmental provision of services defined as human rights. Education was monopolized by the government and private schooling was allowed grudgingly, if at all. Second, reliance on government funding, if not necessarily provision, in the West was based on optimistic visions of ever-continuing economic growth and governments' ability to generate and redistribute revenue. That model favoured a strong state, which 'tends to reduce freedom of choice in participation by the individual, but a weak State tends to result in a highly unequal enjoyment of the benefits resulting from the economic activities'.* The European Social Charter, drafted between 1953 and 1961, reflected the *Zeitgeist*. It guaranteed to any person without adequate resources and unable to secure them, access to assistance. The term 'poor' or 'poverty' was strictly avoided. This marked a departure from 'poor laws' and distinctions between 'deserving' and 'undeserving' poor. The charter insisted that recipients of social assistance should not be deprived of their political rights.[†] Moreover, there was a belief at the time that poverty was eliminated, at least in that privileged niche of the world, and that the challenge for the future would be diseases of affluence. John Kenneth Galbraith set the tone in 1958:

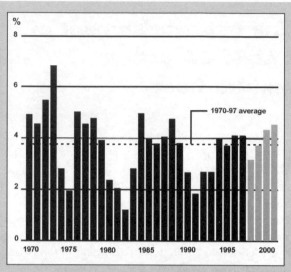

The average global rate of economic growth in % by year

> ... the experience of nations with well-being is exceedingly brief. Nearly all, throughout all history, have been very poor. The exception, almost insignificant in the whole span of human existence, has been the last few generations in the comparatively small corner of the world populated by Europeans. Here, and especially in the United States, there has been great and quite unprecedented affluence, which until now has been the accepted future.[‡]

Thus, the International Covenant on Economic, Social and Cultural Rights, drafted in the 1950s and adopted in 1966, could guarantee the right to an adequate standard of living and 'to the continuous improvement of living conditions'.[§] That optimism was based on the high rate of economic growth at the time. The subsequent downward trend started with the 1973–75 recession which decreased the GDP by more than 3 per cent, and continued with the almost as long and as deep recession in 1981–82. The previous economic optimism was replaced by the return of economics to its traditional role of dismal science.

[*] United Nations, *The Realization of the Right to Development: Global Consultation on the Right to Development as a Human Right*, Centre for Human Rights, Geneva, HR/PUB/91/2, para. 119.
[†] The status of a right to assistance remained an object of dispute: the Independent Committee of Experts interpreted the Charter as laying down such a right, while the Governmental Committee held that no subjective right could be implied. G. Mayer Fabian, 'Social assistance and social services in the case-law of the European Social Charter', in *Proceedings of the Joint Meeting on Human Rights and Social Workers, Strasbourg, 8–10 April 1987*, Doc. DH-ED (87) 13, pp. 31–32.
[‡] J.K. Galbraith, *The Affluent Society*, Houghton Mifflin Company, Boston, 1958, p. 1.
[§] International Covenant on Economic, Social and Cultural Rights, adopted on 16 December 1966, entered into force on 3 January 1976, Article 11 (1).

The plunge in public finance

Consecutive economic crises led to slashed public funding for education in many countries, first developed, then developing. Father Joseph Wresinski, Secretary-General of the Mouvement ATD Quart Monde, described that process as collective arbitrariness.[2] Contrary to what law requires, human rights had the last rather than the first call on public funds. The response to the retrogression in education enrolments which resulted from reduced budgetary allocations was denial that education is a human right.

This need not have happened. Education is not only essential for coping with economic crises but cheap, as it 'makes use of resources which are generally abundant in most developing countries, even during recession and adjustment – labour and locally available materials'.[3] Instead, cutting down fiscal allocations for education was adopted as a global recipe:

> The most serious effect that adjustment can have on primary education is to reduce the central government's allocation to education in general and to primary education in particular. One review found that education's share of total government expenditures declined between 1980 and 1986 in twelve out of thirteen intensely adjusting countries but in only three out of twelve nonadjusting countries with similar levels of economic development. On average, education's share of total government spending declined from 15 to 12 percent in intensely adjusting countries, but increased from 10 to 12 percent in nonadjusting ones. In nine of the twelve intensely adjusting countries, per capita spending on education declined in constant terms.
>
> Another study of countries undertaking structural adjustment from 1979 to 1983 found that a majority (68 percent) reduced government expenditures for education. In 22 percent of the cases, the percentage of spending reduced was less than the aggregate reduction; however, in another 46 percent, education was one of the most vulnerable sectors. Defense proved to be the most protected. In fifteen low- and lower-middle-income countries that underwent structural adjustment programs in the 1980s, public expenditure for education as a percentage of GNP declined from 4.22 percent in 1980 to 3.45 percent in 1985, almost twice the reduction experienced by low- and lower-middle-income countries in general. Other reviews have noted that the greatest impact of adjustment has been felt in Latin America and Sub-Saharan Africa.[4]

Table 6.1 illustrates the drastically decreased allocations for education in 1986 in comparison with 1973, the year before the oil crisis. Decreased public funding for education was possible because it was treated as discretionary. The accompanying calls for the privatization of education were justified by expected budgetary savings. Vito Tanzi of the International Monetary Fund and Ludger Schuknecht of the European Central Bank have warned, however, that 'budgetary savings from more private sector involvement in education are likely to be small'.[5]

Wealthy countries were able to weather the storm as were wealthy families; poor countries and poor children were affected the most. Fees precluded many children from starting school. Budgetary cuts led to what is called *la década perdida*, the lost decade, in South America. Retrogression in education was particularly

Table 6.1 • Allocations for education as % of central government budgets

Country	1972	1986	Country	1972	1986
Argentina	20.0	6.0	Malawi	15.8	11.0
Burkina Faso	20.6	17.7	Mexico	16.4	11.5
Bangladesh	14.8	9.9	Morocco	19.2	16.6
Bolivia	31.3	11.6	New Zealand	16.9	10.9
Brazil	8.3	3.0	Sri Lanka	13.0	8.4
Burma	15.0	11.7	Sweden	14.8	8.9
Chile	14.3	12.5	Tanzania	17.3	7.2
Costa Rica	28.3	16.2	Tunisia	30.5	14.3
Denmark	16.0	9.2	Turkey	18.1	11.9
Italy	16.7	7.2	Zambia	19.0	16.0
Lesotho	22.4	15.5	USA	3.2	1.7

Source: World Bank, *World Development Report 1988,* Oxford University Press, pp. 266–7.

pronounced in Africa. Stephen Lewis, then an advisor for the United Nations Programme of Action for African Economic Recovery and Development, called African education statistics 'a chronicle of despair'.[6] Primary school enrolments declined by 10 per cent.[7]

The new generation was affected by higher rates of illiteracy than the older generations. In Zambia, recorded illiteracy rates grew between 1990 and 1996 to 36 per cent for 14-to-20-year-olds, almost three times higher than the 31-45 age group, whose illiteracy rate was 14 per cent.[8] This retrogression was attributed to global policies on debt servicing and the associated fiscal stringency.

A race towards the bottom line

Although there is disagreement about the optimal level of public funding for education, recommendations converge on around 5–7 per cent of the GNP. The lack of consensus on a specific figure does not undermine agreement that public investment in primary education is necessary and allocations ought to prioritize primary education.

Countries in which public expenditure for education is low (that is, those at the bottom end of Table 6.2, have low enrolments in primary school. They also have young populations and thus a large proportion of school-age children. Low budgetary allocations for education are not correlated solely with their level of poverty. Quite a few have large military expenditure, as Chapter 1 highlighted.

Diminished public funding has led to 'the exclusion of poorer students from education and partial return to educational patterns that perpetuate social inequalities'.[9] Another consequence has been to make parents' duty to educate their children impossible to fulfil due to their inability to afford the cost. Laws on compulsory education were written under the assumption that compulsory

Table 6.2 • Public funding for education in relation to GNP

More than 7%	Barbados, Botswana, Canada, Denmark, Estonia, Finland, Israel, Jamaica, Kenya, Kiribati, Lesotho, Moldova, Namibia, New Zealand, Norway, Poland, Seychelles, South Africa, St Lucia, Ukraine, Uzbekistan, Sweden
6–7%	Congo/Brazzaville, France, Italy, Maldives, Mongolia, Yemen
5–6%	Australia, Austria, Belarus, Belgium, Belize, Costa Rica, Croatia, Czech Republic, Macedonia, Georgia, Iceland, Kyrgyzstan, Lithuania, Malawi, Malaysia, Malta, Mauritania, Morocco, Netherlands, Panama, Portugal, Saudi Arabia, Slovakia, Slovenia, Spain, Switzerland, UK, USA, Venezuela
4–5%	Bolivia, Burundi, Colombia, Comoros, Cyprus, Egypt, Ethiopia, Gambia, Germany, Guyana, Hungary, Iran, Kazakhstan, Kuwait, Mauritius, Mexico, Oman, Thailand, Togo, Trinidad and Tobago, Vanuatu
3–4%	Albania, Argentina, Azerbaijan, Benin, Bulgaria, Chile, Ecuador, Greece, Honduras, India, Japan, Korea, Nepal, Philippines, Qatar, Romania, Russia, Senegal, Singapore, Sri Lanka, St Kitts and Nevis, Uruguay
2–3%	Bangladesh, China, Dominican Republic, El Salvador, Laos, Lebanon, Paraguay, Peru, Tajikistan, Turkey, Zambia, Vietnam
Less than 2%	Chad, Guatemala, Myanmar, United Arab Emirates

Source: UNESCO, *World Education Report 2000*, Paris, 2000, pp 164–7.

schooling would be free. They cannot be enforced when parents cannot afford the cost. Bringing parents to court and imposing fines does not address the underlying problem. Parents cannot afford to pay the fines just as they could not afford the school fees in the first place. Solving the underlying problem necessitates moving upwards, to resource allocation at the local, national and global levels, as well as outwards so as, to integrate human rights into fiscal and economic policies.

The opposite has happened. From a public good protected by public law and public funding, education became a freely traded service. An ideological justification followed: 'We exercise choice when we're going to buy a car or when we're going to buy a box of cereal'[10] and why then would education be any different? Such endorsements of school choice in the US disguise the fact that choice is available only to those with purchasing power. An alternative ideology disappeared with the end of the Cold War, with 'Eastern Europe treated as if it were yet another Third World development problem'.[11] The void created by cutbacks in public funding had profound effects on the losers of the Cold War because no alternative to state-provided services had been allowed. The transition to the free market had one significant omission: 'East European countries have been requested to create capitalism but most people appear to have forgotten that in order to create capitalism you need capital'.[12]

Box 6.2 • What young Europeans learned about the defeat of socialism

In 1995 the 'Youth and History' Survey asked a sample of 31,000 fifteen-year old pupils from 24 countries in Europe, as well as Israel, Palestine, and Turkey, a series of questions about what they had learned about history. A uniform questionnaire with closed questions was administered in order to make results comparable and to start probing into the gap between what is taught, which is fairly well known, and what the pupils actually learn, which is much more important but poorly known. Views about the end of the Cold War revealed an array of pupils' views, many remote from the official curricula:

> We asked, *what do you associate with the changes in Eastern Europe since 1985?* After skipping two items, two stable independent concepts remained: *process of liberation* and *defeat of socialism*. Lithuanian and Spanish adolescents chose a bit above average for *liberation* and *defeat of socialism*. This may be thought to be the best answer, but why in such different states? Was this because one was involved and the other lies far away? Norwegian, Swedish, Finnish and Czech students interpreted the reforms more as *liberation* and less as *defeat of socialism*. Similar interpretations in Nordic social-democrat societies and in post-socialist but neo-liberal countries are not at all trivial. Arabs in Israel and Palestine and Slovenes see little or no *liberation*, but much of *defeat of socialism*.
>
> Perhaps the fact of the small differences between the averages in Russia, Estonia, Ukraine, Bulgaria, Italy and Great Britain is even more astonishing, especially for the societies whose everyday life has changed dramatically since 1985. An enormous proportion of students crossed 'undecided' immediately. For the items *freedom of the member states* (of the Warsaw Pact) and *treason against socialist ideas*, this was 50%. This is much higher than in other item groups. Apparently, they are not indoctrinated by an official version of history but, more surprisingly, there seems no strong social memory in their families and neighbourhoods about the political changes in Eastern Europe. The assumption of fierce and controversial debates about today's crises and improvements, with causal historical attributions of both, was not supported by the students' answers. They reflected a situation of historical oblivion.

Source: J. Van der Leeuw-Roord, *The State of History Education in Europe: Challenges and Implications of the 'Youth and History' Survey*, Edition Körber-Stiftung, Hamburg, 1998, pp. 30–35.

The educational price of the end of the Cold War

The educational retrogression witnessed in Africa in the 1980s was replicated in Eastern Europe and Central Asia in the 1990s. The roots of these retrogressions were identical. The requirement upon the government to finance education was replaced by purchasing power. This resulted, on the one hand, in excellent education for the minority privileged by enrichment and, on the other hand, in less education, or none, for the impoverished majority.

That change was disguised by an altered vocabulary. Education was no longer referred to as a right. *Access to education* became the term of choice as it encompassed the purchase of education. After education entered the realm of trade law in 1995, a dual system emerged. Those who could afford to do so exempted their children from free public education, and only the poorest were left at the mercy of constantly impoverished free education. The dismantling of the Berlin Wall symbolically ended the Cold War at the Brandenburg Gate in November 1989. Its tenth anniversary was marked by 'the Battle of Seattle' in December 1999, a violent protest that forced a temporary halt to the freemarket-ization that had become the hallmark of that decade.

Eastern Europe had consisted of eight countries during the Cold War; subsequently their number increased to thirty; it is possible that the number will grow further. The Hungarian historian Istvan Bibo lamented many times the misery of the small Eastern European states created at the beginning of the twentieth century; now a similar pattern was occurring at the turn of the millennium. Western promises of aid amounted to tens of billions of dollars as the Cold War ended. In 1991, the *Economist* reported that $31 billion had been promised to Bulgaria, Czechoslovakia, Hungary, Poland and Romania; the *Financial Times* cited a promised $45 billion in aid and investment to Eastern Europe.[13] In both parts of Europe, reunification was defined as the former East gaining membership in Western European organizations, first the Council of Europe and then the European Union.[14] In education, that change had to be explained to schoolchildren. What young people actually learned probably differed from what they had been taught. An illustration is provided in Box 6.2.

Literature on the effects of structural adjustment in Africa in the 1980s provided ample evidence that diminishing public funding for education decreased enrolments, and that new generations had less education than their parents. The 1990 World Conference on Education for All, held in Jomtien, Thailand (known as the Jomtien Conference) was convened in the context of a diminishing coverage of primary education in the 1980s, especially in Africa, and of a reduced capacity on the part of the governments to halt further retrogression. The Jomtien+5 meeting noted that 'the downward trend of falling enrolments that we witnessed during the '80s has been reversed'.[15] However, a reversal started in Eastern Europe and Central Asia in the 1990s.

The effects of the diminished ability of the state to generate revenue and finance education are illustrated in Table 6.3. This has led to people valuing education less. Only one in seven young people in Central Europe has rated education as essential for getting ahead in life.[16]

Table 6.3 • Declining schooling for 15-year-olds in the former Soviet Union, 1989–97

Country	15-year-olds in school		Retrogression
	in 1989	in 1997	(%)
Belarus	98	88	−10
Moldova	96	77	−19
Russia	94	88	−6
Ukraine	96	89	−7
Armenia	86	73	−13
Azerbaijan	94	84	−10
Georgia	96	73	−24
Kazakhstan	100	89	−11
Kyrgyzstan	98	85	−13
Tajikistan	99	73	−26
Turkmenistan	96	80	−16
Uzbekistan	98	92	−6

Source: UNICEF Innocenti Research Centre, *Young People in Changing Societies*, MONEE Regional Monitoring Report No. 7, Florence, 2000, p. 44.

Table 6.4 • Development and socio-economic rights at the United Nations Commission on Human Rights

Abbreviated title and number of the resolution	Adoption	Initiators
Right to development (2001/9)	48-2-3	South Africa, Mexico/NAM*
Right to food (2001/25)	52-1-0	Cuba
Unilateral coercive measures (2001/26)	37-8-8	South Africa/NAM*
Structural adjustment/foreign debt (2001/27)	31-15-7	Cuba
Globalization (2001/32)	37-15-1	Pakistan
Access to AIDS medication (2001/33)	52-0-1	Brazil
Toxic waste (2001/35)	38-15-0	Kenya/African Group
Social justice (2001/36)	28-4-21	Cuba
Equitable international order (2001/65)	32-16-4	Cuba
International solidarity (2001/73)	36-16-0	Cuba
Adequate housing (2001/28)	consensus	Germany
Right to education (2201/29)	consensus	Portugal
Economic and social rights (2001/30)	cons./vote	Portugal
Extreme poverty (2001/31)	consensus	France
Women's property rights (2001/34)	cons./vote	Mexico

* NAM = Non Aligned Movement
Source: Commission on Human Rights, Report on the fifty-seventh session (19 March – 27 April 2001), UN Doc. E/CN.4/2001/167 (Parts I and II).

The inverse correlation between freedom of choice and the ability to exercise choice has been typified by UNICEF in an illustrative example from Russia:

> [T]he publication of new children's textbooks and magazines has expanded rapidly. In 1990, 597 different textbooks and 48 children's magazines were published; in 1993 these had risen to, respectively, 807 and 70. Nevertheless, the actual print runs of such publications have plummeted over the same period. For textbooks, they fell by 22 per cent (from 182 to 143 million), and for magazines by 82 per cent (from 22 to 4 million). Therefore, more diversified information may now be available, but fewer children have access to it. [17]

The geopolitical change and the conversion of countries of the former Eastern bloc into aid recipients was reflected in the disappearance of Eastern Europe as a political entity in the United Nations. In the field of human rights, decades of Cold War conflicts were relegated to oblivion. The European Union has become a major actor in human rights, with its policies supported by Eastern European applicants for membership.

Economic and social rights lost their intergovernmental constituency with the end of the Cold War. The continued focus of Western human rights organizations and the media on cold-war human rights agenda aggravated their marginalization. Moreover, the ideological and political battleground is now the right to development rather than economic and social rights. That right is contested for many reasons,[18] and favoured for as many, but its key advantage for many governmental delegations supporting the right to development is that they define it as a right of the state.

As Table 6.4 illustrates, Cuba is the most energetic proponent of development-related human rights, continuing the Cold War within the Commission on Human Rights. A hopeful sign is the emergence of Western European countries as initiators of resolutions addressing economic and social rights. The Commission's preference for consensus means that final texts of resolutions include only those formulations that all governments could endorse. In 2001, resolutions departed from previously used human rights language: 'the right to health' became 'access to health care facilities' while the 'right to housing' became 'adequate housing as a component of the right to adequate standard of living'.[19] These resolutions were critiqued by NGOs as 'meaningless or, worse, negative in both form and contents'.[20]

Notes

1. UNESCO, 'A summary statistical review of education in the world, 1960–1982', Doc. ED/BIE/CONFINTED 39/Rev. 1, July 1984.
2. Speech by Father Joseph Wresinski at an informal meeting with the Committee of Independent Experts (62nd meeting, 21–25 November 1983), 'Social Rights = Human Rights', *Newsletter on the European Social Charter of the Council of Europe*, No. 3, January 1997, p. 4.
3. G.A. Cornia, R. Jolly and F. Stuart (eds), *Adjustment with a Human Face: A Study by*

UNICEF, Vol. I: *Protecting the Vulnerable and Promoting Growth*, Clarendon Press, Oxford, 1987, p. 239.

4. M. Lockheed et al., *Improving Education in Developing Countries*, World Bank/Oxford University Press, Washington, DC, 1991, p. 35.
5. V. Tanzi and L. Schuknecht, *Public Spending in the 20th Century: A Global Perspective*, Cambridge University Press, 2000, p. 184.
6. UNICEF, *The State of the World's Children 1989*, Oxford University Press, New York, 1989, p. 20.
7. C. Colclough and S. Al-Samarrai, *Achieving Schooling for All: Budgetary Expenditures on Education in Sub-Saharan Africa and South Asia*, Institute for Development Studies Working Paper No. 77, Brighton, November 1998, p. 3.
8. D. Atchoarena and S. Hite, 'Training poorly educated people in Africa', International Institute for Educational Planning, Paris, April 1999, mimeograph, p. 62.
9. United Nations, *1985 Report on the World Social Situation*, New York, 1985, No. E.85.IV.2, p. 34.
10. New York City Conference on School Choice, 13 December 2000 (www.manhattan-institute.org/html/nyo_school_choice).
11. G. Merritt, *Eastern Europe and the USSR: The Challenge of Freedom*, Commission of the European Communities and Kogan Page, Brussels and London, 1991, p. 16.
12. M. Glenny, 'Stock-taking of the human rights situation in Europe's emerging democracies', in *Strategies for the Strengthening of Human Rights in Emerging Democracies in Europe: Final Report*, International Helsinki Federation for Human Rights, Vienna, March 1992, p. 17.
13. 'The IMF and the World Bank survey', *Economist*, 12 October 1991; A. Robinson and M. Wolf, 'Europe's reluctant empire-builders', *Financial Times*, 2 December 1991.
14. K. Tomasevski, 'Frontiers to equal rights: New Europe, old divisions', in D. Gomien (ed.), *Broadening the Frontiers of Human Rights*, Scandinavian University Press, Oslo, 1993, pp. 271–86.
15. *Education for All, Achieving the Goal: Mid-Decade Meeting of the International Consultative Forum on Education for All, 16–19 June 1996, Amman, Jordan, Final Report*, p. 7.
16. UNICEF Innocenti Research Centre, *Young People in Changing Societies*, MONEE Project, Regional Monitoring Report No. 7, Florence, 2000, p. 42.
17. UNICEF, *Children at Risk in Central and Eastern Europe: Perils and Promises*, Regional Monitoring Report No. 4, International Child Development Centre, Florence, 1997, p. 56.
18. K. Tomasevski, *Development Aid and Human Rights Revisited*, Pinter Publishers, London, 1993, pp. 45–57.
19. Resolutions 2001/30 and 2001/28, both adopted without a vote.
20. Joint statement by eleven NGOs (endorsed by an additional thirty-two), reproduced in *Human Rights Tribune/Tribune des droits humains*, Vol. 8, No. 1, pp. 15–16.

Unwilling, Unable or
Unlike-Minded? Creators of
Global Education Strategy

Chapter

7

The World Bank's approach to education has created two separate global pathways. The first one, based on international human rights law, has continued, albeit marginalized. As the World Bank has exempted itself from the rule of law and become the largest global source of education finance, its approach has spread quickly and widely. The right to education has been replaced by access to education, government's obligation to ensure free education has been replaced by investment, conditioned by adequate rates of return.

The 1990 World Conference on Education for All (the Jomtien Conference) was a historic event intended to enhance the priority given to basic education through global mobilization around time-bound targets. This mobilization was top-down, in the narrowest sense of this term: international agencies were leading it. Pre-Jomtien developments, including the funding crisis that was largely attributable to the World Bank and wreaked havoc in public education, were relegated to oblivion in the conference. This oblivion was made easy by a new approach and a matching vocabulary.

The Jomtien Declaration did not affirm education as a human right but spoke about 'access to education' and 'meeting learning needs'. Terms with defined meaning, such as 'primary' or 'compulsory' education, were replaced by the term 'basic education'. The previous emphasis on governmental obligations to ensure that education, at least at the primary level, was free and compulsory was replaced by 'societal responsibility' and 'partnership'. The Jomtien Conference followed the Convention on the Rights of the Child within less than a year. An affirmation that all children have the right to education was included in the Convention but not in the Jomtien Declaration. The state-centred model of creating and enforcing law remained confined to the human-rights track. The symmetry between individual rights and the corresponding governmental responsibilities that informs the right to education was excluded from the remit of global education strategy.

Who or what is the 'international community' in education?

The Jomtien Conference marked the World Bank's entry into global education strategy design. The Bank tripled its educational lending during 1988–91, and it soon became the biggest provider of funding for education. As mentioned in Chapter 5, the World Bank finances education through loans, but that difference was obscured by references to the Jomtien Conference as a 'donor-driven process'.[1]

While formally acknowledged as the lead international agency in education, UNESCO was going through a deep crisis at the time:

> As in most other UN agencies, [the] original Western dominance has decreased over the years, especially in the 1960s when dozens of newly independent Third World states joined the organization, the more radical among them forming a tactical alliance with the Soviet bloc. UNESCO as the most 'intellectual' of the UN specialized agencies almost naturally became the battleground of fierce ideological debates, evolving in the mid-1970s into what is usually called 'the UNESCO crisis'.
>
> The issues discussed during the UNESCO crisis [were the] international information and communication order, organizational efficacy and efficiency, and politicization.
>
> The programme of a NWICO (New World Information and Communication Order), which stands in close relation to a New International Economic Order, has brought UNESCO criticism stemming mostly from the Western states. ...Third World governments demanded a new order aimed at obtaining fair shares of communication facilities and of information flows ...
>
> Conflict in the field of organizational efficacy and efficiency focused on Western complaints about excessive budget growth and inadequate financial control. UNESCO was also criticised as being an overcentralized organization. The concentration of staff at headquarters in Paris was considered inappropriate. ...
>
> The Western complaint about excessive politicization was based on the argument that the tasks of specialized agencies were only technical, economic and social in nature. ... The charge of politicization referred predominantly to discrimination against Israel. ...
>
> Already in the early 1970s some of these conflicts brought about changes in the foreign policies of several states, e.g. the temporary withholding of financial contributions to UNESCO by the US Congress and the Israeli cessation in participation. However, in the period from 1978 to 1987, UNESCO went through a severe crisis which threatened its very existence.[2]

In 1984, the United States, United Kingdom and Singapore withdrew from UNESCO, creating 'the tightening of purse-strings'.[3] During the decade of retrogression in education, UNESCO focused on its survival. It was UNICEF's *Adjustment with a Human Face*[4] that exposed the educational cost of structural adjustment. Paradoxically, the World Bank joined key international agencies in preparing and following up the Jomtien Conference.

Those who saw the Jomtien Conference as a donor-driven process were proved right because aid for education increased in its immediate follow-up, as Table 7.1 shows. Nevertheless, that increase was short-lived and did not create a dent in the downward trend of aid. Aid for education has not increased following the 2000 Dakar Education for All Forum, despite pledges that no country committed to attaining education for all would be left without funding. The first meeting of the High Level Group on Education for All, held at UNESCO on 29–30 October 2001, was 'alarmed by the insignificant proportion of overall

Table 7.1 • Basic education in bilateral aid

Country	1995		1996	
	Education % of total aid	Out of which basic	Education % of total aid	Out of which basic
Australia	23.5	2.6	29.0	0.4
Austria	18.1	–	18.7	0.2
Belgium	13.8	0.3	8.6	0.3
Canada	8.8	0.1	7.3	1.2
Denmark	5.2	–	2.8	–
Finland	6.6	–	3.3	1.9
France	21.7	–	31.8	–
Germany	17.8	4.0	15.5	3.6
Ireland	18.0	–	18.0	–
Italy	5.9	–	4.5	0.3
Japan	8.9	0.5	5.5	0.2
Luxembourg	12.2	–	12.2	–
Netherlands	5.5	1.2	7.3	3.3
New Zealand	34.4	0.1	34.4	0.1
Norway	3.0	1.1	6.8	3.0
Portugal	17.6	0.1	24.4	2.5
Spain	8.3	0.9	9.1	0.7
Sweden	8.4	3.1	7.6	4.8
Switzerland	3.0	0.4	4.5	1.0
United Kingdom	10.1	–	9.4	1.4
USA	4.8	1.8	4.6	1.8
DAC average	11.2	1.2	10.8	1.3

Source: OECD/DAC, *Development Co-operation*, 1997 and 1998 Reports.
Note: Data on bilateral aid for education and basic education are included for those donors who made such data available. The figures show that aid for education constituted a little more than one-tenth of total aid, while basic education represented a little more than one-tenth of that. The declared priority for basic education was not translated into corresponding allocations. Aid for education was decreasing while aid for basic education was increasing, though starting from a very small base. For donors such as New Zealand, Australia or France, aid included funding for students from developing countries in the donor country. Australia allocated about 70 per cent of its aid for education to scholarships for foreign university students studying in Australia, while French education aid was used to benefit some 100,000 foreign students in France and 8,000 French teachers working in French-speaking Africa (IWGE, *Education Aid Policies and Practices. Meeting of the International Working Group on Education IWGE, Nice, France, 16–18 November 1994*, pp. 18 and 25). Technical cooperation typically accounted for about two-thirds of aid for education, with '60–80 percent of all education aid commitments spent in recipient countries' (P. Bennell and D. Furlong, *Has Jomtien Made Any Difference? Trends in Donor Funding for Education and Basic Education since the Late 1980s*, Institute of Development Studies, Brighton, March 1997, p. 10).

bilateral and multilateral assistance provided for basic education'.[5] The World Bank decreased its lending for education, from $1.8 billion in the 1990s to just under $1 billion in 2000 and 2001.[6] The downward trend in aid continued and ODA (official development assistance) diminished from $56 billion in 1999 to $53 billion in 2000, and to just over $50 billion in 2001. The European Union's Development Council in November 2001 agreed to increase aid so as to reach the 0.7 per cent target,[7] while in 2002 the US President pledged to double aid within three years.[8] It may therefore be possible to anticipate a reversal of the downward trend in aid, which would be as welcome as it is overdue. The key is G-7. Figure 7.1 shows the performance of the Group of Seven (G-7), the world's leading economies, highlighting the broadening gap between G-7 and the 0.7 per cent yardstick.

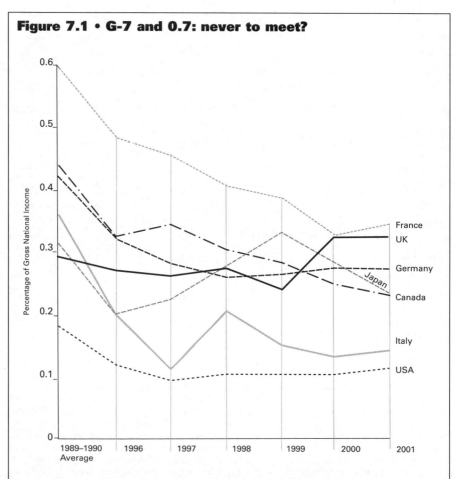

Figure 7.1 • G-7 and 0.7: never to meet?

The recommendation that 0.7 per cent of GNP should be allocated to development aid has been translated into reality by small rather than large donors. Hence, the landscape of aid looks depressing as total aid continues its downward trend. The trend-setters are the largest donors, G-7. With the average 0.2 per cent of the GNP, G-7 countries' aid sank to just above $50 billion in 2002. Raising it to 0.7 per cent would treble annual aid flows.

Consensus as a recipe for inaction

Global summits started with children in 1991, the environment in 1992, human rights in 1993, population in 1994, and social development and women in 1995. Each topic was revisited at the turn of the millennium. If human rights were explicitly addressed by only one of these summits, controversies have spanned them all. Different from law-making, which is a protracted and tedious process, global summits generate political commitments and operate by the rule of consensus.

During the first summit, on children, draftspersons were careful to avoid disputes about the rights of the child. The Convention on the Rights of the Child, which had just come into force three weeks before the summit, was not discussed but taken as a fact.[9] This was not repeated at the follow-up summit on children, in 2002, and the rights of the child were opened for renegotiation. Indicatively, the final text of the Special Session on Children, after eighteen months of consensus building,[10] left two key words to be agreed upon before the meeting could adjourn – *rights* and *resources*.

The Conference on Human Rights in Vienna, in June 1993, created much controversy because the originally expected global endorsement of universal human rights did not happen. The Vienna Declaration and Programme of Action reaffirmed the universality of human rights ('the universal nature of [human] rights and freedoms is beyond question') but added an escape clause:

> ... while the significance of national and regional particularities and various historical, cultural and religious backgrounds must be borne in mind, it is the duty of states, regardless of their political, economic and cultural systems, to promote and protect all human rights and fundamental freedoms.[11]

The term *particularities* derived from the Asia-Pacific Regional Meeting.[12] This new term proved a bone of contention at the Cairo conference one year later. Its final document affirmed universally recognized rights, but posited 'full respect for the various religious and ethical values and cultural backgrounds' and prioritized national sovereignty over human rights, stating: 'the implementation of the recommendations contained in the Programme of Action is the sovereign right of each country'.[13] Moreover, the Cairo document included reservations of twenty-two governmental delegations.[14] The Social Summit in Copenhagen, in March 1995, mentioned human rights sparingly, and government human rights obligations not at all.[15] Such outcomes reflect the minimum that proved acceptable to all, 'pallid, inoffensive wish lists that quickly disappear into bureaucratic oblivion after the signing ceremonies'.[16] Wrongs are listed without pointing to wrongdoers; commitments are written without defining who is responsible for translating words into deeds; accountability for having used the means that defy the professed ends does not get a mention.

The practice of following up each global summit has immensely increased the density of development diplomacy. Each global summit is preceded by preparatory meetings, where a text to be adopted at the summit is negotiated, or even

Box 7.1 • Words worth $300 million: outcomes of Jomtien and Dakar compared

Jomtien (1990)	Dakar (2000)
Every person – child, youth and adult – shall be able to benefit from educational opportunities designed to meet their basic learning needs.	We re-affirm ... that all children, young people and adults have the human right to benefit from an education that will meet their basic learning needs ...
Education is a fundamental right for all people, women and men, of all ages, throughout the world.	Education is a fundamental human right.
Universal access to, and completion of, primary education (or whatever higher level of education is considered as 'basic') by the year 2000.	Ensuring that by 2015 all children, particularly girls, children in difficult circumstances and those belonging to ethnic minorities, have access to and complete free and compulsory primary education of good quality.
Meeting basic learning needs constitutes a common and universal human responsibility. It requires international solidarity and equitable and fair economic relations in order to address existing economic disparities.	Achieving Education for All will require additional support by countries and increased development assistance and debt relief for education by bilateral and multilateral donors, estimated to cost in the order of $8 billion a year.

Note: Negotiation of the final text adopted at Dakar started in 1999 from a thirty-page draft and ended with a five-page text in April 2000. Difficulties in reaching an agreement on collective commitments which the Dakar Conference was to finalize thus must have been considerable. The cost of the process leading to the Dakar Conference was $300 million. There were few financial commitments to carry out whatever would be agreed in Dakar; the $300 million was apparently spent to review the situation and reach an agreement that ultimately could not be reached – what to do after the conference ended to reverse the ill fate of education in the allocation of public funding. Dominique Marlet of Education International obtained the figure of $300 million in an interview with Svein Osttveit, the then Executive Secretary of the Education for All Forum, on 17 August 1999 (www.ei-ie.org) and publicised it within the Global Education Campaign on 9 May 2000 (mailing_list_global_edu_campaign@ei-ie.org). The full text of the five-page final document which was adopted by the Dakar Conference, and the supplementary text (entitled 'Notes on the Dakar Framework for Action') which was subsequently developed by the World Education Forum Drafting Committee on 23 May 2000, are available at http://www2.unesco.org/wef/en-conf/dakframeng.shtm

Sources: *World Declaration on Education for All and Framework for Action to Meet Basic Learning Needs*, Adopted by the World Conference on Education for All, 5–9 March 1990, Jomtien, Thailand, UNESCO, Paris, April 1990. *The Dakar Framework for Action – Education for All: Meeting Our Collective Commitments*, Text adopted by the World Education Forum, Dakar, Senegal, 26–28 April 2000.

finalized.[17] A structure is usually established to follow up the summit, resulting from the iron rule of intergovernmental diplomacy: if you cannot commit yourself, committee yourself. Each global summit sets a price tag on the funding necessary to achieve agreed goals that tend to involve around a ten-fold increase in existing allocations. In education, global estimates of funding needed ranged between 'OXFAM's $8 billion a year and the UNESCO Institute for Statistics's $15 billion'.[18] At the time, aid for education alternated between $700 million, estimated by UNESCO, and $500 million, estimated by the Global Campaign for Education.[19] The abyss between aid needs and aid flows provides a recipe for inaction. Minute funds justify failure to attain posited targets; funds are kept minute because posited targets have not been attained.

Like the global summits, the Jomtien Conference on education was followed by the World Education Forum (known as the Dakar Conference) ten years later. The documents were similar, as Box 7.1 shows. A debate on whether education was or was not a human right was probably a sideshow. On the positive side, the advocates of the selling and purchasing of education lost the battle, as references to education as a right were included in the final document. On the negative side, they won the war, because there was no financial commitment to education for those without purchasing power. The World Bank's statement at the World Education Forum reinforced that slant by referring to free primary education as a long-term plan, to be attained in the year 2015.[20]

Fuzzy vocabulary and governance to match

The vocabulary generated in Jomtien, Dakar, and a host of other global summits requires us to move into the world of Alice-in-Wonderland to remind ourselves that words are weapons rather than labels:

> 'When I use a word,' Humpty Dumpty said in a rather scornful tone,'it means just what I choose it to mean – neither more nor less.'
> 'The question is,' said Alice, 'whether you can make words mean so many different things.'
> 'The question is,' said Humpty Dumpty, 'which is to be master – that's all.'[21]

The difference between having the right to education and purchasing education was eradicated through the term *access to education*. Moreover, language of rights was transposed into that of commercial transactions, using the term *rights* for sharcholders or creditors.[22] UNESCO has highlighted the danger of depleting the language of rights of its original meaning:

> In so far as the 'right to lifelong learning' is understood to include a 'right' to continuing education, it would seem in practice to amount to little more than the 'right' of any citizen to participate, at his or her own expense, in the market for goods and services generally, with more or less encouragement from public funds depending on the situation in individual countries.[23]

The 1990s were a time of linguistic change within the United Nations. Food and agricultural *problems* were renamed 'food and agricultural *development*',[24] 'World *Debt*' tables became as of 1997 'Global *Development* Finance' tables. The new vocabulary of Jomtien and Dakar included terms such as *participation*, that are amenable to widely different interpretations. In Laos the term is used to describe the charging of user fees for education: 'Many communities are significantly involved in school affairs by contributing funds [and] providing labor for construction'.[25]

The Jomtien Conference inaugurated the term *partnership*[26] to depict relations between creditors and debtors, governments and NGOs. This term assumes that the interests of the relevant actors are identical, or at least compatible. Once everybody is allied to everybody else, joint action will flow naturally. The underlying interests, however, tend to be different, often conflicting. *Partnership* does not accurately reflect the relations between a creditor holding a chequebook and a government which desperately needs that cheque. A relation of *partnership* between NGOs and governments is not suggested by the first sentence of Amnesty International's 1993 report: 'Mass murderers are still on the loose. They are called governments and the scale of their crimes defies belief'.[27]

Box 7.2 • What changes would human rights have made?

The term *rights-based development* spread within the donor community at the turn of the millennium. The rights of actors funding and carrying out development interventions (*developers*) had always been protected but not the rights of beneficiaries, who were treated as objects of development interventions (*developees*) with *developers* retaining all the rights. It is against this heritage that the term *rights-based development* was coined.

In the words of Clare Short, Britain's Secretary of State for International Development, three changes are needed to make development aid rights-based:

- 'If we want to work for human rights we must be willing to take risks and reach out where we can, rather than sit smugly at home and feel good about hectoring governments that oppress their people;

- 'This new approach also has implications for the way we work. In our White Paper, the Government commits itself to a rights-based approach to development. This means making people the central purpose of development. Not by speaking or acting on their behalf, but by allowing them to speak for themselves – to articulate their own interests and needs;

- 'Strategies for development should not be a secret deal between governments – done behind closed doors.' *

---

* *All Human Rights for All. A Speech by Clare Short, Secretary of State for International Development to the Law Society*, Department for International Development, London, 3 December 1998, p. 6.

The Jomtien description of governments as natural partners of NGOs in 1990, and their description as mass murderers in 1993, depict two sides of the same coin: governments are the principal protectors as well as violators of human rights. How human rights could have influenced development diplomacy is illustrated in Box 7.2.

Human rights were designed to protect people against abuses of power by their own governments. The role of international agencies was defined as facilitating the implementation of human rights obligations by individual governments. The system was designed as state-centred. UNESCO, the World Bank, UNICEF, the UN Development Programme (UNDP) and the UN Population Fund (UNFPA) were key actors at Jomtien and Dakar, but the heads of these agencies later pointed to the need 'to build leadership and mobilize resources for education'.[28] Who they were addressing remains unknown. Easier to understand, if difficult to accept, was *a chance* for all children to go to school, as they put it in their joint article. The use of the term *chance* suggests a lottery – some children are lucky to have wealthy and committed parents or governments, others have had no such luck. The World Bank had already gone one step further, opting for 'a chance to learn' for African children,[29] making the difference between *the right to education* and *a chance to learn* painfully clear.

Can impoverished basic education help eliminate poverty?

Human rights work focuses on the means to achieve postulated ends and mechanisms to challenge and remedy failures to attain them. The problem in projecting the goals into the future is that it takes away the edge from the need to make a difference now. The duty to today is dodged by projections for tomorrow. A commitment to specified ends without a corresponding commitment to the means necessary to attain them leaves the ends unattained, reflected in strong nouns and weak verbs. Willing the ends entails an obligation to will the means as well. The goal of securing education for all children has not been attained as yet. The year 2015 may record yet another failure unless responsibilities are specified and remedial measures are in place.

The 1990s will be remembered for having converted education from a human right into a development objective, at a time when the key development goal is to halve the number of people living in absolute poverty. But a lottery-based determination of those to be left out clashes with the very notion of rights. Planning to leave half of all poor people still in poverty after the target year necessitates asking who will be left out, by whose criteria, and – most important – why. The human rights approach prioritizes law in holding governments accountable for their pledges, individually and collectively; indeed, it sees law as indispensable. Once a pledge becomes a human rights obligation, failure to attain agreed ends by specified means becomes a violation, to be redressed by compensating the victims and ensuring that it does not happen again.

The *2001 Monitoring Report on Education for All* alluded to problems with both ends and means:

> Though universal primary enrolment remains the principal means of ensuring basic education for all, it is limited to those in the appropriate age group, those for whom schools are accessible and, in many cases, those who can afford the costs of schooling. [30]

Alongside cost, usefulness of education influences parental choices. Disillusionment with education that produces armies of unemployed graduates is well known throughout the world and demonstrates the necessity of adapting education to children's future. When this is not done, parental choice not to send their children to school may look like this:

> People who do not send their kids to school cannot solely be discarded as 'ignorant' but might have made a rational choice. Firstly, education is conducted in French, the official language, which is not spoken by most people. When children come to school, they first have to learn French before they may be able to access other subjects. Secondly, unemployment is common among the youth with years in school. The economic incentive to send children to school is thus less convincing today. A main problem is that many children who go to school do not return to farm work any longer. To send children to school might constitute a double loss: first they cannot participate in farming and herding and thus contribute to subsistence, and, second, they might be able to get a job after school but would be unwilling to accept farming again. [31]

Redesign of formal schooling so as to enable young people to create their livelihood and to make it attractive for them to do so remains a challenge yet to be met. This challenge has been exacerbated by the exclusive focus on basic education, which has eliminated support for secondary and university education in developing countries. All available evidence, however, indicates that the key to reducing poverty is *secondary* rather than primary education. The foundation necessary to enable individuals 'to build up their human capital' is upper-secondary education.[32] South Korea has found that secondary education had the 'crucial relationship with economic growth'.[33] The United Nations Economic Commission for Latin America and the Caribbean (ECLAC) has found that young people have to complete secondary education to achieve an 80 per cent probability of avoiding poverty; its subsequent research has confirmed that 96 per cent of families where the parents have less than nine years of education live in poverty.[34]

Danida's 2001 Education Policy stated that 'much of education offered after basic and primary level is of little utility to the daily lives of people and their income potential'.[35] This harsh indictment assumes that basic education was, is, or will be useful to people's daily lives, but not post-basic education. If children start school at the age of six, and complete their primary education at the age of eleven, how could they possibly help to eliminate poverty while still below the minimum age at which they are allowed to work? Similarly myopic visions were put into practice in Kosovo, revolving around ethnicity and religion, autonomy and statehood, forgetting the price the young have to pay when the survival of their families is jeopardized:

Table 7.2 • Gross enrolment in secondary education, 1995–97

Percentage	Male	Female
Over 100	Australia (150%), Austria (105%), Belgium (142%), Canada (105%), Denmark (120%), Finland (110%), France (112%), Germany (105%), Iceland (109%), Ireland (113%), Korea (102%), Netherlands (134%), New Zealand (110%), Norway (121%), Portugal (102%), Spain (116%), Sweden (128%), United Kingdom (120%)	Australia (155%), Austria (102%), Belgium (151%),Canada (105%), Denmark (122%), Estonia (108%), Finland (125%), France (111%), Germany (103%), Iceland (108%), Ireland (122%), Korea (102%), Netherlands (129%), New Zealand (116%), Norway (116%), Portugal (111%), Spain (128%), Sweden (153%), United Kingdom (139%)
75–100	Bahrain (91%), Barbados (90%), Belarus (91%), Brunei (71%), Bulgaria (77%), Croatia (81%), Cuba (76%), Czech Rep. (97%), Estonia (100%), Greece (95%), Hungary (96%), Iran (81%), Italy (94%), Japan (99%), Latvia (82%), Lebanon (78%), Lithuania (85%), Malta (86%), Poland (98%), Qatar (81%), Romania (79%), Russia (83%), Slovakia (92%), Slovenia (90%), Switzerland (94%), United States (98%), Uruguay (77%)	Argentina (81%), Bahrain (98%), Barbados (80%), Belarus (95%), Brunei (82%), Chile (78%), Croatia (83%), Cuba (85%), Czech Rep. (100%), Greece (96%), Guyana (78%), Hungary (99%), Italy (95%), Japan (100%), Latvia (85%), Lebanon (85%), Lithuania (88%), Luxembourg (75%), Malta (82%), Poland (97%), Qatar (79%), Romania (78%), Russia (91%), Singapore (77%), Slovakia (96%), Slovenia (93%), South Africa (91%), Sri Lanka (78%), Switzerland (88%), United States (97%), Uruguay (92%)
50–75	Algeria (65%), Argentina (73%), Botswana (61%), Cape Verde (54%), Chile (72%), China (72%), Colombia (70%), Ecuador (53%), Egypt (80%), Guyana (73%), India (59%), Indonesia (55%), Iraq (51%), Jordan (52%), Kuwait (65%), Luxembourg (72%), Malaysia (58%), Mauritius (63%), Mexico (64%), Namibia (56%), Oman (68%), Panama (60%), Peru (72%), Philippines (71%), Singapore (70%), South Africa (75%), Sri Lanka (71%), Swaziland (55%), Macedonia (64%), Tunisia (66%), Turkey (68%), Yemen (53%), Zimbabwe (52%)	Algeria (62%), Botswana (68%), Bulgaria (75%), Cape Verde (56%), China (65%), Colombia (75%), Ecuador (55%), Egypt (70%), Iran (73%), Jordan (54%), Kuwait (65%), Malaysia (66%), Mauritius (66%), Mexico (64%), Mongolia (65%), Namibia (66%), Nicaragua (53%), Oman (65%), Panama (65%), Peru (67%), Philippines (75%), Swaziland (54%), Macedonia (62%), Tunisia (63%)

Table 7.2 • cont.

Percentage	Male	Female
25–50	Afghanistan (32%), Albania (37%), Bangladesh (25%), Bolivia (40%), Brazil (31%), Cambodia (30%), Cameroon (32%), Congo (32%), Costa Rica (47%), Côte d'Ivoire (33%), Dominican Rep. (34%), El Salvador (30%), Gambia (30%), Ghana (45%), Guatemala (26%), Honduras (29%), Kenya (26%), Laos (34%), Mongolia (48%), Morocco (44%), Nepal (49%), Nicaragua (45%), Pakistan (33%), Paraguay (42%), Syria (45%), Togo (40%), Venezuela (33%), Zambia (34%)	Albania (38%), Bolivia (34%), Brazil (36%), Costa Rica (50%), Dominican Rep. (47%), El Salvador (35%), Ghana (29%), Honduras (37%), India (39%), Indonesia (48%), Iraq (32%), Lesotho (36%), Morocco (34%), Paraguay (45%), Syria (40%), Turkey (48%), Venezuela (46%), Zimbabwe (44%)
0–25	Benin (24%), Bhutan (7%), Burkina Faso (11%), Burundi (9%), Central African Rep. (15%), Chad (15%), Comoros (21%), Djibouti (17%), Eritrea (24%), Ethiopia (14%), Guinea (20%), Guinea-Bissau (9%), Haiti (21%), Lesotho (25%), Madagascar (16%), Malawi (21%), Mali (14%), Mauritania (21%), Mozambique (9%), Niger (9%), Papua New Guinea (17%), Rwanda (12%), Senegal (20%), Sudan (21%), Tanzania (6%), Uganda (15%)	Afghanistan (11%), Bangladesh (13%), Benin (10%), Bhutan (2%), Burkina Faso (6%), Burundi (5%), Cambodia (18%), Cameroon (22%), Central African Rep. (6%), Chad (4%), Comoros (16%), Congo (19%), Côte d'Ivoire (16%), Djibouti (12%), Eritrea (17%), Ethiopia (10%), Gambia (19%), Guatemala (24%), Guinea (7%), Guinea-Bissau (4%), Haiti (20%), Kenya (22%), Laos (23%), Madagascar (16%), Malawi (12%), Mali (7%), Mauritania (11%), Mozambique (5%), Nepal (24%), Niger (5%), Pakistan (17%), Papua New Guinea (11%), Rwanda (9%), Senegal (20%), Sudan (19%), Tanzania (5%), Togo (14%), Uganda (9%), Yemen (14%), Zambia (21%)

Source: UNICEF, *The State of the World's Children 2001*, New York, 2002.

> Adolescents out of school and work have requested intensive courses for computer and foreign language skills so that they become qualified to work for international organizations [and pinpointed the key issue:] if parents had jobs, adolescents would have to work less.[36]

Table 7.2 reproduces statistics on secondary-school enrolments disaggregated by sex. In the bottom category of countries, where enrolments are low, the future will show whether poverty reduction could be attained with only primary education. There is a close connection between secondary education and the age of marriage and childbearing (dealt with in Chapter 11). The data highlight the current focus on girls' education, but also demonstrate changes in the gender balance, especially in the uppermost right cell. The gender balance in secondary enrolments has moved in favour of females in many countries, as Table 7.2 shows, and the data are similar for universities.

Notes

1. J. Hallak, 'Education for all: high expectations or false hopes?', *IIEP Contributions* No. 3, International Institute for Educational Planning, Paris, 1991, p. 2.
2. P. Billing et al., 'Industrialized countries and the UNESCO crisis', *Cooperation and Conflict*, Vol. 28, No. 2, 1993, pp. 144–6.
3. M.C. Lacoste, *The Story of a Grand Design: UNESCO 1946–1993*, UNESCO Publishing, Paris, 1994, p. 211.
4. G.A. Cornia et al. (eds), *Adjustment with a Human Face. Protecting the Vulnerable and Promoting Growth, A Study by UNICEF*, Clarendon Press, Oxford, 1987.
5. Communiqué from the High-Level Group on Education for All, First Meeting, UNESCO, Paris, 29–30 October 2001, www.unesco.org/education/efa, para. 10.
6. IMF-World Bank Development Committee, 'Education for dynamic economies: Accelerating progress towards Education for All (EFA)'. Paper prepared by the staff of the World Bank, Doc. DC2001-0025, 18 September 2001.
7. 'EU agrees on joint aid target of 0.7 per cent', *Development Today*, No. 17–18/01, 9 November 2001.
8. The pledge was that 'the United States would be increasing development assistance by 5 billion dollars over the next three budgetary years … [to] achieve in the third year of the President's plan an annual level of assistance that would be 5 billion dollars larger than had previously been foreseen'. Press conference transcript, Alan P. Larson, US Undersecretary of State for Economic, Business and Agricultural Affairs, United Nations Conference on Financing for Development, Monterrey, Mexico, 19 March 2002.
9. The summit endorsed the Convention, and UNICEF published it alongside final documents of the Summit. *First Call for Children: World Declaration and Plan of Action from the World Summit for Children. Convention on the Rights of the Child*, UNICEF, New York, December 1990.
10 'Governments "say yes" as agreement is reached on global goals and plan of action for world's children'. United Nations Press release of 11 May 2002, text at www.unicef.org/specialsession/press/02pr28outcome
11. Vienna Declaration and Programme of Action, World Conference on Human Rights, Vienna, 14–25 June 1993, UN Doc. A/CONF.157/23 of 12 July 1993, paras. 1 and 5.
12. The Bangkok Declaration, Report of the Regional Meeting for Asia of the World

Conference on Human Rights, Bangkok, 29 March–2 April 1993, UN Doc. A/CONF.157/ASRM/8 and A/CONF.157/PC/59 of 7 April 1993, pp. 1–7.

13. Programme of Action of the International Conference on Population and Development, Report of the International Conference on Population and Development, Cairo, 5–13 September 1994, UN Doc. A/CONF.171/13 of 18 October 1994, pp. 13–14.

14. Afghanistan, Argentina, Brunei Darussalam, Dominican Republic, Ecuador, Egypt, El Salvador, Guatemala, Holy See, Honduras, Iran, Jordan, Kuwait, Libya, Malta, Nicaragua, Paraguay, Peru, Philippines, Syria, United Arab Emirates and Yemen submitted reservations.

15. Copenhagen Declaration, United Nations Information Centre for the Nordic Countries, March 1995, Commitment 1, para. (f).

16. Eugene Linden, 'Showdown in Cairo', *Time*, 5 September 1994, pp. 40–41.

17. The conference on development finance in Monterrey, in March 2002, led to an NGO protest because 'the adoption of the Consensus in advance of the Conference was undermining the credibility of the process itself'. The NGO Caucus formally declared that it was not part of the consensus since that document 'was not a sound basis for combating poverty or advancing economic, social and cultural rights'. United Nations Press Release, 'Monterrey Conference on Development Financing concludes; Participants resolve to eradicate poverty, achieve sustainable economic growth', 25 March 2002, p. 21.

18. 'Education for All: The price tag'. Leaflet issued by the Dakar Follow-up Unit, Education Sector, UNESCO, December 2001.

19. 'Every Child in School: Are the G8 serious?' Global Campaign for Education Briefing Paper, 23 June 2002.

20. The statement of the World Bank's president, James Wolfensohn, included this remark: 'Here I also want to pay special tribute to the efforts of the NGOs involved in the Global Campaign for Education. They have played an important advocacy role. We fundamentally agree with their call that by the year 2015 free education be a right for all children up to age 15.' J.D.Wolfensohn, 'A time for action: Placing education at the core of development, Presentation at the World Education Forum, Dakar, 27 April 2000', available at http://www2unesco.org/wef/en-news/coverage_speech_wolfen. shtm

21. L. Carroll, *Through the Looking-Glass and What Alice Found There*, (first published in 1871), Victor Gollancz, London, 1986, p. 108–9.

22. The World Bank's two indicators chosen to assess the legal infrastructure underpinning its recent focus on knowledge-based economy have been creditors' and shareholders' rights. World Bank, *Knowledge for Development: World Development Report 1998/99*, Oxford University Press, New York, 1999, pp. 178 and 181.

23. UNESCO, *World Education Report 2000: The Right to Education – Towards Education for All throughout Life*, UNESCO, Paris, 2000, p. 60.

24. UN General Assembly, Food and agricultural development, resolution 47/149 of 18 December 1990.

25. Asian Development Bank, *Lao People's Democratic Republic: Education Sector Development Plan Report*, Manila, Philippines, July 2000, p. 7.

26. At Jomtien, providing basic education for all was 'the unique obligation' of national, regional and local authorities; the declaration added that the authorities could not be expected to carry out that obligation alone and partnerships would be necessary with families, religious groups, local communities, non-governmental organizations as well as the private sector (World Conference on Education for All – *World Declaration on Education for All and Framework for Action to Meet Basic Learning Needs*, Jomtien, 1990). At Dakar, the pledge to achieve the Jomtien goals was assigned evenhandedly to 'governments, organizations, agencies, groups and associations represented at the World Education Forum' (*The Dakar Framework Education for All: Meeting Our Collective Commitments*, Dakar, Senegal, 26–28 April 2000, para. 8).

27. Amnesty International, *Getting Away with Murder: Political Killings and Disappearances in the*

1990s, London, October 1993, p. 1.

28. Joint statement by Koichiro Matsuura (Director-General of UNESCO), James Wolfensohn (President of the World Bank), Thoraya Obaid (Executive Director of UNFPA), Carol Bellamy (Executive Director of UNICEF), and Mark Malloch Brown (Administrator of UNDP) entitled 'For 113 million children, school would be a good start', published in the *International Herald Tribune*, 5–6 May 2001.

29. *A Chance to Learn: Knowledge and Finance for Education in Sub-Saharan Africa*, World Bank, Washington, DC, February 2001.

30. *2001 Monitoring Report on Education for All*, UNESCO/EFA, Paris, October 2001 (www.unesco.org/education/efa).

31. S. Hagberg, *Burkina Faso: Profiles of Poverty*, Sida, Stockholm, June 2000, p. 38.

32. OECD, *Human Capital Investment: An International Comparison*, Paris, 1998, p. 93.

33. South Korean Ministry of Education, *The Development of Education: National Report of the Republic of Korea*, Seoul, September 1996, p. 1.

34. Economic Commission for Latin America and the Caribbean, *The Equity Gap: Latin America, the Caribbean and the Social Summit*, Santiago de Chile, 1997, p. 116; *Equidad, desarrollo y ciudadanía* (Equity, Development and Citizenship), Santiago de Chile, 2000, p. 72.

35. Danish Ministry of Foreign Affairs, *Education, Danida Sector Policies*, Copenhagen, August 2001, p. 25.

36. 'Promoting Kosovar adolescent/youth protection and capacities: Youth-identified problems and solutions', Kosovar Youth Council, June 2000, mimeograph. Text available at http://www.war-affected-children.org/kosovo-e.asp.

Chapter 8

Painfully Visible Loss of the Right to Education: Transfigured University

Rights-based education reaches far beyond the education sector. Budgetary allocations are prioritized: military expenditure often crowds out all civilian items, including education. The hierarchy of expenditure is indicative of the commitment to human rights or the lack thereof. Indivisibility is a human rights principle because denials of some rights lead to concurrent denials of others. The exercise of political rights is a necessary instrument for attaining economic and social rights. Denial of the public right to know and to have a say in budgetary allocations facilitates the prioritizing of military over civilian expenditure, presidential and ministerial perks over teachers' salaries.

Affirmation of the right to know and to have a say in government policy is often denied to universities for obvious reasons. Creating and disseminating knowledge forms part of the very definition of the university. University students and their professors tend to lead in questioning and challenging government policies. In Malaysia, however, the University and University College Act prohibits students from being members of political parties. Their professors may be members of political parties but are not permitted to be politically active.[1] In Chile, Pinochet's education reform was carried out while human rights safeguards were suspended. Looking back, the World Bank has acknowledged that 'the reforms introduced by the military government turned Chile into a laboratory for "Chicago economics"' and that 'these sweeping changes were not accompanied by public information or consultation'.[2] The title of this World Bank retrospective analysis calls that experience a 'lesson in pragmatism'. As it supported Pinochet's military government and its reforms, the title reflects its own pragmatism, then and now. There has been resistance to such 'pragmatism', then and now. One of the pioneers in this battle was Antonio Cassese. Subsequently the first president of the International War Crimes Tribunal for Former Yugoslavia, he was then the author of an unpublished UN report on international financial support for dictatorships. He faulted the increased World Bank lending to Chile following Pinochet's military coup, highlighted the uncritically positive assessments of Pinochet's policy by World Bank staff, and noted the Nordic opposition that led in 1974 to the only non-unanimous World Bank decision of that year.[3] The international donor community split: one part suspended aid to Pinochet's Chile and supported restoration of human rights safeguards, another followed the World Bank's approach.[4]

Attempts to integrate human rights into creditors' and donors' policies have continued ever since, and there is a long way to go. The vicious circle that ensues when the suppression of political rights prevents questioning of education strategies can be illustrated by a story from Laos. On 26 October 1999, thirty young people attempted to organize the first public demonstration since the country became independent in 1975, but were surrounded by policemen before they could even unfurl their posters. The Lao Students Movement for Democracy was crushed. The originator was Thonhpaseuth Keuakoun, who had had to quit studying at Vientiane University because he could afford it no longer; a group had formed around him, united by their shared frustration at being unable to study because it was too expensive.[5] The government denied that their protest had ever been attempted despite eyewitness testimonies – and the detained protesters are feared to have been killed in detention. There has been no sequel as yet. None is likely to take place until human rights are integrated into international financial support to the country's education sector.

Where their voice is not suppressed, university students are politically vocal, but primary school age children are not. This highlights the need for human rights correctives throughout resource allocation and, even more important, protection of *all* human rights so as to enable all involved to know when, how and why such allocations are made. Multiple facets of the suppression of human rights are illustrated in Box 8.1 which summarizes highlights of the battles between gown and gun in Nigeria in 1978–95.

Box 8.1 • Casualties in battles between gown and gun in Nigeria, 1978–95

1978

'Of all the resistance efforts, the Free Education Jihad of 1978 – also known as "Ali Must Go" – stands out. It all started with an attempt by the then military government of General Olusegun Obasanjo to introduce tuition fees for higher education. The Minister for Education at the time was Colonel Ahmadu Ali. The students, organized under the banner of the National Union of Nigerian Students (NUNS), insisted that "education is a right." Their slogan was "Free Education at All Levels." The government maintained that "citizens must educate themselves" and showed no inclination to budge. With the entire weaponry of the Nigerian Army at its disposal, the government was set to have its way by force. For two months – April and May – about 200,000 armed men engaged students who had resorted to lecture boycotts, sit-ins and peaceful processions on several campuses to press their point. The unnecessary invasion of the campuses took the protest to the streets. In the end the government's war against the students left a long trail of deaths, maimings, detentions, expulsions, rustications and suspensions.'*

1990

'In March 1990, the government announced that it had secured a US$120 million university sector loan from the World Bank. The conditions of the loan were not discussed with the university community. They included cutbacks in staffing levels, phasing out departments and courses, the re-introduction of tuition fees, and increased revenue generation through higher levies for hostel accommodation, examinations, medical and sports facilities'.[†]

Details of the loan were revealed when it had been negotiated, two years earlier, as 'the outcome of an agreement reached between the federal government and the IMF/World Bank representatives led by one Nicholas Bannet in Lagos between April 6 and 29, 1988. It said that under the agreement, the federal government, in return for a $120 million World Bank loan, was to reduce the number of faculties and academic and other staff, to introduce tuition fees and "demobilize" unions in universities.'[‡]

1991

In May and June, 200 students were arrested just before their planned protest was to take place, at a time when Nigeria was hosting the OAU Summit. Before their release, they had to sign an *'Undertaking to Be of Good Conduct'*, a copy of which was given the author by one who prefers to remain unnamed after twenty years have elapsed. The text of that undertaking went like this:

'I ... do hereby willingly under my own hand-writing undertake to conduct myself, henceforth, only in a manner that would portray me as a responsible citizen, loyal to the government and mindful of my Civic Responsibilities of maintaining peace at all times.

'By this undertaking, I pledge my gratitude to the government for causing my release on compassionate grounds and, as my expression of this gratitude, I pledge, willingly, wholeheartedly and with total honesty:

(a) Never to issue any press statement ... on any matter relating to detention;

(b) Never to make any indirect allusions to the circumstances or conditions of my detention;

(c) Never to participate ... in any welcome celebrations ...;

(d) Never to institute any legal action against the government ...;

(e) Never to participate ... in activities aimed at or that are capable of evoking student protests.

'I am by this undertaking pledging to conduct myself in a manner agreeable to peace and shall no longer concern myself with student protests. ... I also do

⇨ hereby, on my honour, in deference to my nation and my government and in avowal to my God, promise to concern myself with my studies, my studies alone, and where it is likely that my fellow students are intent on or about to cause trouble, I shall notify this Department of State Services, in good time, well before the manifestation of such intention.'

1995

'Students, like other citizens of Nigeria, were not spared the repression of the regime during the year under review. In furtherance of the discernible agenda of the regime to sap the academia of radical thought and progressive ideas, several students' union leaders were victimized during the year, while the state policy of militarization of campuses by deploying security operatives and policemen was sustained. The trustees of the task of persecuting the students are usually the administrators of these institutions who also exploit the *carte blanche* granted them by the state to "command" their institutions, to victimise students who challenge their official high-handedness, corruption and administrative ineptitude. In 1995, no fewer than 736 students were arrested, 171 either suspended or expelled and 2 killed. During the same period 24 closures of academic institutions were recorded.'§

* O. Ifowodo, 'Academic freedom and the right to education in Nigeria', in X. Arazo et al. (eds.), *Academic Freedom 4: Education and Human Rights*, World University Service/Zed Books, London, 1996, p. 62.
† A.R. Mustapha, 'The state of academic freedom in Nigeria', in *The State of Academic Freedom in Africa 1995*, CODESRIA, Dakar, 1996, p. 108.
‡ Civil Liberties Organization, *Human Rights in Retreat: A Report on the Human Rights Violations of the Military Regime of General Ibrahim Babangida*, CLO, Lagos, 1993, p. 85–6.
§ Committee for the Defence of Human Rights, *1995 Annual Report on the Human Rights Situation in Nigeria*, Lagos, August 1996, p. 116–17.

From free public service to freely traded service

With the shift of international aid to funding basic education, universities have been starved of public funds. Another change happened at the same time: the transfer of education from public to private law and its redefinition from a public good to a freely traded commodity.

Distribution of public funds within education is seen as – by necessity rather than choice – a zero-sum-game. It pits beneficiaries of public funding for education against each other. This makes concerted strategies for halting the decrease of public funding for education even more difficult. There is always too little funding available for all levels and types of education, everywhere. Increased allocations to primary education deplete higher levels of education of public funding, increasing direct costs for students and their families. An acquired right to free university education is criticized as depriving young children of access to any education whatsoever. However, where university students are paying the full cost of their education there is no evidence that primary school children benefit.

Low budgetary allocations are typical for categories that lack a political voice: hence human rights law bestows legal rights upon them. Primary school children cannot form a political party, get elected to parliament and secure budgetary allocations for themselves. International human rights law requires progressive realization of the right to education where primary education ought to be made free of charge, and this should gradually extend to post-primary and, ultimately, university education.

Primary education ought to be free for children because they cannot pay for themselves and nor should they. The key correlate of childhood is freedom from adult responsibilities. For children, education constitutes one of the few globally accepted duties. The very notion of *compulsory* education points to the child's duty to receive schooling. This does not imply that education is free for the parents, community, society or the state. No human right is cost-free – safeguards against police brutality necessitate a well-paid and well-trained police force; freedom of information is illusory without funds needed to access or disseminate information; while the judiciary cannot be independent unless it is properly funded. It is taken for granted that individuals should not have to pay the public authorities for the service of the fire brigade that prevented their house from burning down, and that this service should be funded out of general taxation. Moreover, direct payments to judges in one's own legal dispute are defined as bribery rather than a legitimate charge for a service. However, the global consensus about the services that the government should provide for the whole population has been remoulded in the past two decades. Education was taken out in the 1980s through cost-sharing, and in the 1990s that process went one step further by including education in international trade law.

School vouchers are illustrative of the rationale that underpinned the conversion of education from a free public service to a freely traded service. They were imported into education from economics,[6] and focus on consumer choice and competitiveness.

The Supreme Court of Colombia has ably clarified why education should not be governed by economic arguments:

> ... although the Constitution protects economic activities, private initiative and competition as well as recognizing the right of private entities to establish schools, these liberties cannot negate nor can they diminish the nature of education as public service and its social function; education is also and above all else a fundamental right.
> ... education – even if private – has to be provided in the conditions which guarantee equality of opportunity in access to education, and all forms of discrimination and 'elitism' are thus repugnant to its nature of public service with profound social contents; these, by virtue of excessive economic demands, automatically deny access to intellectually able persons solely because [of] their levels of income.[7]

In 1993, a voucher scheme in Puerto Rico was declared unconstitutional. Some pupils had been provided with a financial grant of $1,500 for transferring from

Tess Peni

Box 8.2 • 'Schools are for kids, not for sale'

The sale of schools has had many facets, from their transfer from public to private management, from free to for-fee, or their conversion into billboards for advertisers. The reason for the commodification of schools has been the constant decrease of public funding, privatization, and public policies advocating public–private partnerships. Because schoolchildren are a captive audience, in-school advertising has blossomed, making children learn how to consume. Government agencies in the USA have been challenging (unsuccessfully thus far) in-school commerce whereby children are taught good nutrition during class but fed sodas and snacks in-between.[*] An editorial in North Carolina has blamed teachers for having 'harbored a prejudice against teaching the benefits of healthy greed'.[†] Unlike US laws, European laws tend to prohibit in-school advertising.[‡]

[*] A. Molnar and J.A. Reaves, *Buy Me! Buy Me! Buy Me! The Fourth Annual Report on Trends in Schoolhouse Commercialism, Year 2000–2001*, Education Policy Studies Laboratory, Arizona State University, September 2001, p. 12.
[†] H. Matthews, 'Sweetening the school budget', *News and Observer*, Raleigh, North Carolina, 1 February 2001.
[‡] I. Brokman, 'L'école, nouvelle terre promise des entreprises', *Le monde diplomatique*, October 1999.

public to private school. The scheme aimed to stimulate financially the transfer of pupils from public to private schools, also transferring tax revenue to private schools. As with all other voucher schemes, the explicit aim was to increase choice. However, the constitutional requirement for public funds to be used solely for public schools prevailed.[8]

Despite such valiant attempts to impede the freemarketization of education, school vouchers have undermined government responsibility to finance all public schools so that all children can enjoy their right to good education. Rather than governments having to ensure that all schools are good, vouchers have enabled parents to shop around with the voucher in hand as payment. The rationale is that schools should be rewarded for attracting learners, and those unable to do so should be deprived of funding. President George Bush (senior) advocated vouchers in 1992 with the justification that schools should not be shielded from competition but should become a marketplace of opportunities. Jonathan Kozol, the author of *Savage Inequalities*, countered:

> They are proposing a voucher of a couple of thousand dollars which at best would allow a handful of poor children or children of color to go to a pedagogically marginal private school. The day that the conservative voucher advocates in America tell me that they would like to give every inner-city black, Hispanic, or poor white kid a $25,000 voucher to go to Exeter, I will become a Republican.[9]

On the other side of the Atlantic, in England, the functional equivalent of Exeter, Winchester, charged £17,442 per pupil in 2001. Will Hutton suggested that that figure should be used as the benchmark for calculating the cost of education for poor children.[10] Neither suggestion is likely to create a dent in what has become the key feature of funding policies: costing education for the poor at one-fifth (at best) of the cost of education for the rich. Michael Barber, chief adviser to the Secretary of State for Education of the UK, has thus summed up the dilemma about the future of funding for education in rich countries:

> The public education system woven into the fabric of 20th century welfare states prepared populations to contribute to society and shaped national identity. But the industrial society and the nation state that prompted their existence have had their day, giving way to the new economy and globalisation.
>
> These powerful new forces could blow public education systems away unless we can develop a clear rationale for their continued existence. More and more parents have greater disposable income: might they decide they want to spend that income on their children, buying an education tailored to their view of the world? If they did, how easy would it be to persuade them to continue to pay taxes for the education of everyone else's offspring?[11]

With such changes in compulsory education, the abandonment of universities to the reign of purchasing power was a foregone conclusion. At the World Trade Organization, resumed negotiations on the liberalization of trade in education services in November 2001 were led by exporters. Exempting at least compulsory education from trade to enable it to continue as a free public service attained increased importance. As noted by New Zealand, at stake is 'the divide between public policy and commercial activity'.[12]

The concept of education as governmental responsibility and public service continues to enjoy the support of the overwhelming majority of governments in the world. The number of commitments on education under the GATS (General Agreement on Trade in Services) is small. Proposals for further liberalization concentrate on post-compulsory education. The key question remains: should trade supplement rather than displace public education,[13] or should the public sector be prevented from 'crowding out private investment in a lucrative sector'?[14]

The US is a key advocate and beneficiary of international trade in education services. In the 2000/2001 academic year, 547,867 foreign students contributed more than $11 billion to the US economy.[15] That amount exceeded the total annual aid from the US and was a hundred times more than the US provided as aid for education ($103 million).[16] As part of its aid policy, USAID's benchmarks included reducing 'dependence of higher education on public funding'.[17]

What is today's price of a university?

The laissez-faire regime for universities has led to private universities being operated as commercial companies whose shares are quoted on stock exchanges.[18] A look back at the era when university education was accessible as a matter of right shows that student enrolments increased sixfold, from 13 million in 1960 to 82 million in 1995. The rupture of that trend was announced by the World Bank in 1994 – universities were in a crisis throughout the world.[19] The Bank objected to

> laws giving all secondary school graduates a legal right to university matriculation ... a system that was, by some accounts, elitist, self-serving, and insufficiently responsive either to the students it served or to the taxpayers who paid.[20]

From an entitlement, university education became a correlate of the ability to afford to study. Few universities in few countries still provide free tuition and even in these the indirect expenses of studying require students to take loans. There is, in addition, an opportunity cost of delayed earnings. A blend of deregulation and privatization has created fertile ground for the mushrooming of private universities. The cost has been removed from the public to the private realm, to individual students, to their families and to corporate sponsorship. The epoch of carefree student life is gone. A university professor has summed up how much student life has changed:

> When last I asked my students, all of them were working at least 10 hours a week and a quarter were working full time. For the past few years my students have squeezed in their education around the more pressing need to pay for it. As a result they rarely read newspapers. I am convinced that the reason governments increase fees and reduce grants is to keep students locked in the halls of commerce in their spare time, thereby removing them from politically inconvenient corridors of power.[21]

Brain-drain and brain-gain

Differences in salary levels at universities have created a migratory spiral: the wealthiest private universities in the wealthiest countries are charging the highest tuition fees and investing the most in staff. In the United States, the difference in salary levels between public and private universities was $1,300 in 1980; it grew to $21,700 in 1998.[23] Alongside the funding necessary to provide quality education, name recognition is key to successful marketing. 'Branding is necessary for market credibility,' as Howard Newby, vice chancellor of Southampton University, in the UK, put it.[24]

Migration goes two ways. Students are seeking the best education money can buy and are travelling to the best university they can afford; universities are establishing campuses in faraway countries, and bringing their services closer to potential buyers, both geographically and financially. The tuition cost for college education in Beijing ranges from 6,000 to 10,000 renminbi, that is, six to ten times the average annual salary.[25] Meanwhile, debilitating austerity furthers outward migratory pressures as in India:

> From a distance, the stately, two-storey, red-brick arts faculty building at the University of Delhi appears impressive. Look a bit closer, though, and the details suggest otherwise: ceilings and walls sport gaping cracks; paint crumbles off in swathes. Inside, it is difficult for students to see the blackboard from their dust-covered benches – light bulbs in many classrooms are burned out and most electrical wires are a tangled, useless mess.
>
> Flaking paint, however, is the least of Vice-Chancellor V. R. Mehta's worries. Classrooms at one of India's most prestigious and oldest campuses are overflowing with students studying outdated courses. Libraries are poorly stocked. The teaching faculty often goes on strike – once or twice a year – demanding better work conditions and higher pay.
>
> That's not surprising considering [the] starting salary for a university instructor is about $280 per month, far less [than] say, a management graduate's pay. Student unrest is a growing problem, too – one that can have serious consequences and end in tragedy. In November, a distressed student at Rajasthan University in Jaipur died after setting himself on fire to protest a three-month delay in exam results – common these days at universities around the country. Without them, he could neither continue his studies nor apply for a job.
>
> India's higher-education system is facing its worst crisis ever. As the government has slashed public funding in recent years, universities are struggling to find other means to support themselves. But therein lies the irony: To reduce its ballooning budget deficit, the government made cuts in educational spending that are shrinking the very force that can propel the economy – educated youth.[26]

International trade in education services has obliterated the previous boundary between aid and trade as the following question illustrates: should tuition fees charged to students from aid-receiving countries in the donor country be recorded as export, or aid, or both? Profit-making was not built into the design of universities. Hence, unanswered questions arise:

A survey by the Australia Institute claims that academics have been pressured to let full-fee-paying international students pass courses they are not equipped for in order not to jeopardize the lucrative international student market, worth over Aus$3 billion a year to the Australian economy. These allegations of soft marking have sparked a deluge of claims and counter-claims as more whistle blowers are coming forward and speaking up.

As government funding has been persistently cut over the last decade, universities have down-sized their operations and turned to money-making ventures to balance their budgets. All students in Australia now either pay into, or run up a debt with, the Higher Education Contribution scheme. Local students who choose to pay full fees are admitted at a lower entrance mark in specially allocated students' places. In addition, universities are engaging in an ever growing number of commercial enterprises.

The fear is that running universities like a business (particularly one strapped for cash) will create a large class divide, on the one hand, and undermine core values on the other. One of the more controversial claims of the survey is that academics are under increasing pressure to give preferential treatment to full-fee-paying students, the majority of whom are international students. Clive Hamilton, director of the Australia Institute, has commented in the *Sydney Morning Herald* that 'while the recent debate has centred on the issue of soft marking for full-fee-paying students, the effects of commercialisation are much broader and go to the heart of traditional notions of academic freedom.'[27]

UNESCO's 1998 Declaration on Higher Education emphasized that higher education should continue to be financed as a public service,[28] but the 1997 Declaration and Action Plan on Higher Education in Africa recommended 'that higher education institutions create structures for the development and management of consultancy activities'.[29] Advocacy of private–public partnership is not costless, as Box 8.4 illustrates.

Box 8.4 • The cost of corporate sponsorship

Public–private partnership became a key phrase for responding to the impoverishment of public education throughout the education ladder, from the nursery to the university. Selfless help by profit-making companies certainly exists, but it is an exception rather than a rule. As a rule, there is no partnership but rather a business deal which, moreover, questions the boundaries between educating and advertising.

There is full agreement between educationists and advertisers that small children can be influenced with a great deal of ease. Early childhood development is prioritized, the starting age of pre-school education constantly lowered. A private provider of education services, KinderCare, promising age-appropriate curricula, starts with six-week-old babies.* Pre-school education has been made compulsory in Venezuela.[†] The beginning of compulsory education has been set as low as two in Togo.[‡] Whether those parents who are getting their children into institutionalized schooling very early are doing this in the best interests of their children is an open question. Whether governments are violating the rights of children and parents by lowering the beginning age of compulsory schooling is a question that courts will soon have to address.

From their side, advertisers have found that one-year-olds are capable of 'brand association', and advertising messages targeting small children have surged. School has been defined as the ideal marketing venue: 'School is the ideal time to influence attitudes, build long-term loyalties, introduce new products, test market, promote sampling and trial usage and – above all – to generate immediate sales.'[§]

Even the wealthiest universities in the wealthiest countries have succumbed to paying the price of corporate sponsorship:

> Business now inhabits the cloisters of even the biggest and richest institutions. The University of Cambridge, for example, possesses a Shell Chair in Chemical Engineering, BP Professorship in Organic Chemistry and Petroleum Science, an ICI Chair in Applied Thermodynamics, a Glaxo Chair of Molecular Parasitology, a Unilever Chair of Molecular Science, a Price Waterhouse Chair of Financial Accounting and a Marks and Spencer Chair of Farm Animal Health and Food Science. Before the acceptance of new tobacco money was banned, it accepted a £1.6m endowment from BAT Industries to establish the Sir Patrick Sheehy Chair of International Relations (Sir Patrick Sheehy was British American Tobacco's Chairman). Rolls-Royce, AT&T, Microsoft and Zeneca have all set up laboratories in the university.
>
> Oxford University has accepted £20m from Wafic Said to build a business school which will bear his name. Mr Said was named in the Commons inquiry into the sale of a supergun to Iraq as the agent responsible for brokering Britain's £20bn arms deal with Saudi Arabia. In 1998, he reached a £2m settlement with the Inland Revenue after investigators found that his companies had not paid the necessary British taxes. Mr Said has appointed six of the business school's ten trustees. Lord Jenkins, the Chancellor of the University, announced that the gift would place Mr Said among those 'to whom Oxford has given immortality.' [**]

---

[*] 'The education market', *Economist*, 16 January 1999.
[†] PROVEA, *Situación de los derechos humanos en Venezuela: Informe anual octubre 2000/septiembre 2001*, Programa Venezolano de Educación-Acción en Derechos Humanos, Caracas, November 2001, p. 127.
[‡] Committee on the Rights of the Child, Initial report of Togo, UN Doc. CRC/C/3/Add. 42 (1996), para. 18.
[§] 'Captive Kids: A report on commercial pressures on kids at school' (1998), available at www.consunion.org
[**] G. Monbiot, *Captive State: The Corporate Takeover of Britain*, Pan Books/MacMillan, London, 2000, p. 287–8.

Notes

1. FORUM-ASIA, *Human Rights in Asia: Annual Human Rights Report 2000*, Asian Forum for Human Rights and Development, Bangkok, August 2001, p. 41.
2. F. Delannoy, *Education Reforms in Chile, 1980–98: A Lesson in Pragmatism*, Education Reform and Management Publication Series, Vol. 1, No. 1, World Bank, June 2000, pp. 8 and 3.
3. Sub-Commission on Prevention of Discrimination and Protection of Minorities, Study of the impact of foreign economic aid and assistance on respect of human rights in Chile, Report prepared by Mr. Antonia Cassese, Rapporteur, UN Doc. E/CN.4/Sub.2/412 (vol. III) of 21 August 1978, paras. 327–39.
4. K. Tomasevski, *Responding to Human Rights Violations 1946–1999*, Martinus Nijhoff/Kluwer, 2000, pp. 111–17.
5. Amnesty International, 'Lao People's Democratic Republic – The October Protestors: Where are They?', *AI Index*, ASA 26/04/00, 31 May 2000.
6. One of the earliest advocates of vouchers was Milton Friedman in his *Capitalism and Freedom*, University of Chicago Press, Chicago, 1962.
7. Supreme Court of Colombia, Request to determine that Article 203 (in part) of the Law No. 115 of 1994 is unconstitutional by Andres De Zubiria Samper, Judgement of 6 November 1997, C-560/97.
8. Tribunal Supremo de Puerto Rico, *Asociación de Maestros v. José Arsenio Torres*, 30 November 1994, 94 DTS 12:34.
9. S. Mondale, and S.B. Patton, *School: The Story of American Public Education*, Beacon Press, Boston, 2001, p. 194.
10. W. Hutton, 'Now is the time for some true class warfare', *Observer*, 25 November 2001.
11. M. Barber, 'Teaching for tomorrow', *OECD Observer*, No. 225, March 2001.
12. World Trade Organization, 'Negotiating proposal for education services: Communication from New Zealand', S/CSS/W/93 of 26 June 2001.
13. World Trade Organization, 'Higher (Tertiary) Education, Adult Education, and Training: Communication from the United States', S/CSS/W/23 of 18 December 2000.
14. J.W.B. Bredie, and G.K. Beeharry, *School Enrollment Decline in Sub-Saharan Africa: Beyond the Supply Constraint*, World Bank Discussion Paper No. 395, Washington, DC, August 1998, p. 15.
15. Institute of International Education, *Open Doors 2001*, Washington, DC, November 2001 (summary at www.iienetwork.org).
16. The budget for fiscal year 2002, p. 1018 (www.whitehouse.gov/omb/budget/fy2002).
17. US Agency for International Development, *FY2000 Performance Overview*, USAID, Washington, DC, 3 April 2001, p. xii.
18. A. Gonzales, 'Philippines', in G. Postiglione and G.C.L. Mak (eds.), *Asian Higher Education: An International Handbook and Reference Guide*, Greenwood Press, Westport, Connecticut, 1997.
19. World Bank, *Higher Education: Lessons of Experience*, World Bank, Washington DC, 1994, p. 1.
20. D.B. Johnstone, *The Financing and Management of Higher Education: A Status Report on Worldwide Reforms*, World Bank, Washington, DC, 1998, pp. 4–5.
21. Letter by Rita Egan from Troy (New York) to *Guardian Weekly*, 8–14 November 2001.
22. P. Jenkins, 'Hotbeds of revolution', *Financial Times*, 14 June 2001.
23. 'University education: The gap widens', *Economist*, 22 April 2000.
24. P. Kingston, 'Distance learning: Britain must push the pace', *Guardian Weekly*, 2 May 1999.
25. 'China embraces the MBA', *Far Eastern Economic Review*, 19 July 2001.
26. P. Mitra, 'Education: Running on empty', *Far Eastern Economic Review*, 21 January 1999.

27. G. Frølund, 'The birth pangs of commercialisation', *Study Abroad: International Education Magazine*, Issue No. 10, March 2001 (www.study-abroad.dk).

28. UNESCO, World Declaration on Higher Education for the Twenty-First Century: Vision and Action, Paris, 5–9 October 1998, Doc. ED-98/CONF.202/3, 9 October 1998, Article 14.

29. UNESCO, Declaration and Action Plan on Higher Education in Africa, adopted by the African Regional Consultation Preparatory to the World Conference on Higher Education, Dakar (Senegal), 1–4 April 1997, UNESCO Office Dakar, para. 27.

PUTTING HUMAN RIGHTS BACK IN

Exposing and Opposing Exclusion

Exclusion is routinely represented through statistics on the millions of out-of-school children in the world. Although meant to be galvanizing, such figures are numbing and, with frequent repetition, they become facts. No chain of accountability can be discerned from such aggregate numbers, and this deflates opposition. Amnesty International began in the early 1960s with a slogan that it is better to light a single candle than to curse darkness. It replaced generalities about the prevalence of abuse of power in the world by exposing specific abuses and pinpointing the chain of accountability so that they could be halted. The point of departure was experience, the testimony of the victim or on behalf of the victim, the human face and the human toll of the abuse of power. Revealing the mechanism for abuse of power indicated what safeguards were needed. Demonstrating that this could be done has created ripple effects outwards and upwards.

At the beginning of 2002, during the bombing of Afghanistan, the Kabul Zoo raised over $10,000 per animal while the UNHCR received less than $0.5 per refugee.[1] This is illustrative of the need to ask *why*. Could it be that the endlessly recited number of millions of out-of-school children is taken for granted because it has been repeated so often? Could it be that the constant visibility of exclusion without corrective action has discredited its messengers? Could it be that the calls to help 'the poor' fail because they portray people in need rather than the obstacles they face and ways to overcome them?

Exposing exclusion: asking the big Why?

Creating information to generate the action needed is a learning process. Reducing complex issues to a simple message is no easy task. Development organizations have gone through a long process of learning, described thus by Lloyd Timberlake in 1986:

> Look at the process that Oxfam's gone through. It started off saying: 'Famine – send food.' Then it said: 'No, wait a minute, famines seem to be about bad development, so we've got to get involved in development, helping villages to be less vulnerable.' Then it was: 'No, hold on a minute, we can't make the villages less vulnerable because of the whole national and international political situation.' So suddenly quiet little Oxfam was mounting a huge march on Parliament to change all that, and getting itself into a situation where it ran up against the Charity Commission. And I think that the public are following the same line of awareness, but more slowly.[2]

Quantifications rather than causal analysis have become a hallmark of every international strategy; education is no exception. But the absence of causal analysis treats poverty like a weather forecast, something to record as a fact beyond anybody's influence. If we fail to ask *why* people are poor, we cannot tackle poverty when it results from denials of human rights. The first step towards eliminating exclusion consists of itemizing its contemporary pattern. Box 9.1 lists the A to W of exclusion from education.

Designing education for war-affected children and designing education for working children, to mention just the two last entries in Box 9.1, require different approaches; thus mere numbers do not indicate what ought to be done.

Box 9.1 • Exclusion from education from A to W

Abandoned children
Abused children
Arrested children
Asylum-seeking children
Beggars
Child labourers
Child mothers
Child prostitutes
Children born out of wedlock
Conscripted children
Delinquent children
Detained children
Disabled children
Displaced children
Domestic servants
Drug-using children
Girls
HIV-infected children, children affected by HIV/AIDS
Homeless children
Illegal alien children
Illegally adopted children
Illiterate children
Imprisoned children
Indigenous children

Institutionalized children
Married children
Mentally ill children
Migrant children
Minority children
Nomadic children
Orphans
Poor children, children of poor parents
Pregnant girls
Refugee children
Rural children
Sans-papiers, children without identity papers
Sexually exploited children
Sold and purchased children
Stateless children
Street children
Trafficked children
Traveller children
Unaccompanied refugee, displaced or migrant children
War-affected children
Working children

Adapted from R. Hodgkin and P. Newell, *Implementation Handbook for the Convention on the Rights of the Child*, UNICEF, New York, 1998, p. 28.

Table 9.1 • Non-registration of children at birth

No data	Benin, Bhutan, Burkina Faso, Central African Republic, Congo/Brazzaville, Congo/Kinshasa, Côte d'Ivoire, Ecuador, Georgia, Haiti, Iraq, Laos, Madagascar, Nepal, Nigeria, North Korea, Saudi Arabia, Senegal, South Africa, Tanzania, Togo, Vietnam
No birth registration system	Afghanistan, Cambodia, Eritrea, Ethiopia, Namibia, Oman, Somalia
Less than 30% of children registered	Angola, Bangladesh, Guinea-Bissau, Lesotho, Liberia, Malawi, Mozambique, Niger, Papua New Guinea, Rwanda, Sierra Leone, Zambia
Less than 50% of children registered	Botswana, Cameroon, Chad, Ghana, Guinea, India, Kenya, Mali, Mauritania, Myanmar, Sudan, Uganda, Yemen, Zimbabwe

Source: UNICEF, *The Progress of Nations 1998.*

Out-of-school children tend to share features such as sex, minority status, the lack of identity papers, or disability. The largest numbers are in countries where no registration of children exists. Although international human rights law mandates registration of all children when they are born, this has not yet been put into practice, as Table 9.1 illustrates. Furthermore, this phenomenon is rarely discussed as a branch of government human rights obligations. Where the certificate of registration is required for enrolment in school, as is often the case, the absence of birth registration leads to access to school being denied. Although the problem is attributed to poverty, there often is a pronounced political distinction between children with and without identity papers. A poem written by Nalaka, a third-grade primary school pupil in Sri Lanka and probably a child of the disappeared, highlights what the lack of identity papers does to children:

> Who do we belong to? who do we belong to?
> Who do we belong to? who do we belong to?
> Kindly find for us documents,
> If there are any documents,
> Showing in which land we were born.[3]

The pattern of exclusion coincides with internationally prohibited grounds of discrimination, combines several of them, and is exacerbated by poverty. The human rights approach requires asking how poverty intersects with discrimination. If children are poor because their indebted families bonded them to upper-caste creditors in repayment of debt, then the origin of the problem is caste-based discrimination. If children are excluded from school because they belong to a

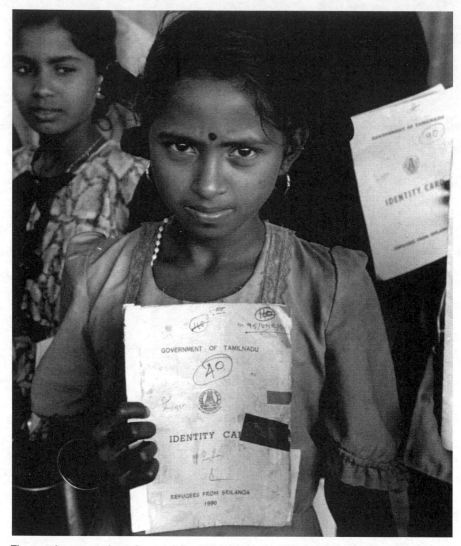

The most important piece of paper. A Tamil girl clutches her identity card   Photo: Howard Davies

frowned-upon minority, additional funding is not likely to be channelled to their education until discrimination against minorities is removed.

Opposing exclusion: pinpointing government obligations

A well-established adage holds that no right can exist without a remedy. Without access to remedies, human rights would be depleted of their core function, to provide safeguards against the abuse of power by the state. Thus, exposing and opposing abuses of power is the main purpose of human rights work. The focus on the state stems from its role in creating and enforcing law, affirming or denying individual and collective rights. Human rights law defines rights as claims addressed to governments; these specify what governments should and should not do. Law is symmetrical, and rights cannot exist without corresponding governmental obligations.

Human rights safeguards were first developed in those areas where the state has a monopoly, such as the use of the armed force, policing and imprisonment. The role of the state in education has been gradually clarified, as Box 9.2 illustrates in the case of India, through the process of making education a constitutional right.

Box 9.2 • What a difference a rights-based campaign can make: Shiksha Yatra in India

From 21 January to 20 June 2001, Shiksha Yatra (India Marches for Education) traversed 15,000 kilometres, 200 districts and 20 states in India; there were more than 50,000 people at its final demonstration in New Delhi. It was one of the last and most decisive building blocks towards the constitutional amendment that in November 2001 made education a fundamental right.

Against fifty years of unfulfilled promises, poor accomplishments epitomized in almost half of school-aged children being out of school and most of them working, and the elusive plan of education for all in 2015, the focus was on making education a right.

The report of Shiksha Yatra highlighted the background and objectives of the campaign thus:

'The facts ... clearly demonstrate that government is rich only in rhetorics and sloganeering. Its half heartedness and lack of political will has put our primary education system in the shambles. Not only government but the civil society in India too has considered education as welfare measure or at best charity. There are several structural/cultural bottlenecks. A very large section of the people is not aware about the importance of education. And, much more in numbers is the category of those people who want to send their children to the school but they don't have access to good quality education for their children.

'It was against this backdrop of state and civil society apathy and gross indifference towards education that Shiksha Yatra was conceived. It aimed at building a mass movement on the question of free, compulsory, meaningful and equal education for all to pressurise government to generate political will to address the problem of education. Based on ground realities Shiksha Yatra aimed at social mobilization for addressing the critical issues in education. The demand included the immediate passage of 83rd Amendment which was to give fundamental-rights status to education. Moreover, the marchers were quite aware of the fact that mere legislation will not suffice as the authority in general have a very poor track record of implementing any pro-poor laws. Therefore, the demand was for a bill with adequate budgetary back-up with sound institutional mechanism to implement the Amendment. For this purpose, the marchers demanded a pumping of 8% of GDP in education.

'Furthermore, apart from putting pressure on the government for generating adequate political and bureaucratic will it aimed at mobilizing people to build positive atmosphere through initiating community process for educating India. In this direction the education marchers also aimed at creating a large army of education volunteers and a vigilant group of public spirited people for the creating of a culture of social audit over education all across the length and breadth of the country. The innovativeness of Shiksha Yatra was that it aimed at redefining education in terms of rights. It wanted to bring out education from charity to rights discourse. The education marchers firmly believed that education ensures upward mobility not only in economistic sense, but armed with the power of knowledge she/he can fight for dignity and rights in our asymmetrical sites of economy, polity, society and culture. It is a tool which empowers hitherto voiceless and marginalized.' *

Why the march

'The Education March was perceived as the only way to reach out to people of diverse ethnic, cultural, and linguistic groups in this vast country. It is a good weapon of mass movement for rallying people together for a common social cause irrespective of religious, linguistic, cultural, social and political affiliations. The mass media, both electronic and print, is not successful in creating awareness, mobilization and sensitization due to illiteracy and non-availability of services in majority of the rural areas. The sensitization through organization of seminars, conferences, press briefings, workshops, etc. only cover the higher echelons of the society and not the grass root level. Moreover such programmes are not only costly and ineffective but also lack strength to mobilize public opinion to translate these activities into action. On the other hand, long marches in this country have had everlasting impact for mobilizing public opinion historically.

Though it is too early to identify the intensity of the reverberations the March has made on the policy makers, there are several initial signs which loudly speak of the efficacy of the March. This is reflected in the fact that no less than 52 questions related to compulsory education and child labour were raised on the floor of the Indian Parliament in the recently concluded Monsoon Session. "Parliamentary Forum on Education" consisting of 163 members of both houses have pledged their support for the passage of the Bill, cutting across party lines. Parents have demonstrated their willingness and power to send their children to school exploding the myth projected by the higher echelons of the society.

'The major strength of the March was its ideological clarity to project education as a fundamental right rather than a welfare issue or a charity issue. Education was a passive and non-issue, but with the March it has become a live issue due to the spontaneous response from the public at large.'[†]

Why the PROBE Team diagnosed education as a political blind spot in 1999

'Why does the government show so little concern for primary education? One answer is that many political leaders are (consciously or sub-consciously) *opposed* to the universalization of education. In some ways, universal education is indeed a threat to privilege and power. As Leo Tolstoy once said, "Education is a matter of enlightenment and no monarch in his senses would like to do that." The context of this statement, however, is quite different from contemporary India. While India, like Russia, does have a history of elite obstruction to the spread of education among the masses, the politics of education today are more subtle.

'Another answer is that, even if they are not opposed to the universalization of elementary education, political leaders have little to gain from it. In other words, there is little political capital to make from getting children to school. Whether this is in fact true is an unresolved question. Indeed, since no major political party has *attempted* to win public support by taking radical steps to universalize education, it is hard to tell whether this strategy would be successful. Getting down that road would require vision and courage, considering that the political gains are uncertain (though possibly quite large), while the costs are more transparent.

'[U]nless the connection between universal education and social justice is more clearly recognized by organizations that claim to represent the under-privileged, the low visibility of elementary education in Indian politics is likely to continue. To some extent, the dominant view that poor people do not 'need' education has influenced even the critics of the establishment. A revision of perspective is long overdue.'[‡]

---

[*] Shiksha Yatra: India Marches for Education Report, prepared by Rajesh Ranjan and presented by Kailash Satyarthi, Chairperson', Delhi, 2001, mimeograph.

[†] B. Zutshi, 'Evaluation of Education March 2001 in India organized by SACCS [South Asian Coalition on Child Servitude] and other partners January – June 2001', Centre for the Study of Regional Development, New Delhi, mimeograph.

[‡] PROBE Team, *Public Report On Basic Education in India*, Oxford University Press, New Delhi, 1999, p. 137.

Much as promises generated by world summits are seldom translated into performance, individual governments tend, once they are elected, to forget the promises made in their electoral platforms. The ability and the willingness of individual governments are often questioned, and they tend to be interrelated. Human rights law requires rights to be precisely defined so that they can be effectively claimed, and their violations exposed, remedied, and prevented, thereby furnishing effective means for holding governments accountable.

Rupturing global inaction

After the lost decade of the 1980s, government commitments to freeing primary education from school fees started with Malawi in 1994; Uganda followed in 1997, Cameroon, the Gambia, Kenya, Lesotho, Nigeria, Tanzania and Zambia at the turn of the millennium.[4] In 2001, the constitutional entrenchment of the right to education in India, summarized in Box 9.2, buttressed this trend. International responses should be supportive if normative statements are used as guidance, but are unlikely to prove supportive if experience is the guide.

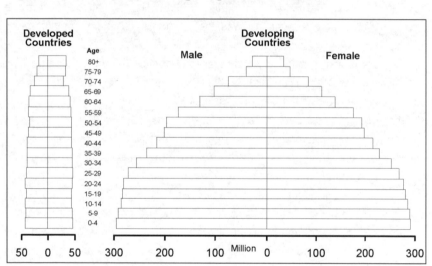

Figure 9.1 • Population Age Pyramids, 2025

Demographic pyramids for the developed and developing countries highlight the difference between the few and the many, the old and the young. The developed-countries' pillar depicts its small and ageing population, the right-hand pyramid the large and young population of the developing world. Children aged 5–15 who should be in school constitute one in ten in the North but one-third or more in the South. The advocacy for lifelong learning in the OECD countries has led UNESCO to observe that there 'the adult population is running out of people to educate' and has switched to prolonging education throughout adulthood for themselves.* In developing countries, meagre funds have to be stretched to school their young populations. Most people will complete eleven years of compulsory education in the OECD countries, while in developing countries all-encompassing primary education has yet to be attained. Eleven years of education for all remains a distant dream.

* UNESCO, *Teachers and Teaching in a Changing World: 1998 World Education Report*, Paris, 1998, p. 29.

The need for international action is evidenced in the different demographic pyramids of the South and the North, illustrated in Figure 9.1. Conservative estimates for the year 2025 predict that one-third of the population in the North will be over 60 years old. In 1950, the proportion was just above 10 per cent, today it is about 20 per cent. Fewer births and longer lives have led to revised population projections, but the process of ageing may be both deeper and faster than anticipated. As a consequence, the rights of the elderly have been added to the human rights agenda in the European Union, and the political voice of the increasing numbers of elderly voters is further slanting governments' priorities towards their entitlements. In contrast, children in the developing world do not have a right to vote and have no say in global decisions about fiscal allocations that should, but do not, prioritize their rights.

Rescuing education from debt bondage

Children who do not win the world rights lottery by being born into wealthy and caring countries and families are deprived of their *chance to learn*, in World Bank language, and are unlikely ever to learn the answer to *why*. Few will be informed about the dynamics of creating and repaying debt, although they are the victims of loans which were squandered but have to be repaid nevertheless. A turning point was the G-7 Cologne meeting, which recognised that debt was unpayable. Jubilee 2000 gave it a boost by education of the public in the creditor countries, especially in Western Europe.[5]

The vicious circle created by lending rather than granting development funding has been an object of fierce criticism for years. Debt relief is much talked about but the conditions are stringent, the process is painfully slow, and the effects are routinely inadequate because indebted countries get in relief much less than they lose through protectionism in trade.

Links between the alleviation of unsustainable debt and increased funding for education became stronger at the turn of the millennium within the HIPC-II (Enhanced Heavily Indebted Poor Countries Debt Relief Initiative). The new requirement for qualification was a poverty reduction strategy paper (PRSP) for each country. Education figures prominently in PRSPs because 40 per cent of debt relief has to be allocated to education and health, and governments have to commit their own funds lest debt relief would be used instead of – rather than in addition to – domestic budgetary allocations. Excerpts from PRSPs are included in Box 9.4, and give an insight into what PRSPs say about education.

Diversion of funds from debt servicing to education was to be conditional on the PRSPs laying out a credible strategy of 'demonstrable results in poverty reduction'.[6] Such demonstrable results are yielded, however, with a long delay, after children become adults, and only where education is not their sole asset. Where access to the labour market is limited or non-existent, the creation of possibilities for the productive use of education requires land ownership, access to credit, or facilitation of self-employment. On its own, education is unlikely to generate income for its beneficiaries or tax revenue for governments, especially if it consists of only five years of general schooling.

Martin Argles

Box 9.3 • Mobilization of shame in creditor countries: 'Haven't we taken enough?'

Helping to launch a poster for the Drop the Debt campaign in London in June 2001, Bob Geldof, a campaign supporter, commented: 'If it takes a shocking image, it's justified'.

'Looking back seventeen years at Live Aid, which raised $70 million for alleviating the Ethiopian famine in July 1995 through mega-concerts watched by 2 billion people in 22 countries, Geldolf acknowledged that celebrity equalled access to the ear of decision-makers and, sometimes, also to their money. 'People go on about us supping with the devil, but what's the point in supping with God; he's already on the side of the angels.'*

* P. Vallely, 'It is 17 years since Live Aid and Bob Geldof is back, telling the world to listen to Africa', *The Independent*, 13 May 2002.

Box 9.4 • Excerpts from PRSPs on alleviating the educational cost of debt

'In Albania, public financing of education is around 10% of the government budget. The share of education in the GDP has decreased from 3.8% in 1995 to 3.3% in 2000. The education sector is one of the six priority fields for public actions in the PRSP. The share of education in GDP is planned to increase from 3.4% in 2001 to 3.7% in 2004.'

'The PRSP of Burkina Faso aims to guarantee access to basic education to the poor. Primary school enrolments rose from 30% in 1990 to 41% in 1999, but the retention rates are low, as is the quality of education. The targets to be achieved within the next four years include exemption of girls in 20 provinces from monthly school fees.'

'In Mauritania, the enrolment rate for girls is 81%; for boys it is 87.6%. Only 56.2% of children complete primary school. Despite the increase in enrolments, the share of education in the GDP has dropped in recent years, mainly because of a freeze on salaries. The PRSP plans to increase budgetary allocations for education from 3,7% of GDP in 1999 to 5% in 2010.'

'Mozambique's PRSP focuses on six fundamental areas for reducing poverty and stimulating growth, including education, which is deemed "a basic human right". Public expenditure on education is planned at 32% of total public spending in 2001–05. The PRSP notes that "the need to establish a system of partial cost recovery must eventually be faced".'

'Niger is one of the few developing countries in the world where education is financed almost entirely by the government. The adult literacy rate is about 20%. Around 51% of the urban population can read and write, compared to only 14% of rural dwellers. Only 10% of women are literate. The PRSP plans increasing education expenditure from 3.4% of GDP in 2000 to 6% in 2015, and allocating at least 20% of the government operating budget to education.'

Sources: Albania, National Strategy for Socio-Economic Development of 21 February 2002; Burkina Faso, Poverty Reduction Strategy Paper of 25 May 2000, endorsed by the IMF/World Bank on 30 June 2000; Mauritania, Poverty Reduction Strategy Paper of 13 December 2000, endorsed by the IMF/World Bank on 6 February 2001; Mozambique, Action Plan for the Reduction of Absolute Poverty (2001-2005) (PARPA) of 1 October 2001, endorsed by the IMF/World Bank on 25 September 2001; Niger, Poverty Reduction Strategy of 31 January 2002, endorsed by the IMF/World Bank on 7 February 2002, texts at http://poverty.worldbank.org/prsp/.

The fragmented nature of the global education agenda – involving not only governments and the UN but also the World Bank and other agencies – has kept the right to education beyond the remit of debt relief, even though the raison d'être of human rights is to act as a corrective to the free market. Governments have human rights obligations precisely *because* primary education should not be treated as a commodity (just as slavery was prohibited, exempting people from being sold and purchased for a price). Despite controversies relating to governmental human rights obligations, their core is clear: governments have a general obligation to enable people to provide for themselves and exceptionally to provide for those unable to do so. Rights of the child are thus prioritized over rights of adults. They entail governmental obligations to create conditions for their realization, that is, an enabling environment.

For this to happen, three separate global processes – debt relief, Education for All and human rights reporting – would have to be merged. PRSPs provide blueprints for the allocation of funds transferred from debt servicing to development, wherein education figures prominently. But PRSPs are assessed by the World Bank and the IMF, excluding their human rights dimensions.[7] These are alluded to, in the PRSPs, in the highlighting of distributional impacts of past education reforms, and would be instrumental in assessing the compatibility of fiscal allocations with human rights obligations. A separate track within this fragmentated global education agenda has been set up following the Dakar Conference, and requires national Education for All (EFA) plans. Few have emerged.[8] Because such plans are often generated in parallel with the process of debt relief, bridging the abyss between two parallel structures and processes would seem useful, indeed necessary. Integrating human rights in national, as well as creditors' and donors' implementing plans, would bridge one more abyss.

Law makes the choices made within debt relief or education strategies sustainable by defining rights and corresponding responsibilities. The reporting process under international human rights treaties includes references to negotiating debt relief and forging education strategies. For example, the UN Committee on Economic, Social and Cultural Rights has recommended that Honduras explicitly take the Covenant into account in relation to its PRSP.[9] The Committee on the Rights of the Child has noted that only 60 per cent of children in Mauritania attend school and has suggested that priorities ensure the realization of the rights recognized in the Convention,[10] which can be facilitated through the PRSP. The linchpin for these three parallel structures and processes of debt relief, EFA and human rights reporting is international cooperation, envisaged as key to the realization of economic, social and cultural rights, especially the rights of the child. The key to diverting debt servicing to education is the commitment of the government and the agreement of key creditors and donors, as the example of Uganda shows.

Uganda's success story

Uganda's government has many times acknowledged its overdependence on external funding, stemming from its debt burden and low revenue. Because the bulk of its debt is owed to the international donor community, Uganda typifies the vicious circle of paying back past debts so as to be able to raise additional funding, but thereby incurring future debts. Although figures differ, aid constitutes about 8 per cent of the GDP, half of the government's budget, and

The New Vision, Tuesday June 29, 1999   23

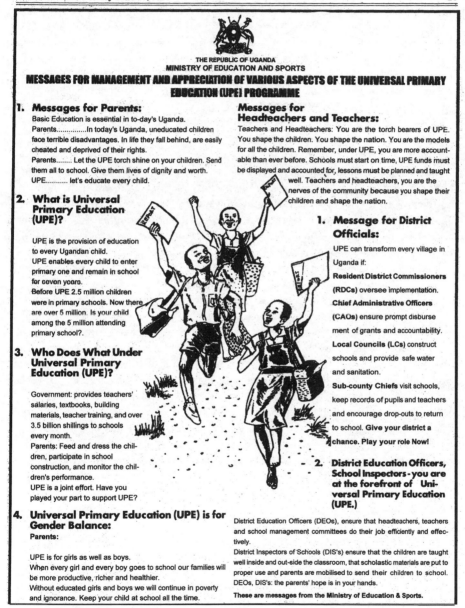

Debt alleviation into education: a government advertisement for Uganda's Universal Primary Education programme

more than half of allocations to education. Since much of the aid is in the form of loans rather than grants, and much of what is nominally labelled 'aid' in fact services previous loans (also labelled as 'aid'), the gap between perception and reality is immense. Many donors are at the same time creditors, and about half of Uganda's annual debt repayments go to international agencies, primarily the World Bank and the IMF. These are faced with the constant conflict of interests between the roles of donor and creditor.

The main actors in decision-making with regard to debt relief are these multilateral creditors which do not consider themselves bound by international human rights law. Groups of creditor countries are not bound by any law. The criteria for debt relief revolve around Uganda meeting the specified benchmarks and performance criteria embodied in documents negotiated between the government and the IMF/World Bank. Uganda's debt servicing was authoritatively assessed as impossible and in 1998 Uganda was the first highly indebted poor country to receive debt relief.[11] The decision was made in April 1997 but Uganda had to wait another year to reach the completion point. Because, as already mentioned, most of Uganda's debt is owed to the IMF and the World Bank, assistance was set at $73 million for bilateral and $273 million for multilateral creditors (of which $160 million was for the World Bank and $69 for the IMF).[12] Some of the budgetary resources released through debt relief were transferred to primary education, increasing by one-third central government's transfers (earmarked for primary education) to districts.

Uganda's Education Strategic Investment Plan 1998–2003 pledged that Universal Primary Education (UPE) was the highest priority, emphasizing in particular the removal of financial impediments to schooling. The Education Policy Review Commission recommended that 20 per cent of the government's budget should be earmarked for education[13] and this target was surpassed by the allocation of 33 per cent of the discretionary recurrent budget, of which 62 per cent was devoted to primary education.[14] Almost half of these funds consisted of teachers' salaries, with the building of classrooms and the purchase of textbooks being the major items in the remainder. Discussions about nominal budgetary allocations are inevitably accompanied by a switch of topic to corruption. One factor that makes this inevitable are double roles – public officials can and do simultaneously pursue their private business. A part of their justification for this are their low salaries. A great deal of attention has been devoted to exposing and opposing corruption.[15] Moreover, military expenditure was assessed as too high, and in March 1999 the IMF delayed an $18 million loan because military expenditure had been reportedly doubled from the planned $150 million to $350 million.[16]

The policy of removing school fees was introduced in January 1997; as a result, enrolment increased from about 2.5 million in 1996 to about 5.5 million in 1998, and to about 6.5 million in April 1999; the officially reported enrolment in primary school thus trebled.[17] The cost of education had previously been the essential obstacle to children's access to school. Families were bearing two-thirds of the cost of primary education, and to pay for schooling for the average seven children born to each women was beyond the reach of most.

The challenge of making schooling available for all Ugandan children can be succinctly portrayed by outlining its major determinants: half of Uganda's population is younger than fifteen, and for each child there is only one adult statistically classified as pertaining to the labour force (aged 15–64). The dependency ratio is thus 1:1. The UPE programme will produce its first generation of 11-year-old graduates in 2003. For most, secondary schooling will be beyond reach, and they are legally prohibited from working. However, UPE is supposed to contribute to poverty reduction and its continuation may depend on donors' assessment by that yardstick.

Will it work in Tanzania?

In the 1970s, Tanzania was a prime example of a poor country with an excellent record in education. The introduction of a basic-needs policy in 1971 had led to a large investment in the public service and the quadrupling of budgetary allocations for its recurrent costs. This had at first been supported by Tanzania's donors and its accomplishments had been applauded; donors' support diminished from 1978, after the first oil crisis and the accompanying recession.[18] In the 1980s, a downward trend started with diminished budgetary allocations and a corresponding deterioration of the previous accomplishments. One striking feature was that, in the 1990s, illiteracy was actually increasing at the rate of 2 per cent per year.[19]

The World Bank has been involved in Tanzania's education for four decades, initially supporting the government's policy of providing free public education for all. Not much can be shown for these loans although, without doubt, they have had to be repaid. The World Bank's standard response to criticism of the orientation of its lending is to point to the government as decision-maker. The government in question often points back to the World Bank. Critics tend to work their way out of that limbo by searching for evidence as to key actors in the forging of specific policies. For Tanzania, the World Bank has found that in the period from the early 1980s to the early 1990s 'both central and local governments were relatively passive toward the initiatives of donor agencies'.[20] This passivity has been described by Perran Penrose as having included the Bank's writing and publishing of Tanzania's social sector policy,[21] although the World Bank's documents duly refer to the government's authorship.

The profound change from the provision of public free-of-charge education to cost-sharing was explained by the World Bank in a statement that 'cost-sharing for social services is politically accepted'.[22] Evidence for this assertion was furnished in the form of results of a survey that inquired into the willingness of parents to pay for the education of their children. In a situation where schools were falling apart due to lack of maintenance, and lack of money to pay teachers' salaries, no alternative was suggested to respondents. Indeed the option of increased generation of revenue by the government through taxation was not even considered in the World Bank's documents. The Bank's *Social Sector Review* (based on 1994 data but, for unexplained reasons, published in 1999) diagnosed 'a public system that is far more extensive than the budget can fund'. Two obvious options presented themselves given this finding – to increase the budget or (further) curtail public provision of free education. The fact that free education is founded upon taxation is well-known, and indeed the World Bank acknowledged that 'households pay taxes which make subsidies possible'. However, it left the question of where additional money should come from unanswered, noting, 'we have no information on the incidence of taxes'. Data showing that the highest income category captured most public free-of-charge services were included in the *Social Sector Review*, but the question of whether they were paying any tax, and if so, whether the tax rate was progressive so as to attain the situation where families and individuals contributed according to their ability, was again not posed.[23] The option of imposing school fees for primary education translates into regressive rather than progressive taxation because an equal financial burden is imposed upon the richest and the poorest, excluding the latter from access to any education whenever they are too poor to bear its cost. This is illegal under Tanzanian law, since the 1995 Education Act defines as an offence the denial of access to education to any child due to, among other things, socio-economic status. Parents are brought to court for the non-payment of fees (and the corollary breach of the legal requirement that education should be compulsory for children aged 7–13) but nothing can be done when they simply have no money to pay the fees. Results of not heeding this rationale in Tanzania are easily illustrated:

- 'The famine of the past three years has caused such a cash shortage that many families can't afford school fees, which for a secondary school place are the equivalent of three months' wages. … Students sent home to bring fees only return after they have found a buyer for a goat or a bag of groundnuts. Although refused admission in classes, they sneak in, or congregate at each other's homes (often a single room rented by those from outlying villages, where they study by candle-light and eke out their food supplies until more arrive from home).'[24]

- 'The annual cost of primary education per child in Kilimanjaro was calculated by Maarifa Ni Ufunguo at 16,950 shillings (almost equally divided between various fees and the cost of uniform and equipment), which prevents a fairly typical family, whose annual income is 48,000 shillings, from educating the typical number of six children. Roman George Saugare, night watchman of Ngumeni primary school, has commented: 'The situation is not good at all. I haven't been paid my salary for a year now because the children do not pay school fees. They come empty-handed. The parents send children to school without money and then the school sends the children back for money which is not there.'[25]

In 2000 the average annual cost of schooling a child was estimated at $80,[26] half of the annual income of poor rural families, which is thus insufficient to keep two or three children in school. In 2000 the net enrolment ratio was 57 per cent and progression from primary to secondary school was 15 per cent. Reduced costs immediately led to an increase in enrolments to 75 per cent.[27] Whether this upward swing will continue to encompass all children depends on the dynamics of debt relief and the priority given to education in all multilateral and bilateral policies towards Tanzania, as well as the domestic priority for translating education into a right.

Notes

1. 'Kabul's lion king', *Economist*, 12 January 2002.
2. P. Harrison and R. Palmer, *News Out of Africa: Biafra to Band Aid*, Hilary Shipman, London, 1986, p. 136–37.
3. B. Fernando, 'Voices of compassionate children', *Human Rights SOLIDARITY*, Vol. 11, No. 12/Vol. 12, No. 1, December 2001–January 2002.
4. Commission on Human Rights, Reports of the Special Rapporteur on the right to education, Katarina Tomasevski, UN Docs. E/CN.4/2000/6, para. 48; E/CN.4/2000/6/Add. 1; E/CN.4/2002/60, para. 13.
5. Commission on Human Rights, Progress report of the Special Rapporteur on the right to education, Katarina Tomasevski, UN Doc. E/CN.4/2000/6, paras. 13–14.
6. World Bank, *Attacking Poverty: World Development Report 2000/2001*, Oxford University Press, New York, September 2000, p. 203.
7. See IMF/World Bank, 'Guidelines for Joint Staff Assessment of a Poverty Reduction Strategy Paper', 18 April 2001, www1.worldbank.org/prsp.
8. The first post-Dakar assessment of progress noted that 66 countries responded to UNESCO's query regarding national plans, with 41 countries stating that they had such plans, out of which 39 had been prepared before the Dakar Forum. UNESCO/EFA, *2001 Monitoring Report on Education for All*, Paris, October 2001 (www.unesco.org/education/efa).
9. Concluding observations of the Committee on Economic, Social and Cultural Rights: Honduras, UN Doc. E/C.12/1/Add. 57 of 21 May 2001, para. 34.
10. Concluding observations of the Committee on the Rights of the Child: Mauritania, UN Doc. CRC/C/15/Add. 159 of 12 October 2001, paras. 45 and 14.
11. An illustrative editorial in the *New York Times* had this to say: '[Uganda] used the money that it saved largely to eliminate fees charged for primary school. The impact was dramatic. While two years ago 54 percent of Uganda's children attended primary school, this year 90 percent do.' 'Out of debt trap', reprinted in *International Herald Tribune*, 4 May 1999.
12. World Bank, *Annual Report 1998*, Washington, DC, 1999, Table 1: HIPC initiative: Status of country cases, p. 5.
13. The relative size of the budgetary allocation for education constitutes 2.6 per cent of GNP, thus one-third of the recommended 6 per cent.
14. Republic of Uganda, Background to the budget 1999/2000 (The challenge of poverty eradication and private sector development), Ministry of Finance, Planning and Economic Development, Kampala, June 1999, p. 20.
15. The actors ranged from the World Bank to Transparency International, from parliamentarians to journalists, while corruption scandals targeted especially Uganda's military intervention in Zaire/Congo which increased military expenditure by 20 per cent and brought about a series of scandals associated with military procurement and involvement in the exploitation of natural resources in Zaire/Congo. C. Sebunya, 'The rise and fall of Salim Saleh, and Uganda's Congolese treasure trove', *New African*, March and May 1999.
16. 'The shine fades on Museveni's Uganda', *Economist*, 1 May 1999.
17. The data of the Ministry of Education place net primary enrolment at 55 per cent in

1994/95, 56 per cent in 1995/96, and the preliminary estimate for 1997/98 was 91 per cent. The rate of completion of the seven years of primary school (P1 to P7) was 30 per cent in 1994/95, 35 per cent in 1995/96 and was estimated at 40 per cent for 1997/98. Republic of Uganda, Memorandum of economic and financial policies, annex to the Letter of Intent dated 28 October 1998, addressed to the Managing Director of the International Monetary Fund by the Minister of Finance, Planning and Economic Development, Table 1: Social outcome indicators, 1994/95–2004/05, p. 13.

18. This is discussed in K. Tomasevski, *Development Aid and Human Rights*, Pinter Publishers, London, 1989, pp. 171–4.

19. Basic Education Master Plan: Medium Term Strategic and Programme Framework 1997–2002, Dar es Salaam, 1997, p. 4.

20. World Bank, *Tanzania: Social Sector Review*, Washington, DC, October 1999, p. 49.

21. P. Penrose, *Cost Sharing in Education: Public Finance, School and Household Perspectives*, Education Research Serial No. 27, Department for International Development, London, September 1998, pp. 38 and 81.

22. World Bank, *Tanzania: Human Resources Development Pilot Project. Staff Appraisal Report*, No. 16519-TA, 26 August 1997, para. 99, p. 37.

23. World Bank, *Tanzania: Social Sector Review*, Washington, DC, October 1999, pp. 10, 44, 58 and 12-13.

24. S. Michell, 'Keeping their eye on the ball: Letter from Tanzania', *Guardian Weekly*, 30 May 1999.

25. Maarifa Ni Ufunguo, 'Cost sharing: A case study of education in Kilimanjaro, Arusha', February 2001, mimeographed.

26. ILO/UNCTAD, 'The minimum income for school attendance (MISA) initiative: Achieving international development goals in African least developed countries', ILO/UNCTAD Advisory Group, Geneva, mimeographed, 2001.

27. Paper by Joseph Mungai, Tanzania's Minister for Education and Culture, entitled 'Sector based educational development funding: strengths and weaknesses as seen from a partner country', mimeograph, p. 10. Presented at the Nordic Solidarity Conference on the Role of Education in Policies for Development Cooperation, Oslo 3–4 June 2002.

Revisiting Segregated Education

I n 1978, UNESCO forged the concept of a right to be different, positing that 'all individuals and groups have the right to be different, to consider themselves as different and to be regarded as such'.[1] This concept was revisited by Albie Sachs in 2000. He took it one step further, affirming 'the right of people to be who they are without being forced to subordinate themselves to the cultural and religious norms of others'.[2] Historically, differences have been accommodated through segregation. The boundaries have followed internationally prohibited grounds of discrimination. Moreover, segregation along religious, linguistic or ethnic lines tends to justify divisions produced on internationally prohibited grounds of discrimination by prioritizing collective over individual rights. Communities are educating *their* children within the boundaries of belonging defined by religion, ethnicity, or language. The model of all-encompassing public education aims to overcome such boundaries and the underlying division of children into *ours* and *theirs*. Although that model is embodied in the spirit and wording of international human rights law, it does not guide education strategies.

A look back at the past half-century shows that powerful movements opposed racial segregation. Their success was marked by prohibitions of racial discrimination and government obligations to eliminate it. Segregation has been changed, however, rather than eliminated. The boundaries of belonging are no longer laid down in law but are determined by the power of the purse, evidenced in the racial profile of residential segregation and the intake of private schools. Different from race, religion has always constituted a boundary of belonging, throughout the history of education. Religious schools are older than secular schools. It is likely that more children attend religious than secular schools today. There are no international statistics, there is no global strategy. Silence prevails. By contrast, there is a great deal of statistics and strategies for children with disabilities. These reveal that there is no shared understanding of 'disability'. The vision embodied in the jurisprudence on the rights of the child provides guidance, but some children are categorized as 'defective' and segregated into 'special schools' regardless of persuasive evidence on the benefits of all-inclusive education.

Mobilization against colonialism and racism

International mobilization against racial discrimination emerged as a response to apartheid in South Africa, which was institutionalized and legalized in the form of so-called 'Bantu education'. The pillar of education in South Africa was segregation and its origin was traced to religious education in Holland, which was transposed to South Africa and explained in 1948 by the need for 'separate schools for non-believers and for Christians, separate schools for Roman Catholics and for the Protestants, separate schools for each of the great religious groups, e.g. Anglican, Lutheran and Calvinistic, and separate schools for each of the national groups'.[3] The 1953 Bantu Education Act rapidly became notorious worldwide as the embodiment of apartheid. One of its aims, as explained by Hendrik Verwoerd of the Ministry of Native Affairs, was to reverse an unintended consequence of the previous openness of educational institutions to the black population, which had created 'the class which has learned that it is above its own people and feels that its spiritual, economic and political home is among the civilized community of South Africa, namely the Europeans'; this should be prevented, he claimed, by not allowing the black population any aspirations except 'having to earn their living in the service of Europeans'.[4]

An endless stream of studies accompanied and strengthened the global mobilization against apartheid and, in education, triggered the first international treaties outlawing racial discrimination. The students' uprising in Soweto on 16 June 1976 in protest against the introduction of Afrikaans as the language of instruction has been celebrated, as of 1995, as Youth Day. Although generally associated with South Africa, racism and educational apartheid were corollaries of colonialism, as Box 10.1 illustrates.

Box 10.1 • Excluding Africans: reports by colonial administrations

Portugal

'In Portugal a distinction is drawn in the census data of certain Overseas Provinces (Angola, Mozambique, Guinea, São Tomé and Principe, and Timor) between the non-civilized and civilized population, the latter consisting of those who follow the European way of life. In the three provinces of Angola, Mozambique and Guinea the indigenous population is still subject to a special regime. ... In the province of Angola there were 4,009,911 persons in the non-civilized population and 135,355 persons in the civilized population, including 78,826 whites, 26,335 of mixed blood, 30,089 Negroes and 105 others, in 1950. The total school enrolment in primary schools in that year was 16,118, including 3,163 Negroes ... in secondary schools 2,582, including 91 Negroes ... in technical and vocational schools it was 1,204, including 50 Negroes.'*

The UK for Tanganyika

'The suggestion that there should be racial unification in primary schools runs counter to the opinion of the majority of educationalists who, throughout the world, emphasize the necessity, in the case of primary education, for schools

⇨ to be related to social and home environments and the advisability of teaching the very young in their mother tongue or in the language they use in their home environment. It is only at later stages that persons from different environments can and should be mixed. There are therefore good grounds for maintaining that the Government's policy with regard to primary education is right and that gradual development towards unification in education from the top is less likely to impede the advance of African education and more likely to be successful than any sudden change or attempt at speeding up this development.'[†]

The UK for Kenya

'Why not provide schools as far as your resources will permit, to be attended equally by children of all races?

'This idea of the multi-racial school is very attractive. It suggests a solution of the political problem of the plural society: children, it is said, have no race feeling, and if you educate them side by side on the same benches they will remain free of it when they grow up. Such schools exist in the United States, and in cosmopolitan cities like Cardiff or Liverpool; why should they not exist in Africa?

'We admit the attractiveness of the idea, and we hope to show that some educationists in Kenya are working towards it. But the case of the United States or the cosmopolitan city in Britain is not a parallel. There, you have a country with a well-established civilization and language of its own, and the problem is to assimilate the alien immigrant – to make the Pole, Chinese or Scandinavian a good American or good Englishman. This is not the problem in Kenya. Nobody suggests that the aim of education there should be to make the European child or the Asian child into a good African.'[‡]

* United Nations, *Study of Discrimination in Education by Charles Ammoun, Special Rapporteur of the Sub-Commission on Prevention of Discrimination and Protection of Minorities*, United Nations, New York, August 1957, pp. 83–4.
† United Nations, Report of the United Kingdom Government for the Year Ending 1952 on Tanganyika under British Administration, Doc. T/1205, para. 434.
‡ The problem of discrimination in education illustrated by experience in the promotion of education in the United Kingdom Territories. Memorandum prepared by the United Kingdom Government for the Study of Discrimination in Education, United Nations, New York, August 1957, p. 26.

In the US, the ideal of the common school aimed to abolish the boundaries of race, sex, caste, ethnicity, language or income and educate all children together. Free public schooling did not encompass the whole population, however: black and Native American children were excluded. Nor did it embrace the whole country. The North led in the nineteenth century and the South followed in the twentieth century. The 1954 *Brown v. Board of Education of Topeka* judgement, summarized in Box 10.2, was a milestone in challenging segregation.

Box 10.2 • Brown v. Board of Education of Topeka

In 1951, Topeka, in Kansas, had four primary schools for black and eighteen for white children. Linda Brown, nine-year-old daughter of the Reverend Oliver Brown, attended Monroe School, five miles away from her home by bus and then on foot through a dangerous part of the town. Moving her to the closest school, just four blocks from home, was impossible because the little girl was black.

Her father sought the assistance of the NAACP (National Association for the Advancement of Colored People) which had started legal challenges of racially segregated schools elsewhere in the United States, and filed a suit before the District Court for Kansas on 28 February 1951. Hearings began about the free bus service provided by the Board of Education of Topeka for black but not white children and the food for undernourished black children. The focus changed, with a witness saying: 'the only way to reach the light is to start our children together in their infancy and they come up together', and with psychologists and psychiatrists explaining the impact of segregation on children, especially its demotivating effects on black children. The verdict was that separate was equal but the question of whether segregation itself could constitute inequality was left open.

The judgement was appealed and five similar cases were pending before the US Supreme Court in 1952, with *Brown* first in alphabetical order. A year passed in which Earl Warren became the new Chief Justice; the NAACP's team included Thurgood Marshall, later to become the first black judge of the US Supreme Court. Another year passed, filled with intense negotiations within the Supreme Court.

On 17 May 1954, the result was made public: separating black children solely because of their race generated a feeling of inferiority, whose effects were 'unlikely ever to be undone'. This explicit opinion declaring racially segregated schools unconstitutional was not enforced immediately. Rather, it was subjected to a lengthy process of translation into practice. A forceful pursuit of racially integrated schooling was resisted with equal force. The Supreme Court had, however, refrained from tackling poverty. The two have remained separated in governmental policies ever since, although they cannot be dissociated in practice.

The 1964 Civil Rights Act prioritized education, as did the 1965 Elementary and Secondary Education Act, which reinforced civil rights guarantees by mandating federal aid to children from poor families. These parallel efforts to tackle race and poverty floundered because they were two sides of the same coin and could

➡️ not be disentangled. In what became known as 'the white flight,' white-and-wealthy families voted with their feet, left cities for suburbs, leaving non-white and poor children in inner-city schools. Racially inclusive schooling included busing, whereby children were transported from one school into another to implement desegregation. Forty years later, the Civil Rights Division of the Department of Justice was involved in more than 200 desegregation cases as well as monitoring the translation into practice of desegregation orders in 500 school districts.* The aim of racially integrated schools was thus undermined by the purchasing power which made 'white flight' possible. The problem is openly acknowledged:

> Largely because of the persistence of residential segregation and so-called 'white flight' from the public school system in many larger urban areas, minorities often attend comparatively under-funded (and thus lower-quality) primary and secondary schools.[†]

* US Department of Justice, Civil Rights Division, Educational Opportunities Section – Overview, text at www.usdoj.gov/crt/edo/overview.htm, September 2001.
[†] Initial report of the United States of America to the United Nations Committee on the Elimination of Racial Discrimination, September 2000, p. 18. The text is available at www.state.gov/www/global/human_rights/cerd_report/cerd_index.html.

The *Brown* judgement was a signpost towards desegregation, but the 'white flight' led in the opposite direction, towards resegregation.[5]

In South Africa, detailed constitutional provisions on education have demonstrated the need to pursue two opposed paths at the same time: to redress effects of racial discrimination while upholding parental freedom of choice, even if it works in the opposite direction. South Africa's Constitutional Court had to rule on the testing of children in Afrikaans as a requirement of access to school. The underlying question was whether the court would challenge the guarantee of parental freedom of choice to educate their children – at their own expense – in a particular language, when the language and racial boundary coincided. The court has noted that the Constitution protects parental freedom to establish schools at their own expense 'from invasion by the state', emphasizing the heritage of Bantu education as background:

> The constitutional entrenchment of that freedom is particularly important because of our special history initiated during the fifties, in terms of the system of Bantu education. From that period the state actively discouraged and effectively prohibited private educational institutions from establishing or continuing private schools and insisted that such schools had to be established and administered subject to the control of the state. The execution of those policies constituted an invasion on the right of individuals in association with one another to establish and continue, at their own expense, their own

> educational institutions based on their own values. Such invasions would now be
> constitutionally impermissible ...

The obligation to respect parental freedom to establish schools based on, among other things, language, favours those able to afford it. Since income remains racially stratified, allowing the testing of children for their linguistic competence in Afrikaans could perpetuate racial segregation, defying the constitutional requirement whereby 'the right to establish educational institutions based on common culture, language or religion cannot be exercised in a manner that discriminates against pupils on the grounds of race'.[6]

Religious and secular schooling

International human rights law accommodates parental preferences concerning education of their children. It requires states not only to allow establishment of schools but also to adjust public schools to the parental preferences. The guarantee of freedom of religion in international human rights law does not have a counterpart that would guarantee freedom *from* religion. A complaint against 'compulsory instruction for atheists in the history of religion and ethics' as a human rights violation has been rejected, with an explanation that 'given in a neutral and objective way and [if it] respects the convictions of parents and guardians who do not believe in any religion' it does not violate human rights.[7]

Respect for religious convictions has emerged with particular frequency with regard to Jehovah's Witnesses. The European Court of Human Rights examined a complaint concerning a girl who was suspended from school because of her refusal to participate in a parade. She regarded it as a commemoration of war. Her religious convictions prevented her from participating in an event that would glorify warfare. The court took note of the parents' pacifist convictions (not saying anything about the girl's own) but found no human rights violation.[8] The Supreme Court of the Philippines has taken the opposite approach and affirmed that children who are Jehovah's Witnesses have the right to be exempt from the flag ceremony (consisting of the singing of the national anthem, saluting the flag and reciting a patriotic pledge) because their freedom to exercise their religious beliefs could only be limited on the grounds of a danger to public safety.[9] These two different decisions demonstrate the lack of a globally shared yardstick for assessing how far public secular schools should accommodate the religious beliefs of their pupils. Jurisprudence in this area is evolving, as is the search for balancing the rights in conflict and their conflicting interpretations. It is likely, even without growing Islamophobia in the United States and Western Europe in the aftermath of September 11th, that Islam will continue questioning that balance. The reason is that international human rights law was founded on the Western heritage of separation between church and state. The original assumption that religion would remain confined to the private sphere did not, however, stand the test of time.

The ripple effects of
the 1979 Islamic revolution in Iran

Iran ended the centrality of the Cold War on the global human rights agenda. Following its 1979 revolution, it launched a formidable challenge to the legitimacy of secular − including human rights − law. This challenge, which has subsequently been amplified, questioned the very normative basis of international law, especially regarding human rights. A decade later, after the Cold War had ended, this led to negative publicity for Islam, which intensified in the aftermath of September 11th. Islam became a convenient ideological foe to replace communism. The line of reasoning was that Islam was hostile to human rights, Islam was equated with fundamentalism, and fundamentalism was equated with terrorism.[10]

The 1979 revolution ousted Shah Reza Pahlavi − not known for his commitment to human rights − and brought to life the Islamic Republic of Iran. The US embassy in Teheran was the first and most publicized target, typifying the change from a Western-supported to an anti-Western regime. In that tense atmosphere, the new Islamic Republic of Iran in 1981 challenged the Universal Declaration of Human Rights for being secular. Iran argued that religious (divine) law had precedence over secular (man-made) law, that secular bodies were not qualified to interpret religious law.[11] UN human rights bodies objected to 'the lack of transparency and predictability in the application of Iranian domestic law'[12] resulting from the powers of religious bodies to determine the contents of the law.

Such a challenge by Iran had not been anticipated. Controversy intensified when Iran questioned the powers of UN human rights bodies to assess its human rights law and practice. In 1981, Iran's ambassador to the UN stated that the United Nations was a secular body and should not address religious matters.[13] One year later, Iran dissociated itself from the Universal Declaration of Human Rights and international human rights treaties, although it did not formally renounce them.[14] Separation between church and state was rejected with the following rationale:

> God has assigned his prophets to guide people to salvation. The Shiite Imam, as the true successor to the Prophet Muhammed, has the responsibility to create a favourable atmosphere for the furtherance of moral values based on faith and righteousness and to struggle against all manifestations of corruption. It is for this reason that in this last monotheist divine religion there is no separation between the State and religion.[15]

Controversies intensified and the UN Special Rapporteur on Iran noted in exasperation that 'there are no accounts of situations or specific cases whose accuracy and veracity are not disputed'.[16] The UN's response was also exasperating. The subsequent Special Representative on Iran, Maurice Copithorne, found 'the politicised tone [of] the dialogue so pervasive that human rights are in danger of becoming a vehicle rather than an end in themselves'.[17]

Creationism *versus* evolutionism in the USA

Religion constitutes an immensely important issue in the United States because, unlike most Western and/or Northern countries, the majority in the United States declare themselves to be religious. The turbulent history of conflicts between different religious communities in public schooling led to the separation between church and state in the US Constitution. This had initially been interpreted to require that public education be secular; but this was subsequently reversed, and further change is likely to ensue.

The text of the US Constitution provides a deceptively simple recipe: 'Congress shall make no law respecting an establishment of religion, or prohibiting the free exercise thereof.' The US Supreme Court initially interpreted this as 'the ideal of secular instruction and political neutrality'.[18] After religion was defined to include secularism,[19] it became impossible to advocate freedom *from* religion as a counterpart to freedom *of* religion. The focus gradually shifted from the initial preference for secularism to equal status for religion and secularism, and to the challenging of 'discrimination against religion'. Moreover, freedom-of-speech safeguards equated the 'religious perspective' and 'secular perspective'.[20] This has facilitated the entry of religion into school activities, programmes and curricula.

Science thirsts for empirically based knowledge; religious beliefs involve decisions about right and wrong. Such beliefs are often used to challenge empirically based knowledge. Disentangling the two was mandated by the US Supreme Court when it posited that government should avoid entanglement with religion. This recipe has not been heeded.

Darwin's *The Origin of Species* created a stir by demonstrating how natural selection occurs. This prompted opposition from many religious communities whose belief in design by the Creator was challenged by the discovery. US courts became involved in 1927, when a teacher was dismissed for teaching evolution, an anti-religious doctrine positing that human beings evolved from other species.[21] (The trial was dubbed 'the monkey trial'.) The US Supreme Court revisited the issue in the 1960s, and a law banning the teaching of evolution was declared unconstitutional: '"creationism" represented a religious dogma which hampered scientific education'.[22] The issue was not settled, however, and the US Supreme Court had to rule on whether school curricula should include the theory of evolution or the biblical account of human creation, or both. It upheld evolution, emphasizing the need for effective teaching of science.[23] The Supreme Court's judgments are delivered far away from school boards which make decisions by majority vote. These are political choices. The autonomy of universities prevents such political choices from moulding the curriculum, as does respect for academic freedom, but students enter university after twelve years of schooling governed through such political choices and influenced by associated advertising.[24]

Kansas was a target of worldwide attention when its school board opted for 'creationism' in 1999. Elections in 2000 altered its composition, making reversal of that decision possible. Decision-making involved consultations with the public,

Christian Rights campaigners lobby to overturn the second law of thermodynamics © the Onion 2002

encompassing actors with opposite viewpoints such as Kansas Citizens for Science, the Intelligent Design Network, the University of Kansas, and the Creation Science Association of Mid-America. The board appointed a Kansas Science Education Standards Writing Committee, which suggested restoring evolution in the curriculum, and the board's majority voted in favour.[25] The fate of school curricula may have been thus decided until the next round of elections for the school board.

Overcoming the heritage of *defectology*

Unlike decisions on what children should learn, which are seen as political choices, education for children with disabilities is viewed in terms of funding. Increasing the teacher–pupil ratio from 1:30 to 1:2 elevates the cost. While determining the curriculum and contents of education is seen as a costless political choice, children with disabilities are defined as costly, as if the definition of disability was not itself a political choice, as well as the consequent denial of education or segregation.

Terms 'learners with special needs' or 'exceptional learners' were driven by guilt associated with the pejorative reference to 'the disabled'. In the former Soviet Union, a scientific discipline was created – *defectology*. Children categorized

151

as having 'defects' were segregated into separate institutions, never to join the mainstream, doomed for life to institutions endowed with fewer and fewer resources.[26] The Supreme Court of Canada has defined non-discrimination with regard to persons with disabilities thus:

> Exclusion from the mainstream of society results from the construction of a society based solely on 'mainstream' attributes to which disabled persons will never be able to gain access. Whether it is the impossibility of success at a written test for a blind person, or the need for a ramp access to a library, the discrimination does not lie in the attribution of untrue characteristics to the disabled individual. The blind person cannot see and the person in a wheelchair needs a ramp. Rather, it is the failure to make reasonable accommodation, to fine-tune society so that its structures and assumptions do not result in the relegation and banishment of disabled persons from participation, which results in discrimination against them. The discrimination inquiry which uses 'the attribution of stereotypical characteristics' reasoning as commonly understood is simply inappropriate here. It may be seen rather as a case of reverse stereotyping which, by not allowing for the condition of a disabled individual, ignores his or her disability and forces the individual to sink or swim within the mainstream environment. It is recognition of the actual characteristics, and reasonable accommodation of these characteristics which is the central purpose of [non-discrimination].[27]

The proportion of schoolchildren with special needs varies internationally between 1 per cent and 41 per cent.[28] Finland reports 18 per cent, Greece, Italy and Spain less than 2 per cent of children with special educational needs.[29] Such disparate figures demonstrate the lack of a shared notion of what special needs are, and the blurring of difference between the three Ds – disability, difficulty, and disadvantage. Disability is commonly defined by reliance on the medical model. Learners with visual, hearing, physical or mental impairments are segregated into special schools or provided with teaching and learning aids in mainstream schools. Learning difficulties are differently diagnosed. Immigrant or minority children, unfamiliar with the language of instruction, may be diagnosed as having learning difficulties.

One line of argument follows equal rights and the best interests of each child, arguing that schools should adapt to each child rather than rejecting those labelled difficult-to-educate. Another argument acknowledges openly and honestly that 'the reason why so many pupils with disabilities do not attend ordinary schools is that ordinary schools cannot cater for them'.[30] The reason is insufficient resources – space, time, teaching staff, teaching and learning aids – which budgetary stringency and increased competitiveness are making worse. However, denials of education are rarely based on cost alone.

The Czech government reported to the UN Committee on the Elimination of Racial Discrimination in April 2000 that 75 per cent of Roma children are routed to special schools, which means that they cannot continue education in secondary schools, nor can they acquire vocational qualifications.[31] The story is, unfortunately, typical, and there have been repeated denunciations of the racial segregation of the Roma in education in the Czech Republic, as well as in the neighbouring Slovak Republic.[32] The background has been explained in more detail in the *Central Europe Review*:

'Our children grow up in mud, in settlements that are often segregated not only from the rest of the village but also cut off from the water and electricity.' Several elementary schoolteachers told CER [Central Europe Review] that Roma children from the settlements have no idea how to peel a banana or an orange before eating it when they first come to school.

Since the attendance of Romani children at kindergarten is relatively low their knowledge of the Slovak language is minimal by the time they enroll at the elementary school. The mental capacity of a six-year-old Roma child, as argued by staff at the State Pedagogical Institute, is equivalent to a two- to three-year-old non-Roma child. This is evident from their drawings and paintings in the first grade of the elementary school.

An elementary schoolteacher told CER that, because the Romani child does not usually understand Slovak at the time of enrollment into the elementary school, they are unable to follow first grade lessons. Whilst their knowledge of the Slovak language improves over the first school year, the child can miss key topics and usually falls behind in the second grade.

The trend continues into the third and the fourth grades so by the time Romani children reach their fifth grade they are unable to catch up. As a result, the school arranges the transfer of the child to the special school for mentally handicapped. ...

A director of a special school for mentally handicapped told CER that in many cases the Roma children who are transferred for having poor schooling results are certainly not mentally handicapped.

The state that is responsible for the elementary education of all children has been shifting Roma children, who come from bi-, sometimes tri- or quatro-lingual families, into special schools for mentally handicapped for years. In these institutions children cannot complete the elementary education necessary for pursuing secondary school or university. Instead of pursuing their studies, Romani children that finish special remedial schools for mentally handicapped at best find themselves a place at a special occupation training school for blue-collar workers. At worst, they see another side of social exclusion – long-term unemployment.[33]

When it does not entail less education, diagnosis of special needs does – as it should – lead to compensation of disability, difficulty or disadvantage. In the UK, entitlements for learners with special needs to additional help depend on their being individually 'statemented'. This denotes that such pupils are issued with a statement which formally affirms their special educational needs that then ought to be met.[34] If the yardstick for funding schools was that they should meet all the needs of all pupils the problem would not arise. This is not the case anywhere in the world, and hence there is a universal struggle for funds:

- Parents want as much funding for their child with special needs as possible.

- Both special and mainstream schools want as much funding as possible.

- Schools generally prefer the funds and not the difficult-to-handle pupils.[35]

Conceptually the most far-reaching judicial interpretations of the meaning of the right to education have dealt with children with disabilities. It is indeed the best illustration of the strength and vigour of the notion of the rights of the child to see courts in a variety of countries affirming that education has to be adapted to each child rather than that children should be forced to adapt to whatever schooling has been designed for them.

Inclusiveness, that is, integration of learners with disabilities into main-stream schools, has created the need to adapt to learners with divergent abilities, placing costs into the human rights framework. The jurisprudence has affirmed that 'admission of a severely handicapped child to an ordinary school, with the expense of additional teaching staff or to the detriment of other pupils' is not an entitlement when education can be provided in a special school.[36] This has been amplified by the German Federal Constitutional Court, which has held that inclusiveness does not diminish the need to review each individual case, giving particular weight to the views of the child and his or her parents:

> The current state of pedagogical research does not indicate that a general exclusion of disabled children from integrated general schools can be constitutionally justified. The education should be integrated, providing special support for disabled pupils if required, so far as the organizational, personal and practical circumstances allow this. This reservation is included as an expression of the need for the State to consider all the needs of the community in carrying out its duties, including the financial and organizational factors.[37]

These photographs of teaching and learning chicken-and-egg in sign language show how much fun education can be.

Box 10.3 • Bridge or fence between communities? Prospects for desegregating education in Sri Lanka

*Since the 1970s in Sri Lanka, history has not been taught as a separate subject, but incorporated into the social studies curriculum. In Sinhala-medium schools the texts used for teaching Buddhism, Sinhala language and social studies were found to contain the most damaging messages for ethnic relations, conveying negative images of Tamils as the historical enemies of the Sinhalese and celebrating ethnic heroes who are presented as having vanquished Tamils in ethnic wars. In Tamil-medium schools, ethnic antagonism was not conveyed in the school texts themselves, however. Government textbooks do not contain anti-Sinhala attitudes. Texts used in teaching Hinduism and the Tamil language are mostly mono-cultural in content, with very few references at all to the Sinhalese or other ethnic groups. Social studies was the subject in which prejudice was most strongly conveyed, despite the fact that Tamil-language social studies texts themselves contain primarily a Sinhalese version of Sri Lankan history.

In Sinhala-medium schools, a considerable amount of history is taught in the Buddhism curriculum. It emphasizes Sinhalese confrontations with Tamils in defence of Buddhism. Teachers of Buddhism generally supported such use of history. They felt it important for their students to know about "struggles that the leaders of the country undertook to preserve the faith". Positive lessons from history are not included. No attempts are made to teach about the contributions that certain Tamil kings made to Buddhism, or the links that existed between Sri Lankan kingdoms and Buddhist centres in south India, for example.

In the case of social studies teaching in the Tamil medium, ethnic prejudice and antagonism was conveyed despite its absence in the school textbooks themselves. Tamil teachers and students alike saw the official history contained in the textbooks as erroneous, but necessary for passing exams. In addition to the official history, Tamil reinterpretations were taught and discussed which conveyed a reverse image of the same long history of conflict.*

"Just as much as Tamil is my mother tongue I want Sinhala to be my father tongue. To be clever, I must know English too," says 14-year-old Siva from one of Sri Lanka's tea-growing estates. His personal language plan, and ployglot optimism, is evidence that Sri Lanka's attempt to heal decades of bitter language politics through trilingual education is bearing fruit. Yet, there are few countries in the world where the consequences of government language policy have been so serious and so disastrous.

After independence in 1948, Sri Lanka embarked on a remarkable roller coaster of language politicisation. In 1956 Prime Minister Bandanaraike's

> ⇨ government made Sinhala the sole official language. Through the 1960s Tamil objections to the Sinhala Only policy eventually established the "right to an education" in the two national languages, but also segregated the school system.'†
>
> * E. Nissan, *Sri Lanka: A Bitter Harvest*, Minority Rights Group International, London, 1996, p. 36.
> † J.L. Bianco, 'Sri Lanka's trilingual peace, Learning English Supplement', *Guardian Weekly*, November 1999.

Notes

1. UNESCO, Declaration on race and racial prejudice, adopted by the General Conference of UNESCO on 27 November 1978, Article 1 (2).
2. Constitutional Court of South Africa, *Christian Education South Africa v. Minister of Education*, Case CCT 4/00, Judgement of 18 August 2000, para. 24.
3. B. Rose and R. Tunmer, *Documents in South African Education*, A.D. Donker, Johannesburg, 1975, p. 118.
4. A. N. Pelzer (ed.), *Verwoerd Speaks: Speeches 1948–1966*, APB Publishers, Johannesburg, 1966, p. 77.
5. Commission on Human Rights, Report submitted by Katarina Tomasevski, Special Rapporteur on the right to education: Mission to the United States of America 24 September – 10 October 2001, UN Doc. E/CN.4/2002/60/Add.1.
6. Constitutional Court of South Africa, *The Gauteng Provincial Legislature: Dispute concerning the constitutionality of certain provisions of the School Education Bill of 1995*, CCT 39/95, 4 April 1996, para. 5.
7. Human Rights Committee, *Erkki Hartikainen v. Finland*, Communication 40/1978, Views of 9 April 1981.
8. European Court of Human Rights, *Efstratiou v. Greece* and *Valsamis v. Greece*, Judgements of 18 December 1996.
9. Supreme Court of the Philippines, *Ebralinag v. The Division Superintendent of School of Cebu*, G.R. Nos. 95770 & 95887, 1 March 1993 and 29 December 1995.
10. K. Tomasevski, *Responding to Human Rights Violations 1946–1999*, Martinus Nijhoff/Kluwer, 2000, pp. 156–83.
11. Statement of Ambassador of Iran to the United Nations before the Third Committee of the General Assembly, UN Doc. A/C.3/36/SR.29 of 26 October 1981, pp. 4–5.
12. Comments of the Human Rights Committee following its consideration of the second periodic report of the Islamic Republic of Iran, UN Doc. CCPR/C/79/Add. 25 of 3 August 1993, para. 6.
13. Statement of Ambassador Khorasani before the Third Committee of the General Assembly of 26 October 1981, UN Doc. A/C.3/36/SR. 29, pp. 4–5.
14. T. Meron, 'Iran's challenge to the international law of human rights', *HRI Reporter*, Vol. 13, No. 1, Spring 1989, pp. 8–10.
15. United Nations, Core document forming part of the reports of States parties: Islamic Republic of Iran, UN Doc. HRI/CORE/1/Add. 93 of 30 June 1998, para. 8.
16. General Assembly, Situation of human rights in the Islamic Republic of Iran. Note by the Secretary-General, UN Doc. A/45/697 of 6 November 1990, para. 265.
17. Commission on Human Rights, Report on the situation of human rights in the Islamic Republic of Iran, prepared by the Special representative of the Commission on Human Rights, Mr Maurice Copithorne, UN Doc. E/CN.4/1996/59 of 21 March 1996, para. 2.

18. US Supreme Court, *Barnette*, 319 US 637.
19. Religion includes 'secular humanism' (*Torcaso v. Watkins*, 367 U.S. 488 (1961)) or else a 'religion of secularism' (*Abington School District v. Schempp*, 374 U.S. 203 (1963)).
20. *Lamb's Chapel v. Center Moriches Union Free School District*, 113 S. Ct. 2141 (1993).
21. Supreme Court of Tennessee, *Scopes v. State*, 154 Tenn. 105, 289 S.W. (1927).
22. US Supreme Court, *Epperson v. Arkansas*, 393 U.S. 97 (1968).
23. US Supreme Court, *Edwards v. Aguillard*, 482 U.S. 578, 19 June1987.
24. Fliers around shopping malls include texts such as this: 'The theory of evolution is just a theory, yet our public school's texts do not mention the significant amount of scientific evidence against it. Why the censorship?'
25. The science standards as recommended by the Kansas Science Education Standards Writing Committee (albeit after numerous alterations) were adopted by 7 votes to 3, overriding arguments by members who were 'personally not ready to accept the idea that nature was solely responsible for the origin of life'. Kansas State Board of Education Meeting Minutes, 13 February 2001, (www.ksde.org/commiss/bdmin/Feb01mins.html).
26. Mental Disability Rights International, *Children in Russia's Institutions: Human Rights and Opportunities for Reform*, Washington, DC, February 1999, p. 9
27. Supreme Court of Canada, [1997] *Eaton v. Brant County Board of Education*, 1 S.C.R., 241, para. 67.
28. *Education at a Glance: 2001 OECD Indicators*, Paris, 2001, p. 174.
29. European Commission, *Key Data on Education in Europe 1999/2000*, Office for Official Publications of the European Communities, Luxembourg, 2000, pp. 141 and 149.
30. S. Hegarty, *Educating Children and Young People with Disabilities: Principles and the Review of Practice*, UNESCO, Paris, [n.d.], p. 49.
31. Committee on the Elimination of Racial Discrimination, 'Fourth periodic report of the Czech Republic', UN Doc. CERD/C/372/Add. 1 of 14 April 2000, para. 134.
32. Committee against Racial Discrimination, Concluding observations relating to Slovakia, UN Doc. A/55/18 of 14 August 2000, paras 9 and 11.
33. E. Sobotka, '1+1=3: Roma in the Slovak educational system', *Central Europe Review*, Vol. 3, No. 2, 15 January 2001.
34. The UK government has openly acknowledged that parents seek statutory statements because this may be 'the only route to funding to meet children's needs'. Department for Education and Employment, *Excellence for All Children: Meeting Special Educational Needs*, Green Paper, October 1997, Appendix 2, para. 1.
35. European Agency for Development in Special Needs Education, *Financing of Special Needs Education. A Seventeen-Country Study of the Relationship between Financing of Special Needs Education and Inclusion*, Middelfart, November 1999, p. 157.
36. European Commission on Human Rights, *Martin Klerks v. the Netherlands*, Application No. 25212/94, Decision on admissibility of 4 July 1995, *Decisions & Reports*, Vol. 82, 1994, p. 129.
37. Federal Constitutional Court of Germany, Decision of 8 October 1997, 1 BvR 9/97.

Chapter 11

Rights-based Education as a Pathway to Gender Equality

Improved access of girls to school has been prioritized in global education strategies by setting 2005 as the target year for the elimination of gender disparities. This is the earliest time-bound goal agreed at Dakar in 2000, and hence it will be a test case for others. Table 11.1 reproduces data collected by UNESCO's International Institute of Statistics on the gaps that ought to be closed by the year 2005. The record thus far has been mixed. Gender disparity in access to school continues in many parts of the world, while girls outnumber boys in some countries, among them Botswana, Lesotho, Mongolia and the Philippines. Disparity may be reduced for a while but the accomplishment then proves unsustainable. Furthermore, education alone is insufficiently attractive to be self-sustaining. What girls can do with their education determines the attractiveness of schooling. If women cannot be employed or self-employed, own land, open a bank account, get a bank loan, if they are denied freedom to marry or not to marry, if they are deprived of political representation, education alone will have little effect on their plight. The principle of indivisibility of human rights necessitates looking at education in relation to all other rights and freedoms. Indeed, it is the recognition of all other rights – or the lack thereof – that affects education.

Why basic education for all girls may not make much difference on its own

Attempts to remedy the unequal enrolments of girls have included both inducements to their parents and increases in the availability of schools and access to them. The latter has included requirements upon primary schools to enrol a specific percentage of girls, establishment of special schools for girls, and the recruitment and training of female teachers. Experiences have shown that such initiatives yield results, but these are patchy and often not sustained. The mid-decade review of Education for All found in 1995 that 'the gender gap in age-specific net enrolment ratios actually grew worse in the 1990s, except in the Arab states'.[1] Subsequently, gender disparity increased in the Arab states in 1995–2000 with proportionally fewer girls having had access to schooling.[2] Reasons why improved enrolments did not prove sustainable point to the importance of what girls can do with their education.

An illustrative question has been voiced in Saudi Arabia:

Table 11.1 • Countdown to the year 2005: gender disparities in primary school enrolment

Reverse gender gap: Lower enrolment of boys	Enrolment % Girls	Boys	No gender gap, or less than 2% difference	Enrolment % Girls	Boys	Less than 10% difference in enrolments favouring boys	Enrolment % Girls	Boys	More than 10% difference in enrolments favouring boys	Enrolment % Girls	Boys
Bahrain	98	96	Argentina	100	100	Algeria	92	96	Burkina Faso	28	40
Botswana	82	79	Bolivia	100	100	Angola	53	61	Central African R.	43	64
Cuba	97	96	Chile	87	88	Brazil	96	100	Chad	42	68
Dominican Rep.	88	87	China	100	100	Burundi	34	41	Côte d'Ivoire	51	67
Jordan	83	82	Costa Rica	92	92	Comoros	46	54	Djibouti	27	37
Lesotho	64	56	Fiji	100	100	Congo/Kinsh.	31	33	Ethiopia	30	41
Madagascar	63	62	Kuwait	67	68	Egypt	89	95	Guinea	37	54
Namibia	90	83	Malaysia	98	98	El Salvador	80	82	Guinea-Bissau	44	62
Paraguay	92	91	Maldives	100	100	Eritrea	31	36	Iraq	74	85
Rwanda	92	90	Mauritius	93	93	Gambia	57	65	Liberia	35	46
Samoa	98	95	Mexico	100	100	Guatemala	80	85	Mali	34	49
Swaziland	78	76	Nicaragua	80	80	Indonesia	82	86	Morocco	73	85
Tanzania	49	47	Peru	100	100	Iran	78	81	Niger	20	32
Uruguay	92	92	Qatar	85	86	Laos	73	79	Papua N. Guinea	78	91
Zimbabwe	91	90	Sri Lanka	100	100	Lebanon	77	79	Senegal	54	64
			United Arab E.	82	83	Mauritania	58	62	Togo	78	99
			Vanuatu	100	100	Mozambique	37	45	Yemen	44	77
			Venezuela	88	88	Oman	65	67			
						Philippines	97	99			
						Saudi Arabia	57	61			
						Sierra Leone	55	60			
						Sudan	42	50			
						Syria	89	96			
						Thailand	76	78			
						Tunisia	96	99			
						Zambia	72	74			

Note: The data have been collected by the UNESCO Institute for Education within monitoring of Education for All. Most figures refer to 1998, the most recent year for which education statistics are available. Many do not reflect precise measurements but are estimates.

> Is there any logical justification for spending huge amounts of money on women's education when thousands of female graduates face the prospect of either remaining at home or entering a single profession, girls' education, which is already overcrowded?[3]

In Saudi Arabia, girls' education was transferred from the religious authorities to the ministry of education in March 2002, following a tragedy in which fifteen girls burned to death in a girls's school in Mecca, prevented from escaping because they had not been properly veiled.[4] Underlying an education policy which posits that girls should become good housewives, wives and mothers is the wives' status as property of their husbands. In the words of Sheikh Abdul-Aziz al-Aqil, 'the Muslim woman is a precious jewel whom only her rightful owner can possess, for he has paid dearly for that'.[5]

Box 11.1 • The price parents pay for having their daughters schooled

Girls' right to education is inextricably linked with the rights they can gain through education; these lie beyond education strategies. A glimpse into the detrimental effects of formal schooling on girls' marital prospects in Uganda and Nepal demonstrates the need for mainstreaming all human rights in education strategies. The intrinsic value of education, which is so optimistically assumed, clashes with social norms which confine girls to early marriage, negotiated between their parents and those of the prospective bridegroom. The price which a girl can fetch amongst the Karimojong in Uganda is reduced if the girl has gone through formal schooling. The price which the girls' parents have to pay to the bridegroom's family, as lamented by a Nepali mother, increases with the girl's formal schooling.

In Uganda, the Moroto district Assistant Chief Accounting Officer Abdul Aziz has depicted education as an obstacle to girls' marital prospects: 'Educated girls do not fetch the 100–120 head of cattle for bride-price. Myth has it that education turns them into prostitutes, they lose virginity which is culturally treasured.' On average an educated Karimojong girl fetches bride-price as low as 5–10 cows.*

Sukhiya Yadav of Armani village in Rautahat district in the Tarai [in Nepal] has four daughters and two sons. She married off her three daughters before they were 12 to avoid having to pay a high dowry price (*lilak*). Times changed, and seeing other people in the village sending their daughters to school, Sukhiya wanted to educate her youngest daughter. So she enroled her little girl along with her son in the local primary school. Now the daughter is 14 and has passed the fifth grade. But this is not a proud moment for the mother, who is constantly worried about her daughter's future. Sukhiya's daughter has passed the primary level but cannot continue going to school because the secondary school is far away and it is not proper for an adolescent girl to be sent such a distance. And her marriage will be a very expensive proposition because it takes more dowry to get older girls married. Sukhiya is not sure any more whether she did the right thing by sending her daughter to school.

'In my zeal to educate my daughter I have brought devastation to my family because now I'll have to sell off all my land to pay the *lilak* for her wedding. If only I had married her off before sending her to school.'[†]

---

* T.W. Kakembo, 'Karimojong choose pen over virginity', *The Monitor* (Kampala), 29 June 1999.
[†] CWIN, *Voice of the Child Worker*, Issue No. 24, March 1995.

Table 11.2 • Women aged 20–24 married before 20 by years of schooling

Country	Less than 7 years of schooling (%)	More than 7 years of schooling (%)	Country	Less than 7 years of schooling (%)	More than 7 years of schooling (%)
AFRICA			**ASIA**		
Botswana	26	15	Indonesia	70	23
Burundi	45	25	Pakistan	57	19
Cameroon	90	49	Philippines	50	23
Ghana	73	55	Thailand	47	14
Kenya	70	36			
Liberia	74	42	**LATIN AMERICA**		
Mali	93	79	Bolivia	53	30
Namibia	32	12	Brazil	53	24
Niger	92	28	Colombia	52	26
Nigeria	83	33	Dominican		
Senegal	75	28	Republic	77	36
Tanzania	80	54	Ecuador	63	30
Togo	71	28	El Salvador	73	33
Uganda	79	55	Guatemala	67	28
Zambia	85	48	Mexico	66	26
Zimbabwe	75	28	Paraguay	53	24
			Peru	64	21
MIDDLE EAST			**OECD**		
Egypt	69	21	France	52	28
Jordan	47	27	Japan	27	2
Morocco	38	11	USA	45	16
Sudan	52	17			
Tunisia	25	9			
Yemen	68	26			

Source: S. Singh and R. Samara, 'Early marriage among women in developing countries', *International Family Planning Perspectives*, Vol. 22, No. 4, December 1996, p. 153.

That women in many countries in the world still face the obstacle of being treated as property is something we prefer to forget because it is difficult to tackle. That obstacle cannot be wished away when devising education strategies because it penalizes parents for having educated their daughters by increasing the dowry they need to pay or decreasing the bride price they would have otherwise obtained, as Box 11.1 illustrates.

Box 11.2 • What AIDS prevention message for schoolchildren?

The UN Secretary-General has urged the case for girls' education by linking it to the empowering of girls to protect themselves against HIV/AIDS: 'Prevented from going to school, [girls] are denied information about how to protect themselves against the virus. Without the benefit of an education, they risk being forced into early sexual relations, and thereby becoming infected. Thus, they pay many times over the deadly price of not going to school.'* At school, they may not be allowed access to information necessary for self-protection. The curriculum is usually designed to accommodate what the closely involved adults, principally parents and teachers, are comfortable with rather than what children need and have a right to get. The Children's Charter, adopted on 1 June 1992 by the Children's Summit of South Africa, posited that all children have the right to adequate education on sexuality.[†] This was a courageous and ambitious statement. School messages tend to be different. The model family presented to Uganda's schoolchildren in 1987 had little resemblance to the Ugandan family: the average number of children was seven, the average number of wives was not known, and polygamy was prevalent.

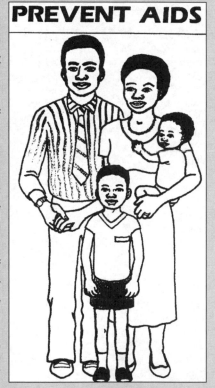

PREVENT AIDS

From a Uganda school health kit on AIDS control

* Address by Kofi Annan, Secretary-General of the United Nations, launching the Girls' Education Initiative at the World Education Forum on 26 April 2000, mimeograph.
† The Children's Charter of South Africa, Pretoria, June 1992, Article 8.

The expectations placed upon girls' education in global and national education strategies are often immense. A few years of schooling alone are expected to make all the difference, and that on their own. The association between women's education and their fertility is a particular focus, because education is generally expected to result in fewer and healthier children. Empirical research shows, however, that education has no statistically visible effect on fertility levels in Africa unless it is for longer than seven years.[6] This is reinforced by data on the linkage between early marriage and education, reproduced in Table 11.2. The data show that it is secondary rather than primary education that has discernible effects on postponing marriage.

Conflicting expectations of girls can deprive them of access to school. If they are required to work in the household, the school schedule has to be adapted to the seasonal and daily rhythm of family life. Since poor families depend on the work of each member of the family for their survival, combining school and work often proves necessary. Parental motivations for not sending children to school are much more pronounced for girls than boys: 'Since girls cannot get jobs if they have only primary education, parents ask: why pay for them to sit six years in a classroom, when they could be at home working?'[7]

Two faces of gender disparity

The interplay between non-availability of schools and parental choice often impedes the schooling of girls. There is a great deal of research targeting parental choices, but a scarcity of information about schools that are available, accessible and acceptable to girls as well as adapted to them. Available schools may be accessible only to boys, by law or in fact. One reason is the teachers.

Table 11.3 summarizes data compiled by UNICEF on the gender imbalance in net enrolments in primary school. (These differ from the data in Table 11.1 because they were reported by different actors for different purposes.) It confirms that gender imbalance victimizes girls but also illustrates the other side of the coin, namely the surplus of girls in some countries. In the Caribbean, UNICEF has noted difficulties in attracting and retaining boys particularly where teachers are female.[8] Table 11.4 reproduces data from UNESCO which illustrate the absence of female teachers in some countries and their prevalence in others.

Both facets of gender disparity point to the need for adaptability. Many international and domestic strategies have been developed to increase the number of female pupils and teachers, but few have been developed to address the other extreme. Few countries in the world have established a policy of gender balance, namely the objective that the representation of one sex should not exceed 40 per cent without corrective measures being automatically triggered off. Table 11.4 shows that women constitute more than two-thirds or even more than four-fifths of primary school teachers in some countries. That pattern was detected in the very first report on discrimination in education produced within the United Nations. This 1957 report highlighted three factors in women's destiny to be primary-school teachers: 'The idea that women are particularly well suited to teach young children, the fact that teaching offers an outlet to women to whom

Table 11.3 • Girls' enrolment in comparison with boys'

More than 10% of girls	Lesotho (11%), Trinidad and Tobago (11%)
+3% to +9%	Mongolia (3%) Nicaragua (3%), Bahamas (4%), Dominican Republic (4%), Botswana (5%), Namibia (7%)
+1% to +2%	Albania, Bahrain, Costa Rica, Denmark, Ecuador, El Salvador, Estonia, Fiji, Georgia, Haiti, Honduras, Hungary, Korea, Luxembourg, Malaysia, Panama, South Africa, USA, Yugoslavia
−1% to −2%	Belize, Bulgaria, Canada, Chile, China, Croatia, Guyana, Libya, Macedonia, Madagascar, Malta, Oman, Peru, Philippines, Poland, Qatar, Samoa, Saudi Arabia, Slovenia, Tanzania, United Arab Emirates, Zambia
−3% to −5%	Belarus, Eritrea, Indonesia, Kenya, Kyrgyzstan, Latvia, Tunisia, Turkey, Vanuatu, Venezuela, Somalia
−6% to −9%	Congo/Brazzaville (6%), Uganda (7%), Algeria (8%), Bangladesh (8%), Bolivia (8%), Burundi (8%), Syria (8%), Ethiopia (9%), Djibouti (9%), Iraq (9%), Mauritania (9%)
−10% to −20%	Cameroon (10%), Comoros (10%), Mozambique (10%), Mali (11%), Papua New Guinea (12%), Senegal (12%), Burkina Faso (13%), Egypt (13%), Iran (13%), Laos (14%), Niger (14%), Gambia (18%), Guinea (18%), Morocco (19%)
More than −20% of girls	Congo/Kinshasa (21%), Central African Republic (22%), Guinea-Bissau (26%), Togo (26%), Afghanistan (27%), Chad (29%), Benin (31%), Nepal (39%)

Source: UNICEF, *The State of the World's Children 1999*, pp. 106–9.

Table 11.4 • Percentage of female primary school teachers

More than 90%	Armenia, Bahamas, Georgia, Kazakhstan, Mongolia, Czech Republic, Italy, Latvia, Lithuania, Moldova, Russia, Slovakia, Slovenia, Ukraine
75%–90%	Australia, Austria, Azerbaijan, Botswana, Bulgaria, Colombia, Croatia, Cuba, Dominica, Estonia, France, Germany, Guyana, Hungary, Ireland, Israel, Jamaica, Kyrgyzstan, Lesotho, Malta, New Zealand, Nicaragua, Qatar, Romania, San Marino, Seychelles, Sri Lanka, Suriname, St Kitts and Nevis, St Lucia, Swaziland, UK, Uzbekistan, Venezuela, USA, Yugoslavia
50%–75%	Albania, Bahrain, Belgium, Belize, Brunei Darussalam, Canada, Cape Verde, Chile, Cyprus, Denmark, Dominican Republic, Ecuador, Egypt, Fiji, Greece, Grenada, Honduras, Indonesia, Iran, Iraq, Japan, Jordan, Kiribati, Korea, Kuwait, Macedonia, Madagascar, Malaysia, Myanmar, Namibia, Netherlands, Paraguay, Peru, Samoa, Saudi Arabia, South Africa, Spain, St Vincent and Grenadines, Sudan, Sweden, Switzerland, Syria, Tajikistan, Tonga, Trinidad and Tobago, United Arab Emirates
25%–50%	Afghanistan, Algeria, Burundi, Cambodia, Cameroon, China, Congo, Djibouti, Eritrea, Ethiopia, Gabon, India, Kenya, Laos, Malawi, Mauritius, Morocco, Niger, Nigeria, Oman, Papua New Guinea, Tanzania, Tunisia, Turkey, Uganda, Vanuatu, Zambia, Zimbabwe
Less than 25%	Benin, Burkina Faso, Chad, Côte d'Ivoire, Congo, Equatorial Guinea, Gambia, Guinea, Mali, Mauritania, Mozambique, Nepal, Pakistan, Senegal, Togo

Source: UNESCO, *World Education Report 1998*, pp. 144–7; the figures refer to 1995.

many other careers remain closed, and the fact that men are attracted towards better paid professions'.[9]

Child-mothers

Early marriage and childbearing conflict with primary education and are often the main reasons for girls not completing primary education. The Charter on the Rights and Welfare of the African Child requires states to ensure that girls who become mothers before completing their primary education 'have an opportunity to continue with their education on the basis of their individual ability'.[10] Translating this obligation into practice requires affirmations that pregnant girls and child mothers have the right to education. The Supreme Court of Colombia has confirmed that school regulations which envisaged penalization of pregnancy by suspending pregnant girls from education and rerouting them into tutorials should be altered. The court has defined pregnant girls' right to education thus:

> Although a suspension from school attendance does not imply a definitive loss of the right to education, it does imply the provision of instruction to the pregnant schoolgirl in conditions which are stigmatizing and discriminatory in comparison with other pupils in her ability to benefit from [the right to education]. Surely, the stigmatization and discrimination implied in the suspension from school attendance have converted this method of instruction into a disproportionate burden which the pupil has to bear solely because she is pregnant, which, in the opinion of the Court, amounts to punishment.
>
> The conversion of pregnancy – through school regulations – into a ground for punishment violates fundamental rights to equality, privacy, free development of personality, and to education.[11]

Pregnancy as a disciplinary offence does not affect boys. They cannot get pregnant and risk punishment. Expulsion of pregnant girls typifies unacceptable school discipline. Education should, in theory, enhance girls' ability to make informed choices. Lack of access to information that would have enabled the girl to make any choice, least of all an informed one, forms the background to much schoolgirl pregnancy. There are frequent clashes between societal norms which pressurize girls into early pregnancy and legal norms which aim to keep them in school. Moreover, the practice of expelling pregnant teachers from school forms part of recent history and points to the heritage of precluding school-children from being exposed to pregnancy by being in the company of pregnant teachers. If a teacher is not married, she may still be dismissed for the offence of pregnancy.[12]

Information about pregnancy as a disciplinary offence leading to expulsion from school is fragmentary, scarce and outdated. Pregnant girls are reportedly expelled from primary and secondary schools in Liberia, Mali, Nigeria, Swaziland, Tanzania, Togo, Uganda, and Zambia, while change has been introduced in Bolivia, Botswana, Chile, Côte d'Ivoire, Guinea, Kenya, and Malawi.[13] Such information is usually collected as the first step towards change.

Change does not come easily. Parents, teachers and community leaders all tend to support the expulsion of pregnant girls from school, rationalizing this punitive choice by the need to uphold moral norms which prohibit teenage sex, with pregnancy treated as irrefutable proof that this norm was breached. Adult men, including teachers, who seem to be responsible for most teenage pregnancies, have remained beyond the remit of punitive measures.

Societal norms are not automatically changed through the adoption of international or domestic guarantees of the equal right to education of girls, nor are they altered through democratic decision-making in which girls would not have a voice anyway. Law provides only a starting point for the process of change. In Africa, Botswana led the way towards readmitting girls expelled from school because of pregnancy,[14] dealing with many obstacles in turn:

> **Rule:** No pregnant girl can write an examination in any school. **Practice**: Affected girls find this rule extremely punitive. If they have prepared for an examination before becoming pregnant (or knowing that they were pregnant), they have to wait two years until they are allowed to take that examination.
>
> **Rule:** The girl-mother should not be above the age limit for admission. **Practice**: Girls who leave school because of pregnancy can apply for re-admission two years thereafter (after pregnancy, delivery and the expiry of another year, defined as mandatory maternity leave), and are certain to be above the age criteria for the class they should be continuing in.
>
> **Rule:** A testimonial and school report from the previous school are required for re-admission. **Practice**: For all girls who left their previous school without informing the head teacher about the reason for leaving (which is often the case), it is unlikely that the head teacher would agree to give any testimonials.
>
> **Rule:** The girl-mother has to furnish her own identity card and the birth certificate of her baby for re-admission. **Practice**: The process of getting a birth certificate is so long and cumbersome that this would delay re-admission even further, while those without identity papers may take even longer to obtain them.[15]

Countering denials of women's rights

It was because of Afghanistan that the issue of denials of women's rights was raised, for the first time in history, before the United Nations Security Council. The military victories of the Taliban in 1994–96 gave effective military control over most of the country; subsequently the Taliban became the *de facto* governing regime. Although Afghanistan had been proclaimed an Islamic state in 1992, the then government did not advocate denial of human rights to women. Explanations for the Taliban's exclusion of girls from schooling were sought in a mixture of restrictive interpretations of Sharia law, and customary practices in parts of Afghanistan.[16] The Taliban's official pronouncements in the areas over which it had gained military control denied women freedom of movement as well as the rights to education and to work.[17] Since this happened just after women's rights were brought into the mainstream through the 1993 Vienna Declaration and Programme of Action, and a commitment to gender equality had been forged during the preparations for the Beijing Conference, international attention on women's rights was at a high point. The Taliban's model of legislating and enforcing denials of women's rights represented an open and explicit defiance of the evolving international commitment to equal rights for women. Foreign and international reactions were rapid and vehement. The human rights of women were mentioned for the first time by the Security Council, which denounced discrimination against girls and women. While it noted 'with deep concern possible repercussions on international relief and reconstruction programmes in Afghanistan', it called upon 'all States and international organizations to extend all possible humanitarian assistance to the civilian population of Afghanistan'.[18] UNICEF had suspended assistance in areas under the Taliban's control, where discriminatory practices against girls and women prevented them from having access to education, and where foreign humanitarian agencies were required not to employ female staff. Even the UN Special Rapporteur on human rights in Afghanistan, whose report detailed those developments, had been prevented from bringing along a female human rights officer.[19]

The banning of education for girls placed the Taliban at odds with the whole world, including other countries applying Sharia law, which were all trying to increase and improve education for girls. Possibly because of many international protests, one subsequent interpretation was 'that the education of Afghan girls had not been banned but only suspended until a segregated system could be organized'.[20] Another interpretation was that both boys and girls could be sent to school up to the age of twelve.[21] Against this heritage, the language of rights was finally introduced to 1.5 million Afghani children who started school in April 2002, and the 3 million who were in school by the following August. The process may prove easier because 30 per cent of teachers are women.[22]

Box 11.3 • Controversial headscarves

Turkey's commitment to secularism in education has brought about a ban on the wearing by girls of headscarves, whose breach entails denial of access to education, or expulsion. The Constitutional Court found in 1998 that headscarves should not be allowed as this 'might adversely affect the public security and unity of the nation because the headscarf or turban shows who belongs to which religion'. Hasan Celal Guzel, a former Minister of Education, was imprisoned for having objected to the exclusion of girls and women from education because of their headscarves. Mass dismissals of university teachers and students for wearing or supporting headscarves occurred in 1998 and 1999, affecting up to 30,000 students and teachers. The International Labour Organization (ILO) has associated headscarves-related restrictions and expulsions with girls' and women's unequal access to education, requesting the government to ensure that such restrictions do not affect the rights of Muslim women:

> The potential discriminatory effect of the ban on headscarves takes on particular significance when viewed in the light of information supplied by the Government

indicating that women's level of education is very low in Turkey (one out of every two women jobseekers has only a primary school education), as is their level of participation in the workforce.[*]

In the Netherlands, a refusal by Muslim girls to participate in physical exercise although it was part of the compulsory curriculum was brought before the Equal Treatment Commission. It has found that the refusal of a school to allow Muslim girls to wear long-sleeved T-shirts, long trousers and headcaps constitutes discrimination. In another case, the efforts of a school to accommodate a Muslim girl by offering to allow her to wear clothing adapted to her religious convictions, and a separate dressing room, have been judged sufficiently accommodating. In yet another case, the Equal Treatment Commission determined discrimination. As part of her practical training at a teacher training college, involving teaching in a primary school, the young woman wanted to teach at her former primary school but was rejected, having answered the question whether she would wear a headscarf in the positive.[†]

In France, courts alternately quashed and upheld the expulsion of girls wearing headscarves. The Conseil d'État, the functional equivalent of a constitutional court, has thus drawn the line between tolerating the display of religious symbols and inhibiting provocation or proselytizing:

> In educational institutions, displaying symbols whereby learners manifest that they pertain to a particular religion is not by itself incompatible with secularism as long as it is confined to exercising their freedom of expression and manifesting their religious beliefs; such freedom does not, however, permit the learners to display religious symbols which, due to their very nature, or to the particular circumstances in which they are displayed, individually or collectively, or to their ostentatious or demonstrative character, constitute an exercise of pressure, provocation, proselytizing or propaganda.[‡]

In Switzerland, public education is secular and ought to respect the religious convictions of every individual child and her or his parents. In a case involving a Muslim teacher wearing a headscarf, the Swiss Federal Court ruled against such a display of religious convictions. It feared disputes amongst children belonging to different religions (and their parents) which the introduction of various religious symbols could engender at school. Moreover, because teachers are a role model for learners, the Court has affirmed the necessity that they be religiously neutral.[§]

[*] Commission on Human Rights, Report submitted by Katarina Tomasevski, Special Rapporteur on the right to education: Mission to Turkey 3–10 February 2002, UN Doc. E/CN.4/2002/60/Add. 2, paras. 57–8.
[†] Equal Treatment Commission of the Netherlands, Rulings No. 1998–79 of 6 July 1998; No. 1997–149 of 24 December 1997; No. 1999–106 of 23 December 1999; No. 1999–103 of 22 December 1999.
[‡] Conseil d'Etat, Case *Kherouaa, Kachour, Balo and Kizic*, decision of 2 November 1992.
[§] *X v. Etat du Canton de Genève*, Arrêt du Tribunal Fédéral, 123 I 296, 12 November 1997.

Adapting education to girls' equal rights

Reviews of school curricula and textbooks promise to change the image of girls and women and to help the new generation avoid the stereotypes that we have been raised with. Studies of school textbooks reveal that they present women at home while men are presented as out in public, making history. A survey of the portrayal of women in textbooks used in primary education in South America has revealed that in Peru, for example, women are mentioned ten times less often than men.[23] In Croatia, a study of secondary school textbooks has shown a focus on adults rather than children. When children are portrayed, they are sons rather than daughters. Sons span 30 per cent of the material on family life and daughters 15 per cent. In secondary school textbooks, it is 42 per cent for sons and 17 per cent for daughters.[24] A study of school textbooks in Tanzania has shown that girls doing domestic chores are a favourite topic in learning English and Kiswahili grammar. A primary school textbook for Kiswahili depicts a girl on her school-free day thus:

> Today is Saturday.
> You don't go to school on Saturday.
> You will work here, at home.
> First, you will wash your school uniform.
> After that, fetch the water.
> Then you clean the compound.
> After we have finished eating, you will wash the dishes.
> Then you will go to the shop to buy sugar and rice. [25]

Father serving tea, mother reading newspapers

It's Sunday, it's Sunday
Holiday and fun day.
No mad rush to get to school
No timetable and strict rule.
Mother's home and so is father
All of us are here together.
Father's like a busy bee
Making us hot cups of tea.
Mother sits and reads the news.
Now and then she gives her views.
It's Sunday, it's Sunday
Holiday and fun day.

Promoting change: new forms of family life
(Verse taken from *Dhamak-Dham*, a book of alternative children's rhymes in Hindi)

This type of analysis is the first step towards change, and such change is taking place rapidly. There is another way of prompting change, illustrated above. Presenting to schoolchildren a family where the father is cooking and serving tea while the mother is reading newspapers and commenting on world politics reflects family life as at least as some children know it today.

Notes

1. *Education for All: Achieving the Goal. Mid-Decade Meeting of the International Consultative Forum on Education for All, 16-19 June 1996, Amman, Jordan, Final Report*, p. 36.
2. Country reports prepared within the Education for All 2000 Assessment are available at http://www2.unesco.org/efa/wef/countryreports/home-html.
3. A.R. Al-Rashid, editorial, *Arab News*, 7 February 1999, quoted from: Amnesty International, 'Saudi Arabia: Gross human rights abuses against women', Doc. MDE 23/57/00, London, September 2000.
4. A. Gresh, 'Balbutiments de l'opinion publique en Arabie saoudite', *Le monde diplomatique*, May 2002.
5. D. Hirst, 'Educated for a life of enforced indolence', *Guardian Weekly*, 19–25 August 1999.
6. *Women's Education and Fertility Behaviour: Recent Evidence from the Demographic and Health Surveys*, UN Doc. ST/ESA/SER.R/137, United Nations, New York, 1995, p. 30.
7. T. Jackson, *Equal Access to Education: A Peace Imperative for Burundi*, International Alert, London, June 2000, p. 29.
8. UNICEF, *The State of the World's Children 1999*, New York, 1998, p. 58-9.
9. United Nations, Study of Discrimination in Education by Charles Ammoun, Special Rapporteur of the Sub-Commission on Prevention of Discrimination and Protection of Minorities, UN Doc. E/CN.4/Sub.2/181/Rev. 1, Sales No. 1957.XIV.3, New York, August 1957, p. 43.
10. Organization of African Unity, Charter on the Rights and Welfare of the African Child, Article 11 (6).
11. Supreme Court of Colombia/Corte Suprema de Colombia, *Crisanto Arcangel Martinez Martinez y Maria Eglina Suarez Robayo v. Collegio Cuidad de Cali*, No. T-177814, 11 November 1998.
12. The ILO Freedom of Association Committee has dealt with the expulsion of unmarried pregnant teachers in Saint Lucia. According to a 1977 regulation 'an unmarried teacher who becomes pregnant shall be dismissed upon becoming pregnant a second time if still unmarried'. The case revolved around a collective agreement which aimed to alter that regulation. The regulation itself was a consequence of the policy to portray to schoolchildren 'the ideal of married family life' for which teachers were expected to serve as role models. Freedom of Association Committee, 270th Report, Case No. 1447 (Saint Lucia).
13. *School Drop-out and Adolescent Pregnancy: African Education Ministers Count the Cost. A Report on the Ministerial Consultation held from 15 to 18 September, 1994, Mauritius*, organized by the Forum for African Women Educationalists (FAWE) in collaboration with the Government of Mauritius, pp. 23-4 and 58-60.
14. E.L.M. Bayona and I. Kandji-Murangi, *Botswana's Pregnancy Related Educational Policies and Their Implications on Ex-pregnant Girls' Education and Productivity*, Research Priorities for the Education of Girls and Women in Africa, Abridged Research Report No. 16, Academy Science Publishers, Nairobi, undated, p. viii.
15. Summarized from 'Botswana re-entry policy', *FAWE (Forum for African Women Educationalists) News*, Vol. 8, No. 3, July–September 2000, pp. 18–20.
16. The Taliban-specific interpretation of Sharia law is reportedly related to Pashtun

customary law (*Pashtunwali*) rather than solely to the Qu'ran.

17. This denial challenged Afghanistan's twentieth century development from the un-veiling of women in 1959 by Afghanistan's king of the time, Zahir Shah, and the secularization associated with the Soviet-supported regime in 1978–89 which, *inter alia*, entailed equal rights for girls and women as well as measures to decrease the high illiteracy rate among women (an estimated 80 per cent).

18. Security Council resolution 1076 (1996) of 22 October 1996, paras. 11 and 12.

19. Commission on Human Rights, Final report on the situation of human rights in Afghanistan submitted by Mr Choong-Hyun Paik, Special Rapporteur, UN Doc. E/CN.4/1996/64 of 27 February 1996, paras. 69, 70, 72–3, 76, and 86–7.

20. Commission on Human Rights, Final report on the situation of human rights in Afghanistan submitted by Mr. Choong-Hyun Paik, Special Rapporteur, UN Doc. E/CN.4/1997/59 of 20 February 1997, para. 80.

21. Commission on Human Rights, Final report on the situation of human rights in Afghanistan submitted by Mr. Choong-Hyun Paik, Special Rapporteur, UN Doc. E/CN.4/1998/71 of 12 March 1998, para. 31.

22. A. Rashid, 'Afghanistan: A revolution', *Far Eastern Economic Review*, 1 August 2002.

23. T. Valdes and E. Gomariz, *Latin American Women: Compared Figures*, Instituto de la Mujer and FLASCO (Facultad Latinoamericana de Sciencias Sociales), Santiago de Chile, 1995, p. 105.

24. Summarized results of the research project entitled Portrayal of Women in Croatian Textbooks, carried out by a team led by Branislava Baranovic of the Institute for Social Research, are available on the website of the women's human rights group B.a.B.e. (Be active, Be emancipated) at htpp://members.tripod.com/~CRWOWOMEN/august00.htm

25. D.A. Mbilinyi, 'Women and gender relations in school textbooks', in D.A. Mbilinyi and C. Omari (eds.),*Gender Relations and Women's Images in the Media*, Dar es Salaam University Press, Dar es Salaam, 1996, pp. 93–4.

Chapter 12

Human Rights Safeguards in Education

The right to education is a bridge to *all* human rights: education is indispensable for effective political participation and for enabling individuals to sustain themselves; it is the key to preserving languages and religions; it is the foundation for eliminating discrimination. It is the key to unlocking other human rights. The rationale for human rights safeguards is that power is easily abused, hence safeguards against its abuse are always necessary. Children are the easiest victims of abuses of power by their parents, teachers, or governments. Domestic laws which force indigenous peoples to abandon their identity as the price of access to school, deny their rights, as Box 12.1 illustrates.

Box 12.1 • From hispanicizing to educating in Latin America

Regarding the discrimination that still affects the indigenous woman, in her traditional skirt, the Vice-President of the Bolivian Republic, Victor Hugo Cárdenas, made his views clear in a press interview:

'Cárdenas recognizes that progress is slow, though tangible, and does not deny that indigenous communities still suffer from marginalization and racism. For example his wife, Lidia Katari, a teacher by profession, is unable to teach because she dresses in the traditional Indian skirt, shawl and bowler hat. "Years ago they told her that she either got rid of that attire or stopped working. She asked for leave and is now in the battle for her own rights and the rest of the indigenous population." The experience of Cárdenas's grandfather was far more bloody: his boss ordered his hand to be cut off because he considered it insolence that he should be able to write. Cárdenas's father had to change his Aymara family name and adopt a Spanish family name from his mother's line.'*

'For many decades, the education offered by Latin American governments was uniform and took no account of students' local, regional, ethnic or linguistic culture patterns. From the time mass primary education was introduced in [the nineteenth] century, school was considered essential to the formation of the nascent Latin American nations. Thus school was supposed to 'hispanicize'

▷ the population, teach basic civics and provide the conceptual tools necessary for people to function in society. In [the twentieth] century, mass schooling in rural areas made education an important instrument of linguistic and cultural unification. During the 1930s, the view was that isolation and lack of linguistic communication were the main problems that caused discrimination against indigenous communities. In many Latin American countries special educational programmes were set up for the indigenous communities with the aim of improving their command of Spanish (or Portuguese). This process was called 'bilingual education', meaning that the indigenous language was used as a communicative bridge with the new language, the country's official language; today, in technical terms, this approach is called 'transitional bilingual education', since once the official language has been learnt, the vernacular or mother tongue is abandoned. In the 1970s, a new bilingual education movement began in Latin America, known as 'intercultural bilingual education', the aim of which is that indigenous children should master both languages simultaneously and create a dialogue of respect between the indigenous culture and the dominant national culture; many programmes of this kind have been implemented, reflecting the highest level of non-discrimination in the educational system.' †

* Committee on the Elimination of Racial Discrimination, Thirteenth periodic report on Bolivia, UN Doc. CERD/C/281/Add. 1 of 12 July 1995, para. 38.
† Sub-Commission on Prevention of Discrimination and Protection of Minorities, Joint working paper on article 7 of the International Convention on the Elimination of All Forms of Racial Discrimination prepared by Mr José Bengoa, Mr Ivan Garvalov, Mr. Mustafa Mehedi and Mrs Shanti Sadiq Ali, UN Doc. E/CN.4/Sub.2/1998/4 of 10 June 1998, paras. 135–7.

Education is often defined as a message carrier.[1] Whether children understand the message depends on three key factors: the language of instruction, teachers, and books. Hence, human rights safeguards have been prioritized in these three areas.

The majority of children in the world may be educated in a language different from their own, but there is too little information available about language as an obstacle to learning. Whether the message will be understood further depends on the principal messengers, teachers. Education consists of two parallel processes – teaching and learning. Thus, the role of teachers is crucial in facilitating the learning process. Alongside parents, it is teachers who translate the abstractly defined aims and purposes of education into messages that children can recognize and internalize. With the advent of human rights education, it is teachers who are expected to adapt the orientation, contents and methods of education to human rights requirements. And yet, their own rights are often denied or violated, and teachers introducing human rights education may be criminally prosecuted. Schoolbooks result from a process that may be defined as 'technical' but is inherently political. This process should be open to public scrutiny, and guarantees of freedom of information should apply. However, such *shoulds* are conspicuous by their non-implementation.

The medium is the message: the language of instruction

One can easily imagine failing an exam in a language of which one does not understand a single word, in a script which one cannot read. Adding insult to injury, the failure to pass that exam may entail a diagnosis of a severe learning disability. This is the fate of millions of children who are instructed in a language they cannot understand. Their going to school is equated with learning, although the choice of the language of instruction can preclude them from learning anything. The UNESCO/UNICEF Monitoring Learning Achievement Project has found that more than 70 per cent of African schoolchildren are taught in a language other than their mother tongue.[2] For one refugee child from Zaire who continued his education in London, language proved a huge barrier to integration:

> When I began primary school, I had to learn English from the beginning. So I had a special teacher. This caused a lot of jealousy with my class mates. To add to my problems, I spoke French, which was the language that our favourite primary school teacher also spoke. When we spoke to each other nobody else could understand. The other children turned violent towards me. I would regularly go home with bruises on my back, hungry because they would spit in my lunch box.[3]

While foreignness is commonly defined by how people look, speaking a foreign language is as much a symbol of foreignness. The French-speaking African boy may have had a particularly hard time in London because Eurobarometer surveys have shown that English young people are both the least able in Europe to speak another language and the least willing to learn.[4]

Adaptation to linguistic diversity conflicts with unilingualism, if it is a pillar of nation-building. In the United States, English is not the official language of the country, but English-only usage is heavily promoted to hasten a shift to English-only usage for immigrants. This shift sometimes fails to acknowledge the variety of languages that pupils speak; there is no one and only 'foreign language' from which pupils have to be converted to English. A New York teacher who failed the test required for a bilingual teaching certificate described the reason for having failed thus:

> I passed both the Spanish and English written tests and the Spanish oral. I don't think I failed because of the quality of my English, it was my answers. He didn't like them. My interviewer asked me why I wanted to be a bilingual teacher and I told him I wanted to help the Spanish-speaking children in the city. He seemed unhappy with that answer

and asked me what I'd do if I were assigned to a school where the children were Chinese. I asked him why they would send someone who was bilingual in Spanish to a school where the children speak Chinese when there are so many children who speak Spanish. That did it, I think.[5]

A survey by Advocates for the Children of New York has revealed that just below half (49 per cent) of bilingual teachers spoke the same language as their students, while 35 per cent spoke a language that some students could understand.[6] Studies that demonstrate how bilingual education fails in order to encourage English-only education have indeed ample evidence to draw upon. Reasons why bilingual education fails are seldom revealed.

The language of instruction has always created a great deal of controversy and this controversy is not likely to diminish. On the contrary. It encompasses decisions about the official language of instruction for public schools, the teaching of, as well as teaching in, minority and indigenous languages (as well as the recognition thereof), and the teaching of (as well as in) foreign languages. Few countries in the world are officially multilingual, and only a slightly larger number have several rather than only one language of instruction. The European Court of Human Rights has affirmed the right of the state to determine the official language of the country, which is then also the language of instruction in public schools, but it denied that there was a right to education in a language of one's choice.[7]

States have been required to respect the right of minorities to set up their own schools in minority languages since the time of the League of Nations. In 1919 the precedent was set by Poland, which affirmed, alongside education in minority languages in public schools, the right of citizens who were members of minorities to establish, manage and control schools at their own expense, 'with the right to use their own language and to exercise their religion freely therein'.[8] Minority rights preceded human rights in Europe, where minorities created by the many intra-European wars acquired rights under international law between the two world wars. The right of minorities to own-language schools at their own expense was reaffirmed by the Permanent Court of International Justice.[9] Thereby, problems have been diminished rather than solved. Even in Europe, which started elaborating guarantees for minority rights much earlier than other regions, the refusal of individual states to recognize minorities keeps these rights in the realm of the yet-to-be-conquered. In a series of cases the Human Rights Committee has affirmed that no right to education in a minority language exists when a state has explicitly declined to undertake any international human rights obligations entailing the recognition of minorities and corollary guarantees for their rights.[10]

Thus, almost a century after the first international guarantees for minority languages, problems have increased rather than diminished. Demands that minority schools be state-financed are often made but seldom granted. The right to be educated in one's mother tongue has been on the international human rights agenda since the 1950s; controversies and conflicts have intensified with time. The wisdom of unilingual education, even in one's mother tongue, has been challenged, adding a new item to this endless controversy. The financial implications of multilingualism in education have further exacerbated existing controversies.

The language of instruction affects the right to education in two major ways:

- Compulsory instruction in a language which children do not understand constitutes an obstacle to their enjoyment of the right to education;

- Education in a language which prevents children from mastering the official or dominant languages, making them unable to continue education or obtain employment, is discriminatory, as it prevents them from full development and integration in society.

In Laos, schooling is unilingual. School enrolments reflect the linguistic obstacles: non-Lao-speaking minorities are in practice excluded from school. More than 90 per cent of children in the smallest linguistic groups have never attended school:

> Lao, the official and instructional language, is the first language of about 50 percent of the population. Children from homes where Lao is not spoken enter school with a significant handicap, a condition partly accounting for the high dropout rate. Changing the language of instruction would be a complex political and technical problem, and is unlikely in the foreseeable future.[11]

In Canada, detailed guarantees have been adopted with regard to education in English and French which specify entitlements for these two linguistic communities. In the words of Canada's Supreme Court, these language rights are based on political compromise. They cannot be extrapolated to other countries as they are 'quite peculiar to Canada'.[12] Nevertheless, Canada's judicial determination of language rights in education offers a sliding-scale approach to entitlements. Depending on the actual and potential number of learners, these range from minority language instruction to minority language educational facilities, and to the minority's management and control of education. Language rights 'are granted to minority language parents individually. Their entitlement is not subject to the will of the minority group to which they belong, be it that of a majority of that group'.[13] Further, the Supreme Court has clarified the linkage between language and culture:

> [A]ny broad guarantee of language rights, especially in the context of education, cannot be separated from a concern for the culture associated with the language. Language is more than a mere means of communication, it is part and parcel of the identity and culture of the people speaking it. It is the means by which individuals understand themselves and the world around them. Language is not merely a means or medium of expression; it colors the content and meaning of expression. It is ... a means by which a people may express their cultural identity.[14]

Shooting the messengers?
Obstacles to teachers' rights

In the words of the Supreme Court of Canada, 'teachers are seen by the community to be the medium of the educational message', and their position of trust and influence requires that they be held to high standards both on and off duty. The younger their learners, the more vulnerable they are to teachers' abuse of trust and influence. The teachers' conduct in the classroom is an object of scrutiny, as is their out-of-school behaviour:

> A school is a communication centre for a whole range of values and aspirations of a society. In large part, it defines the values that transcend society through the educational medium. The school is an arena for the exchange of ideas and must, therefore, be premised upon principles of tolerance and impartiality so that all persons within the school environment feel equally free to participate.
>
> Teachers are inextricably linked to the integrity of the school system. Teachers occupy positions of trust and confidence, and exert considerable influence over their students as a result of their position. The conduct of a teacher bears directly upon the community's perception of the ability of the teacher to fulfil such a position of trust and influence, and upon the community's confidence in the public school system as a whole.[15]

During the 1980s the West German government excluded members of the Communist Party from the teaching profession. An ILO Commission of Inquiry concluded:

> A teacher obviously has a duty not to abuse his function by indoctrination or other improper influence on his pupils. Further, in activities and statements outside his service, he must bear in mind the compatibility of what he does and says with his responsibilities. When he violates these duties, he can be subject to disciplinary measures quite apart from any general duty of faithfulness to the basic order. Whether a breach of duty has been committed must however be determined on the basis of the actual conduct. There can be no justification to assume that, because a teacher is active in a particular party or organization, he will behave in a manner incompatible with his obligations.
>
> The Commission recognizes that public activities undertaken by a teacher and known to his pupils may exert an influence on the latter. That, however, applies to all teachers, whatever their political orientation, and raises the wider issue of the role which it may be appropriate to permit teachers to play in public life. Guidance on this question is provided by the Recommendation concerning the Status of Teachers, adopted in October 1966 by a Special Intergovernmental Conference convened by UNESCO, in collaboration with the ILO. According to paragraphs 79 and 80 of this Recommendation, 'the participation of teachers in social and public life should be encouraged in the interests of the teachers' personal development, of the educational service and of society as a whole' and 'teachers should be free to exercise all civic rights generally enjoyed by citizens and should be eligible for public office'.[16]

Despite their importance, teachers get no more than a casual nod in global education strategies. It is much too easy to define them as a production factor in the manufacturing of human capital and forget that they are people with rights (alongside having much to say about education). Probing into teachers' fate can reveal that neither their labour rights nor their trade union freedoms are recognized and that their salaries may be much too low to enable them to teach. Furthermore, they are often unable to teach because they had too little education themselves. René Préval, the President of Haiti at the time, described the quality of the teaching profession in the country in 1997:

> This year, we have had a success rate of about 10% in our *baccalauréat* results. In parallel, we made 1,500 teachers sit exams. Only 400 of them were able to put ten words in alphabetical order and just 41 were able to list ten fractions in increasing or decreasing order. [17]

For education that takes place without a school building, without water, sanitation, desks or chairs, books, blackboards, pens or paper, a teacher makes all the difference. To be able to make a difference, the teacher's role needs to be recognized. This is often not the case, as Box 12.2 illustrates for Ethiopia.

For rich teenagers who have replaced socialization by surfing the worldwide web, there is no evidence that this benefits their social skills, tolerance or even basic literacy. A Korean mother of a twelve-year-old complains: 'We're really concerned. We want him to learn from the real world, not the cyber world'. The government of South Korea has set up the Centre for Internet Addiction Counselling. Its work has shown that the average age of the internet addict is 11–13. [18] In the United States, Jane Healy has questioned the role of computers in learning:

> They can hurt children's personal skills, work habits, concentration, motivation, the development of social skills and also I think that they can stand in the way of mental development because so much of the software has been designed by technicians aiming to sell, not child development specialists trying to educate. What you end up with are very consuming and mindless games. This often takes place at critical periods of mental development when kids need to interact with human language in social settings. They need to learn to use their own brains creatively and imaginatively and independently instead of being run through a series of tricks by a software program. [19]

The advantage of teaching being labour-intensive is that the employment of large numbers of people is necessary to educate the millions of children and young people in the world. Since teachers are locally trained, hired and paid, the additional benefit is that there is no need for foreign exchange; this is not the case for the schools or schoolbooks that may be financed through loans which will have to be repaid. It seems, however, that instead of being seen as indispensable for schooling, teachers tend to be perceived as an enemy of their own vocation.

Box 12.2 • Teachers' rights fare ill in Ethiopia

Excerpt from a 1999 UNESCO book on aid for education:

... the World Bank recently sent a group of fourteen experts to Ethiopia to explore the feasibility of an education sector programme. This is a country where more than 100,000 professionals from the civil service, technical establishments and institutions of higher learning have been retired or expelled on political pretext, but using World Bank and IMF structural adjustment justifications. These include over fifty of the university's experienced and seasoned professionals who, from my personal knowledge of a large number of them, could do as good a job, if not better than the World Bank in response to the country's needs.*

Concluding remarks of the ILO Freedom of Association Committee in 2000:

During its previous examinations of this case, the Committee addressed very serious allegations of violations of freedom of association, in particular the Government's refusal to continue to recognize the Ethiopian Teachers' Association (ETA), the freezing of its assets and the killing, arrest, detention, harassment, dismissal and transfer of ETA members and officials.

... the Committee wishes to underline that the trade union situation in Ethiopia in general has been discussed several times during the last eight years ... and that the teachers' and ETA's case in particular have been discussed during three consecutive years by the Conference Committee, which expressed deep concern at the trade union situation in Ethiopia.[†]

Excerpt from 2001 report of the Special Rapporteur on the right to education:

The Special Rapporteur brought to the attention of the Government of Ethiopia an apparently related series of events which targeted officials of the Ethiopian Teachers' Association (ETA). One of them, Dr Taye Wolde-Semayat, was sentenced in June 1999 to long-term imprisonment. Another, Essefa Maru, was killed in 1997; he was the President of ETA at the time.[‡]

* A. Habte, 'The future of international aid to education: a personal reflection', in K. King and L. Buchert (eds.), *Changing International Aid to Education: Global Patterns and National Contexts*, UNESCO Publishing, Paris, 1999, p. 56.
† ILO Freedom of Association Committee, Complaint against the Government of Ethiopia presented by Education International (EI) and Ethiopian Teachers' Association (ETA), Case No. 1888, Interim report, 17 November 2000.
‡ Commission on Human Rights, Annual report of the Special Rapporteur on the right to education, Katarina Tomasevski, UN Doc. E/CN.4/2001/52, para. 19.

One reason teachers are viewed as a burden rather than an asset is the proportion of education budgets allocated to teachers' salaries. In a country where school-age children represent one-third of the population, a ratio of one teacher for every fifty children makes teachers almost 1 per cent of the population. They tend to constitute about 5 per cent of the labour force and their salaries form the bulk of the education budget. The consecutive crises through which education has passed have triggered a constant effort to cut down education budgets. Teachers' salaries were the obvious first target for budgetary cuts, and ideological rationalizations followed.

Trade union freedoms and labour rights for teachers, much as for other professions, form part of basic international labour standards, which are legally enforceable in many countries as well as internationally. Cases such as the denial of the right to form trade unions, dismissal of striking teachers (or their punishment by internal exile, transfer, or reduced salaries), anti-union discrimination, or the harassment, arrest or murder of trade union leaders, have affected teachers as much as other professions. There are, in addition, many issues specific to the teaching profession. Non-discrimination constitutes the key human rights principle and applies to all individual rights and freedoms, those of teachers and learners alike. Discrimination against teachers takes many forms, and ranges from their access to teachers' training, to recruitment, and to dismissal. In the field of teacher training, the Equal Opportunity Commission of the Netherlands, for example, faulted a teacher training college for not preventing its employees from acting in a discriminatory manner. A learner of Surinamese origin had been advised to terminate his studies with the justification that his skills were inadequate. The Commission inquired into the process whereby this conclusion was reached, only to determine that one of the evaluators had made a racist remark; it faulted the teachers' college for failing to protect the applicant against such racist remarks.[20] The Commission has similarly held that the dismissal of a female music teacher, justified by the assertion that male and female music teachers perform differently due to their physiological differences, constituted a human rights violation.[21]

The ILO Freedom of Association Committee has consistently rejected governments' assertions that teaching is an essential service, and has affirmed that teachers have the right to strike: 'the right to strike can only be restricted and even prohibited in the public service (public employees being those who act as agents of the public authority) or in the essential services in the strict sense of the term (i.e. those services whose interruption would endanger the life, personal safety or health of the whole or part of the population)'.[22] The Committee has explained:

> The Committee has been faced with many cases over recent years involving restrictions on the freedom of action of teachers, be they teachers employed in the private sector, as non-titular public employees or having the status of civil servants. ... The Committee reiterates that it has always held the right to strike to be one of the fundamental rights of workers and their organizations; it is one of the essential means through which they may promote and defend their occupational interests.[23]

Moreover, the ILO has affirmed that trade unions 'should be able to have recourse to protest strikes, in particular aimed at criticising a government's economic and social policies'.[24] The Human Rights Committee has examined a case of two university teachers who had been arrested for the offence of lèse-majesté ('outrage au Chef de l'État dans l'exercise de sa fonction'). They were refused reinstatement in their jobs upon release from prison as they had 'deserted' their posts, not having been able to teach while in prison. The Committee confirmed that 'the freedom to engage in political activity individually or through political parties, freedom to debate public affairs, to criticise the Government and to publish material with political content' applies to university teachers, whether they are part of the public service or not.[25] The limits of what can be taught are, however, much narrower than what international human rights law requires.

Censorship of textbooks

The *Ienaga* case in Japan (1965–97) revolved around descriptions in school textbooks of Japanese atrocities during the Second World War.

The court cases were started by Professor Saburo Ienaga, who challenged alterations to his history textbooks. These included deleting of references to the rape of Chinese women by Japanese soldiers, and to bacteriological experiments by the notorious Unit 731, as well as changing 'Japan's aggression against China' to 'Japan's advance into China'. Japan's Supreme Court upheld the constitutionality of the institutionalized screening of school textbooks, that is, the government's 'competence to decide the content of education for children to the extent that is necessary and reasonable' so as to make the contents 'accurate, neutral and fair'. The Supreme Court found that the process leading to the authorization of school textbooks determined whether the contents were, among other things, 'fair and non-biased concerning politics and religion; whether the contents were accurate; and whether the contents were suitable for the stage of children's mental and physical development.' The underlying rationale was that:

> children and students do not have enough capability to criticise the content of class education and they can hardly choose a school or a teacher. In addition, to guarantee equality of opportunity in education, content of education is required to be accurate, neutral and fair, and to have a certain national standard regardless of region and school.[26]

Having examined the controversies regarding descriptions of Japanese atrocities during the Second World War, the Supreme Court found that Professor Ienaga's reference to the 731 Unit had been unjustifiably deleted:

> At the application for authorization of the revised textbook under consideration in 1983, the Minister of Education attached a comment of modification on the description newly adding the issue of 'the 731 Unit' to delete the description entirely with the reason that it was too early to take up the issue in textbooks without having reliable studies at the time. The comment shall be considered as an illegal act as a deviation of his discretion since there were unacceptable mistakes in the process of his judgment on the recognition of theories at the time and on the evaluation that the description infringed the former standard of authorization.[27]

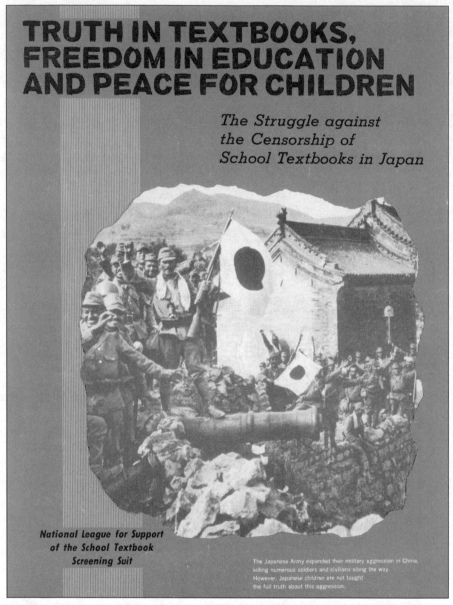

TRUTH IN TEXTBOOKS, FREEDOM IN EDUCATION AND PEACE FOR CHILDREN

The Struggle against the Censorship of School Textbooks in Japan

National League for Support
of the School Textbook
Screening Suit

The Japanese Army expanded their military aggression in China, killing numerous soldiers and civilians along the way. However, Japanese children are not taught the full truth about this aggression.

The front page of a pamphlet produced as part of the campaign against the censorship of schoolbooks in Japan triggered by the Ienaga case.

Josep Fontana, a Spanish historian, has claimed that efforts by governments to brainwash children tend not to produce the intended results. 'Patriotism is irrational and it is not formed through education,' he has held, adding that the stultifying mass of facts which children have to memorize does not have much of a chance to instil in them enthusiasm.[28] Nevertheless, bouts of rewriting history

Box 12.3 • Is geography about knowledge or power?

Gearóid Ó. Tuathail uses the first sentence in his book about the uses and abuses of geography to state that 'geography is about power'.* We are taught that the geographical maps which depict the world reflect facts, and we have to learn them as such. Questions come much later, as another author describes:

> I know that, in my own case, as a child of the empire learning about Canada's place within the Commonwealth in the 1950s, I felt a certain pride sitting before the once and former empire, done up in pink in the Oxford Junior Atlas. I was like Marlow in Joseph Conrad's *Heart of Darkness*, who as 'a little chap would look for hours at South America, or Africa, or Australia' and lose himself 'in the glories of the exploration'. Year after year, we studied the great British and French explorers, tracing their journeys with different colored dotted lines across oceans and continents, in ship and on snowshoe, as they trod across what they took to be lands that were theirs for the civilizing.
>
> We spent long hours coloring the nations of Africa and South America, saving our pinks (the mapping color of a healthy and robust white domination?) for the British Empire and the Commonwealth, in what seemed to me until recently the most innocent of school busywork. The shading of mountain and coastline along boundary after borderline added a therapeutic moment to the school day. Maps were an art form that even the artistic underachievers could reasonably achieve, all the while bringing us along on this great historical ride that left the world a colorful mosaic, with consequences that we might spend the rest of our lives figuring out and living through.†

* G. Ó. Tuathail, *Critical Geopolitics: The Politics of Writing Global Space*, Routledge, London, 1996, p. 1.
† J. Willinsky, *Learning to Divide the World: Education at Empire's End*, University of Minnesota Press, Minneapolis, 1998, pp. 145–6.

frequently follow changes of government or governance and victories in political or armed conflicts. The rewriting of history to blank out atrocities that are likely subsequently to be defined as human rights violations has been condemned by El Hadji Guissé and Louis Joinet as an attempt to exclude specific events or phenomena from the category of crimes against humanity.[29] There has been a series of disturbing findings about abuses of education relating to every and any recent armed and political conflict – and some not so recent. The Special UN Committee on Israeli Human Rights Practices in the Occupied Territories has been alerted to the portrayal of Arabs 'either as shepherds or invaders' in school textbooks.[30]

The idea that many different views about the same event could be legitimate, although different or contradictory, is difficult to reconcile with the single-version history which all children in the world are taught. Colliding perceptions and interpretations of the same event are common in real life but are expunged from history textbooks. A one and only, objectively and/or scientifically true version is as impossible as it is widespread (there may be a few exceptions in experimental schools and pilot programmes, altering the image of history from factual to subjective). The same can be said about geography, as Box 12.3 illustrates.

Laurent Wirth has proposed that schoolchildren should be exposed to historical examples of abuses of history in order to enable them to recognize manipulation and protect themselves from it.[31] Marc Ferro has suggested that any study of history should 'begin by drawing up a list of conflicts and taboos and looking at them through the eyes of other people'.[32] The Council of Europe has tackled abuses of education twice, the first time after the Second World War and the second time after the end of the Cold War. As is typical in human rights work, mobilization was each time triggered by abuses of history. It found that, in 1914, historians had 'placed their scholarship at the service of the war effort',[33] and concluded that 'all political systems have used history for their own ends'.[34]

The objective towards which education should be directed is often defined as tolerance. Setting the limits of the intolerable is the first necessary step towards creating space for tolerance. Primary-school curricula are similar worldwide and devote the highest percentage of time in school, 28 to 49 per cent, to language instruction.[35] Too little is known about translating human rights messages into a language that children can understand; few would be able to cope with terms such as 'human rights' or 'tolerance'. Moreover, the messages used in language instruction may conflict with human rights education, which becomes part of the school curriculum much later, if at all. And what a child hears in school may conflict with out-of-school messages.

In most countries, domestic law protects individuals against being publicly insulted, but prohibitions of 'group defamation'[36] are rare. Maligning 'foreigners' can be deemed an expression of patriotism and is often a vote-winner. This has been emphasized by the ECRI (European Commission against Racism and Intolerance) which has, in the case of Denmark, pointed out that negative stereotypes and prejudices 'are promoted by public opinion leaders, including political elites from across the political spectrum'.[37] Their inevitable influence on children and young people undermines human rights messages in school-based education. In addition, David Coulby has pointed out that schools and universities 'are being involved in the encouragement of xenophobia as a mode of state-building'.[38] Eliminating obstacles to the full enjoyment of the right to education is therefore necessary, from the local to the global level, throughout the world.

Notes

1. R. Cowen, 'Fine-tuning educational earthquakes?', in D. Coulby et al. (eds), *Education in Times of Transition: World Yearbook of Education 2000*, Kogan Page, London, 2000, p. 5.
2. 'Going for quality education in Africa', *Countdown: UNESCO Education News*, No. 23, December 2000–February 2001.
3. R. Warner (ed.), *Les voix du Zaire/Mingongo ya Zaire/Ndinga ya Zaire/Voices from Zaire*, Minority Rights Group, London, 1995, p. 33.
4. European Commission, 'European Report on Quality of School Education: Sixteen

Quality Indicators', May 2000, mimeograph, p. 20.

5. D. Tapper, 'Swimming upstream: The first-year experiences of teachers working in New York City Public Schools', Education Priorities Panel, May 1995 (www.edpriorities.org/Pubs).

6. 'Report from the front lines: What's needed to make New York's ESL and bilingual programs succeed', 7 February 2001 (www.advocatesforchildren.org/pubs/ELLteachRepFINAL).

7. European Court of Human Rights, *The Belgian Linguistic Case*, Judgement of 23 July 1968, Series A, Vol. 6, p. 31.

8. Article 8 of the Polish Minorities Treaty of 1919, reproduced in *Protection of Linguistic and Racial Minorities by the League of Nations*, Geneva, 1927.

9. Permanent Court of International Justice, *Minority Schools in Albania*, Advisory Opinion of 6 April 1935, Series A/B, No. 64.

10. Human Rights Committee, *Dominique Guesdon v. France*, Communication No. 219/1986, Views of 25 July 1990; *Yves Cadoret and Herve Le Bihan v. France*, Communications Nos. 221/1987 and 323/1988, Views of 11 April 1991; *Herve Barzhig v. France*, Communication No. 327/1988, Views of 11 April 1991.

11. Asian Development Bank, *Lao People's Democratic Republic: Education Sector Development Plan Report*, Manila, Philippines, July 2000, p. 3.

12. Supreme Court of Canada, *Société des Acadiens du Nouveau-Brunswick Inc. v. Association of Parents for Fairness in Education* [1986], 1 S.C.R., 549, p. 578; *Mahe v. Alberta* [1990], 1 S.C.R., 342.

13. Supreme Court of Canada, Reference *re* Public Schools Act (Man.), s. 79(3), (4) and (7) [1993], 1 S.C.R., 839, p. 12.

14. Supreme Court of Canada, *Mahe v. Alberta* [1990], 1 S.C.R., 342.

15. Supreme Court of Canada, *Ross v. New Brunswick School District No. 15* [1996] 1 S.C.R., 825, paras. 44, 45 and 42–3.

16. Report of the Commission of Inquiry appointed under article 26 of the Constitution of the ILO to examine the observance of the Discrimination (Employment and Occupation) Convention, 1958 by the Federal Republic of Germany, Geneva, 26 November 1986, paras. 568–9.

17. H. Goutier, 'President of last resort. Interview with René Préval', *Courier*, No. 161, January–February 1997, p. 40.

18. 'The dark side of Korea's cyber world', *Far Eastern Economic Review*, 18 June 2002.

19. T. Cramptom, 'A shortsighted fad: Interview with Jane Healy', *International Herald Tribune*, 16 October 2000.

20. Equal Opportunity Commission of the Netherlands, Ruling 1999-79 of 9 September 1999.

21. Equal Opportunity Commission of the Netherlands, Ruling 1999-50 of 9 June 1999.

22. Freedom of Association Committee, 272nd Report, Case No. 1503 (Peru), para. 117.

23. Freedom of Association Committee, 277th Report, Case No. 1528 (Germany), para. 285.

24. Freedom of Association Committee, 304th Report, Case No. 1863 (Guinea), para. 358.

25. Human Rights Committee, *Adimayo M. Aduayom, Sofianou T. Diasso and Yawo S. Dobou v. Togo*, Communications No. 422/1990, 423/1990, and 424/1990, Views of 12 July 1996.

26. Supreme Court of Japan, *Ienaga v. Japan*, (O) No. 1428 of 1986, Judgement of 16 March 1993, para. 2.

27. Supreme Court of Japan, *Ienaga v. Japan*, (O) No. 1119 of 1994, Judgement of 29 August 1997, para 4 (3).

28. F. Valls, 'La Academia no está legitimada para censurar,' *El País*, 2 July 2000, pp. 12–13.

29. Commission on Human Rights, Progress report on the question of the impunity of perpetrators of human rights violations prepared by Mr Guissé and Mr Joinet, UN

Doc. E/CN.4/Sub.2/1993/6 of 19 July 1993, para. 91.

30. United Nations, Report of the Special Committee to Investigate Israeli Practices Affecting the Human Rights of the Palestinian People and Other Arabs of the Occupied Territories, UN Doc. A/54/325 of 8 September 1999, paras. 235–6.

31. 'Facing misuses of history, general report by Laurent Wirth', in *The Misuses of History: Learning and Teaching about the History of Europe in the 20th Century, Oslo (Norway), 28-30 June 1999*, Council of Europe Publishing, Strasbourg, July 2000, pp. 52–3.

32. Keynote address by Marc Ferro at the symposium 'Towards a Pluralist and Tolerant Approach to Teaching History: A Range of Sources and Didactics', 10–12 December 1998, Brussels (Belgium), Council of Europe Publishing, Strasbourg, November 1999, p. 125.

33. Keynote address by Georg Iggers, in *The Misuses of History. Learning and Teaching about the History of Europe in the 20th Century, Oslo (Norway), 28-30 June 1999*, Council of Europe Publishing, Strasbourg, July 2000, p. 13.

34. Council of Europe, Recommendation No. 1283 on history and the teaching of history in Europe, Parliamentary Assembly, 22 January 1996.

35. UNESCO/IBE, *World Data on Education: A Guide to the Structure of National Education Systems*, Paris, 2000, pp. 170–5.

36. T.D. Jones, *Human Rights: Group Defamation, Freedom of Expression and the Law of Nations*, Martinus Nijhoff Publishers, The Hague, 1998.

37. European Commission against Racism and Intolerance, Second Report on Denmark adopted on 16 June 2000, Doc. CRI (2001) 4 of 3 April 2001, para. 28.

38. D. Coulby, 'Education in times of transition: Eastern Europe with particular reference to the Baltic states', in D. Coulby et al. (eds.), *Education in Times of Transition: World Yearbook of Education 2000*, Kogan Page, London, 2000, p. 17.

Summing Up: Human Rights through Education

Chapter 13

There is no simple recipe whereby full enjoyment of the right to education, human rights safeguards in education, and human rights through education could be translated into practice. Full integration of human rights in education is a process best described as a three-dimensional chess game:

- On the top chessboard, strategies and law define who should be educated, by whom, how and for what. But strategies may be in conflict with the law. A funding strategy may undermine legal guarantees. The key human rights requirement is that education should be a public responsibility. This does not mean a taxpayer-funded monopoly, however. Freedom of choice is part and parcel of every human right; education is no exception. Budgetary allocations reflect the real (as distinct from the rhetorical) priority of education at all levels, from the global to the local. Rights-based education is much more difficult than it was in the past because education is not only a free public service but also a freely traded service. This has led to the vicious circle of decreasing budgetary allocations, deteriorating public education, and the consequent exodus to private education of those who can afford it. Human rights are key to halting that trend, positing that education is a public good and a public responsibility.

- On the middle chessboard, formal pledges and priorities are translated into reality through actual power structures. Informal goals often override formal pledges; the pattern of relationships and influences moulds, often distorts, officially set priorities. Schools and universities are built fast and well, or slowly and badly, depending on effective monitoring and enforcement. Teachers may receive their salaries or these may have disappeared if funds destined for education have been made to flow through a labyrinthine bureaucracy. The curriculum may be incomprehensible to both pupils and teachers because too few understand the language of instruction.

- The bottom chessboard is the realm of the people. The education sector is, for the most part, people. They are not the numbers through which number-crunchers and bean-counters routinely portray education, but people endowed with human rights. Fully integrating all their rights in the parallel processes of teaching and learning is an ongoing process, worldwide.

This three-dimensional chessboard encompasses vertical and horizontal linkages. Budgetary allocations ought to be adjusted to the diversity of pupils entering education. The languages spoken by pupils ought to be matched with those in which teachers can teach. School textbooks can be very pretty and immensely expensive, or simply not available. Textbook authors can be involved in court cases combating censorship or defending themselves against racism. School-children can be raped or beaten to death by their teachers. As if this was not sufficiently difficult to cope with, every so often the chessboard is turned upside down and it is difficult – but essential – to remember where all the pieces were. Changes have been many, within education, and at the intersection of education and society. Looking back at the road travelled thus far, progress is evidenced in the adaptations that education has undergone in order gradually to accommodate key human rights requirements. The road ahead is long and winding. It is helpful, however, that signposts have been identified at major crossroads.

A look back

The history of human rights can be depicted through two broadening concentric circles, the first showing a gradual extension of recognized rights and the second an incremental inclusion of those previously excluded. Gradual extension of the right to education is embodied in its very definition, in the principle of progressive realization. This entails prioritizing all-encompassing free and compulsory educa-tion, and extending entitlement as widely and quickly as possible. The rights first bestowed upon adult, propertied, white men were gradually extended to women, then to non-white adults, later to non-citizens, then to people with disabilities, and most recently to children. From its first recognition, the right to education has advanced along this path through four main stages:

- The first stage involved recognizing education as a right. Even this very first stage has not yet been attained in the whole world. One notable exception is the United States of America.[1] Where the right to education is recognized, non-citizens such as asylum-seekers or undocumented migrant workers may be explicitly excluded: prevented from sending their children to school. Domestic servants may not be recorded as bearers of human rights. Hence, the process of incremental inclusion is ongoing. Education statistics encompass those already included, but rights-based education necessitates a focus on those who are still excluded. Box 13.1 provides an example, using Kuwait's education statistics as a case in point.

- When primary education at least has become all-encompassing, the second stage often entails segregation. Newly admitted categories, such as girls, minor-ity and indigenous children, or children with disabilities, have been provided with education but confined to separate, routinely inferior, schools. In the memorable words of the US Supreme Court, 'separate is always unequal'. Human rights challenges are gradually desegregating education along gender, racial or diverse-ability lines, but segregation remains institutionalized and legalized in many countries on many grounds.

- The third stage in the process of adjusting education to the requirements of the right to education entails shifting from segregation through assimilation to integration. Categories newly admitted to mainstream school have to adapt,

Box 13.1 • Education statistics for Kuwait examined using the human rights yardstick

The difference between human and citizens' rights is pronounced in Kuwait because only 34 per cent of the population are citizens.* The majority cannot claim rights which are confined to citizens. In the labour force, an even larger proportion – 65 per cent – are non-citizens. The government guarantees a job to each citizen: hence 94 per cent of public sector employees are citizens while only 1.3 per cent in the private sector are.[†]

The absence of citizenship particularly victimizes the *Bidun*, who do not possess citizenship and cannot claim rights due to statelessness. The *Bidun* cannot meet the citizenship criteria of settlement in Kuwait prior to 1920 and continued residence until the citizenship legislation was promulgated in 1959. The possibility of attaining citizenship through naturalization is also foreclosed due to the requirement of a twenty-year-long uninterrupted residence. The parallel processes of law reform and budgetary stringency due to the collapse of oil prices in the mid-1980s and the Gulf War in the early 1990s led to the classification of the *Bidun* as illegal residents, although they have been inhabitants from times immemorial.[‡] The requirement of administratively certified links with one particular state as the basis for claiming rights will continue to render them rightless. It will continue to exclude *Bidun* children from education.

The *Bidun* represent only a fraction of the population that is classified as foreign in Kuwait. The population of Kuwait was estimated at 2 million before the Iraqi occupation; it diminished to 1.2 million in 1992, with a reported number of 800,000 non-citizens.[§] The estimated size of the population again reached 2 million in 2000. The *2000–2001 World Development Report* used 2 million as the estimated size of the population and 1.9 million for calculating the labour force. The difference of 100,000, or 5 per cent, illustrates the arbitrariness of such estimates. The number of domestic servants in the Gulf region is estimated at 3 million; all are foreign, and most are girls and women.[**] Their plight comes to light only when individual cases illustrate the impact of their lack of any rights, but publicity tends to focus on one isolated case while the plight of all other domestic servants goes unchallenged.

The *Bidun* are a minuscule fraction of the officially recorded labour force in Kuwait.[††] Women are also a tiny minority in the labour force. Little is known about *Bidun* girls and women. Questions would probably elicit the following answer:'Women count but are not counted.'[‡‡]

* United Nations, 'Concluding observations of the Committee on the Rights of the Child', UN Doc. CRC/C/15/Add. 96, paras. 5 and 17, 26 October 1998.

† International Organization for Migration, *World Migration Report 2000*, International Organization for Migration/United Nations, Geneva, 2000, p. 109.

‡ United Nations, Final observations of the Human Rights Committee, UN Doc. CCPR/CO/69/KWT, para. 15. The name *Bidun*, instead of the previous *Bedouin*, is derived from Arabic *bidun jinsiya*, which denotes statelessness and/or lack of citizenship related to their nomadic way of life. There is no standard transliteration in English, hence alongside *Bidun* one finds also *Bedoon* as well as *Bédouin* in French. These differences are not merely linguistic. The Kuwait delegation, in its dialogue with the Human Rights Committee during the consideration of its report under the International Covenant on Civil and Political Rights, differentiated between '*Bidun*', classified as illegal residents and defined as citizens of other countries trying to fraudulently benefit from Kuwait's generous social services by claiming to be stateless, and '*Bedouins*', defined as a nomadic population indigenous to the Gulf and genuinely stateless (UN Doc. CCPR/C/SR.1853).

§ P. Stalker, *The Work of Strangers: A Survey of International Labour Migration*, International Labour Office, Geneva, 1994, p. 245.

** 'A survey of the Gulf', *Economist*, 23 March 2002.

†† World Bank, *Attacking Poverty: World Development Report 2000/2001*, World Bank, Washington/New York, 2001, pp. 274 and 278.

‡‡ Economic and Social Commission for Western Asia, *Survey of Economic and Social Developments in the ESCWA Region 1996–1997*, United Nations, New York, 1997, p. 139.

abandoning their mother tongue or religion. Girls are admitted to schools whose curricula were designed for boys, indigenous and minority children are placed in schools that provide instruction in an alien language and teach them history that denies their very existence. This process is often underpinned by inclusionary goals, albeit interpreted differently. Assimilation entails imposition of uniformity, integration acknowledges diversity but only as a departure from the 'norm'. Hence, newcomers may be temporarily granted some form of minority status but have to adjust to a 'norm' which extrapolates key features of the earliest self-granted bearers of rights – male, white, adult, property owners – the model for all others.

- The fourth stage necessitates adaptation of education to the diversity of subjects of the right to education. The previous requirement upon children to adapt to mainstream school is replaced by adapting education to everyone's equal right to education and equal rights in education.

There is no country in the world that has put in place enforceable guarantees for *all* components of rights-based education for *all* diverse categories into which we have split the human race. Adaptation of education to each child is a dream as yet unfulfilled. The task of monitoring *all* dimensions of rights-based education *all* the time is challenging enough. The need for well-resourced corrective mechanisms to investigate and remedy all departures from human rights standards is costly, in every sense of this term. The requirement to recognize the rights of *all* involved by providing them with access to effective remedy for their grievances illustrates the scope of the changes still to be made.

Recognizing human rights violations in education

Often it is difficult even to begin questioning differences between education and rights-based education. The key reason is not the absence of human rights violations in education, but the paucity of experiences in exposing and opposing them. Three decades of human rights work are short enough. Thus far, the focus has been on torture, disappearances and summary executions. In education, attention has been directed to extending the coverage of education. Education involves a larger number of people than any other institutionalized activity and this may well be the reason for emphasizing its *hardware* at the expense of *software*. Because school reaches the largest number of children and young people at their most impressionable age, the purpose of schooling is more often to instruct children in what they should think than to teach them *how* to think. Moreover, the orientation and contents of schooling may be classified as 'technical' issues if only quantitative targets are defined and monitored.

Box 13.2 • The purpose of schooling as determined in Saudi Arabia, China and Cuba

In Saudi Arabia 'education aims at the implantation of the Islamic creed in new generations and the development of their skills so as to enable them to contribute to the building of their society.'* On this basis, the general objectives of education are defined as follows:

> The purpose of education in Islam is to have student understand Islam in a correct and comprehensive manner; to plant and spread the Islamic creed; to furnish student with the values, teachings and ideals of Islam.
>
> Promoting the spirit of loyalty to Islamic law by denouncing any theory or system that conflicts with this law and by honest conformity with general provisions of this law.[†]

The 1995 Education Law of the People's Republic of China demands adherence by educational institutions to 'Marxism, Leninism, Mao Zedong Thought and the theory of building socialism with Chinese characteristics', adding that 'education must serve the socialist modernization drive' and learners should be educated in 'patriotism, collectivism, socialism as well as education in ideals, morality, discipline, legality, national defence and national unity'. Furthermore, all citizens have not only a right but also an obligation to receive education.[‡]

A similar specification of the framework within which the young generation should be educated is found in Cuban legislation, which stipulates that the coming generations ought to be educated as communists. The law mandates loyalty to Cuba's Communist Party ('la fidelidad ... al Partido Comunista de Cuba').[§]

* Saudi Arabia's Constitution of 1 March 1992, Article 13.
† *Development of Education in the Kingdom of Saudi Arabia. National Report prepared by the Ministry of Education*, Centre for Statistical Data and Educational Documentation, Riyadh, 1996, p. 24.
‡ *The Laws on Education of the People's Republic of China* compiled by the Ministry of Education, Foreign Languages Press, Beijing, 1999.
§ The title of the second section of the 1978 Law on Children and Youth (Codigo de la niñez y la juventud) is 'The process of educating the young generations as communists' (El proceso de formación comunista de la joven generación).

In many countries, the purpose of education is cast in stone; the syllabus, curriculum and textbooks are beyond challenge. Box 13.2 provides three typical examples.

What children are taught can amount to indoctrination, advocacy of racism or sexism, war propaganda, or stultifying regurgitation of useless bits of information. The variety of purposes for which education can be used has led human rights campaigners to press for congruence between the orientation and contents of education and human-rights values. Education moulds the child's perception of human rights. Human rights education ought to be located at the top of the educational ladder. It is unlikely to be effective if the child was earlier taught about its own unworthiness because the child happens to be female, or disabled, or simply young and playful.

Small children perceive only one side of everything, their own experience. One important educational step for any child between the ages of three and five should be learning to perceive a viewpoint different from the child's own. Missed opportunities in childhood are difficult to remedy later, in conflicts that revolve around each side perceiving only one side of everything. Suzanne Goldenberg has furnished one example:

> [D]espite the proximity in which they live and die, Israelis and Palestinians, in the main, are interested in knowing only their strand of the story. [They] appear not to be suffering from doubts but from certainties.
>
> Increasingly Israelis are resistant to hearing or seeing anything that challenges their version of events, a national cant that basically says: 'We are the victims, they are terrorists, and the whole world is against us.'
>
> Palestinians, naturally, see themselves as universal victims as well. The competition for victimhood reached its apogee a few days after September 11, when the Palestinians and Israelis held candlelight memorials with astoundingly similar placards: 'We know how you feel, we are victims of terrorism too.'[2]

Individuals as well as countries tend to remember the pain they have suffered, not the pain they have inflicted on others, making the self-perception of victimization one-sided. History textbooks epitomize what David Tyack calls 'the pedagogy of patriotism',[3] rarely describing abuses committed by one's own government against populations of other countries or the people in one's own country, although history abounds with such examples. An early US Supreme Court case, which affirmed parental rights in education,[4] revolved around the prohibition on teaching any subject in a language other than English. The background involved a ban on teaching in German, triggered by anti-German hysteria after the First World War. For many, the victimization of Arab Americans, Muslim Americans, and Sikh Americans after September 11th evoked memories of the internment of 120,000 Japanese Americans (then referred to as 'people of Japanese ancestry') following the 1941 attack on Pearl Harbor. The country's self-perception of victimization had led to the collective victimization of its citizens of Japanese ancestry. The US government apologized five decades later, with compensation for the victims.[5] The human rights safeguards developed during the past six decades forbid collective as well as individual victimization on the grounds of ethnicity, origin and/or religion. Moreover, governmental human rights obligations also include the prevention of scapegoating. Indeed, in 2000 Congress adopted the Wartime Violation of Italian American Civil Liberties Act, emphasizing the need to 'discourage the occurrence of similar injustices and violations of civil liberties in the future'.[6] One could anticipate that an apology for the victimization of people identified as Arab, Muslim or of Middle Eastern origin will follow in fifty years. Or else, take a cue from Maya Angelou, and admit that history cannot be unlived but, if faced with courage, need not be lived again.

Violence and education, violence in education

In New York, exposure to violence may have been aggravated by September 11th and its aftermath. Schoolchildren are continuously reminded of the pervasiveness of violence as they pass through metal detectors at school gates, have their lockers searched for guns, and hear sirens and alarms. The first person at the doorway of a public school is likely to be a uniformed police officer. The *2000 Indicators of School Crime and Safety* noted that in the school-year 1996–97 one in ten schools reported at least one serious violent crime and almost one in ten students carried a weapon to school.[7]

If education is defined in the broadest sense of this term, as the sum total of what children learn from their parents and peers, from the mass media as well as from the hugely developed advertising and entertainment industries – much of whose products are specifically targeted at children – in-school and out-of-school messages often conflict. Studies into violence have revealed that 'youth who observe adults accepting violence as a solution to problems are apt to emulate that violence'.[8]

Children victimized by violence are likely to become violent adults, but this early clue to the causation of violence is seldom explored. School-based programmes for the prevention of violence, where they exist, tend to be an optional add-on to the compulsory curriculum. Catherine Bonnet has argued that violence against children was a taboo until the 1960s because it revealed the shameful behaviour of adults.[9] The Committee on the Rights of the Child has highlighted the need to take into account children's life experiences when focusing on the aims of education, especially in international policies and programmes on education.[10] The Madrid Conference on School Education in Relation with Freedom of Religion and Belief, Tolerance and Non-Discrimination has prioritized 'school curricula, textbooks and teaching methods'.[11] Controversies regarding the teaching of wars, conflicts and associated abuses occur daily, worldwide. Croatian textbooks have been found to have included descriptions of 'Serbian aggressors' as 'merciless barbarians who ran amok'.[12] In Serbia, the same events were described as 'enforced expulsion of the Serbian population' from Croatia, reminiscent of the 'genocide fifty years earlier'.[13]

The need to rethink how violence is presented to schoolchildren goes much beyond the teaching of history. Violence is part of schooling where corporal punishment is routinely used in the administration of school discipline. It can be used to underpin the instrumentalization of schooling – to generate 'cookie-cutter test takers', as this is called in South Korea[14]

Forcing children to memorize information that may or may not be useful is part of education-in-practice worldwide and is reinforced by testing. It is relatively easy to design tests for items which have to be memorized and accurately repeated, with little alteration between different languages and cultures. Internationally comparable data are easily generated for mathematics and science. Recent tests placed at the very top of the performance table Singapore, South Korea, the Czech Republic, Japan and Hong Kong.[15] The anxiety in the Western world was considerable. On the one hand, the expectation that any ranking must place the West at the top was shattered, with East Asia and Eastern Europe outperforming the West. On the other hand, any such ranking kindles competitiveness among national economies. The background is a vision of education as the driving force of international competitiveness.

The underside of excellent performance is not assessed in any form of international performance table, although the price for children in the best-performing state, Singapore, is high:

Just ask the boy who was caned by his mother for scoring 83% in a science exam – despite being the fourth highest scorer in the class. In an earlier incident, he was caned for scoring 73% in a maths exam, according to *The Straits Times*.

Now the nine-year old gets so anxious over exams that he suffers from asthma, cold sweats and diarrhoea. His mother makes him spend six hours a day on homework, the paper reports. During school holidays he spends eight hours a day on revision and preparation for the next term's work. His mother isn't apologetic, saying she maintains the pressure because she wants him to get into a prestigious secondary school and to succeed in life.

The tale has many Singaporeans upset. 'The mother should be caned,' says one irate educator.' Kids like this are traumatized every time they have to take an exam.'

According to a recent survey of 1,742 children aged 10 to 12 commissioned by *The Straits Times*, students are more afraid of exams than of their parents dying.[16]

That the worst fear of 10–12-year-olds is failing examinations, followed by their parents dying, and followed by not scoring high marks in examinations,[17] may have been a motive for the ongoing revision of the objectives of education in Singapore. Children themselves cannot challenge the ends and means of education because their rights remain largely unrecognized. This task is left to their parents. They tend to follow two different paths – some wish corporal punishment to be banned, others want it preserved.

An attempt by a group of parents whose religious doctrine posited that physical punishment of children was legitimate and necessary, to challenge Sweden's policy against corporal punishment of children, forced the European Commission on Human Rights to revisit an issue which had already been the object of considerable litigation. The parents complained against the encroachment upon their 'ability to express and implement their own convictions in the upbringing of their children' embodied in Sweden's 1979 law, which was 'intended to encourage a reappraisal of the corporal punishment of children in order to discourage abuse'.[18] The Commission did not find that a general policy against corporal punishment amounted to a threat of indoctrination of children against their parents' conviction that corporal punishment was legitimate and necessary. An excerpt from an editorial which hailed the banning of corporal punishment in Thailand in 2000 points in the opposite direction:

> Psychological studies bear out the connection between the violent treatment of children, whether at the hands of teachers or parents, and their propensity for violence and aggression in later life.
>
> The more violence they suffered as a child, the more violence-prone they become as adults. Not everyone who has been caned or smacked at school will become a Pol Pot, but there is no escaping the fact that violence begets violence. The difference is only a matter of degree.
>
> Caning may be effective in stopping pupils from doing what the teacher forbids. But it is a short term solution. After being caned, children will behave ... until the next time. More importantly, the lesson that they learned will be a highly negative one. It is that human interaction is based on force, that might is right. The more they are exposed to such treatment, the more likely they are to deal with others not by reason but by force.[19]

Confronting the transmission of discrimination through education

Education can be a means to retain or to eliminate inequality. As it can serve two mutually contradictory purposes, two opposite results may ensue. Literature on discrimination abounds with assertions that prejudice breeds discrimination, yet the reverse is also true. Discrimination as a medium of indoctrination breeds prejudice; it is meant to do so. Children learn through observation and imitation. They are likely to start perpetuating discriminatory practices much before they can understand the term *discrimination*. By the time their curriculum includes the word *discrimination* they are likely to have internalized the underlying prejudice.

Prejudice is formed in late childhood and adolescence and is sustained from one generation to another through social usage. When it favours individual and group self-interest, it is easy to rationalize. Having domestic servants makes life easy for the family. Accepting the equal rights of servants entails the family doing the washing, cleaning, cooking, and gardening while the servants go to school. Discriminatory practices can be countered by changing the rules of behaviour, but their underlying rationale usually remains unexplored. It is customary to label this underlying rationale as irrational, but it often includes many rational, if unstated, arguments concerning preserving an assumed superiority, keeping existing privileges, or fear of competition. In 1957, the first United Nations study into discrimination in education highlighted thus the underlying rationale of discrimination:

> A policy based on fear of losing a privileged position necessarily entails measures to deny education to an entire population group, or to allow it access only to education at a lower level.[20]

Box 13.3 • Asking politically incorrect questions: how schoolchildren learn about racism

In 1975, David Milner published in England his findings on pre-school children's racial preferences.[*] He used white and black dolls and found that all white five-year olds preferred a white over a black doll, 80 per cent of African-Caribbean children showed the same preference as did 30 per cent of children of South Asian origin. He repeated the experiment two years later, after the children had undergone two different types of education. One group had a mixture of teachers and students from all three categories, including as diverse a curriculum as could be mustered at the time. The second one, the control group, had none of this. After two years, the repeated experiment showed that half of African-Caribbean pupils retained their preference for the white doll, while the preference by Asian pupils for white dolls diminished by half. What would have happened if children had been exposed to inclusive education for ten, fifteen or twenty-five years was a question which David Milner would have liked to explore. He could not do so because his experiment created too much of a stir at the time, as it would today. Fear, and corollary self-censorship, impede tackling questions which are crucial – what children learn and how they learn.

Few people are at ease when addressing differences in race, colour, sex, religion, provenance, or disability. We have been taught *what* we should think, or at least say in public, and shy away from asking how and why so many children and young people in countries with all-encompassing and well-funded education systems exhibit self-professed racism and xenophobia.

A pupil observed that anti-racism messages start too late: 'If you start to teach them when they are very young it would be better than to start giving them information by Year 11 when they already have their minds made up about it.'[†] How their minds have been made up for them is a question asked when the outcome looks something like this:

> Early in September I listened as a group of Australian students in an upper high school class in Perth talked about the recent movement of asylum-seekers towards this country. A girl was loudly declaring. 'I wish we had nuclear bombs 'cause then

we could bomb 'em all, and that'd be the end of it. It'd serve 'em right. They should just all go to hell. I don't want them and their diseases and violence in our clean country.' Most students in the group were vocal in support. One who appeared to have some sympathy for the asylum-seekers was abused and ended up defending himself with, 'Well, don't get me wrong: it's not like I want the boat people or anything.' Curiously, a Muslim was in the group. When asked about her own family, she replied.'We came here legally, not like those scum.'[‡]

* D. Millner, *Children and Race*, Penguin, Harmondsworth, 1975.
† C. Hamilton et al., *Racism and Race Relations in Predominantly White Schools: Preparing Pupils for Life in a Multi-Cultural Society*, Special Report, Children's Legal Centre, University of Essex, Colchester, n.d., p. 4.
‡ N. Cheesman, 'In danger of ourselves', *Human Rights SOLIDARITY*, Vol. 11, No. 12/Vol. 12. No. 1, December 2001 – January 2002, p. 20.

Box 13.4 • Creating exclusion of migrant workers

'The technique – in all cases – is simple:

(1) Bring in a large number of people when they are needed and subsequently complain that they are here.

(2) Push them into inferior jobs (jobs which the natives refuse) and then complain that they are inferior; the jobs they do are clear evidence of that.

(3) Keep them down and condemn them for being incapable of rising.

(4) Deprive them of education and condemn them for being uneducated.

(5) Force them into overcrowded houses and condemn them for creating slum conditions.

(6) Condemn them for being different: a grave offence, since your own behaviour and attitudes are so obviously the right ones.

(7) And finally reject them because of language difficulties. If a Turk or Albanian speaks less fluent Schwitzerdeutsch than a child from Appenzell, this is a clear indication that he is not much good.'

Source: G. Mikes, *Switzerland for Beginners*, André Deutsch, London, 1975, pp. 50–1.

The lack of opportunity for victims of discrimination is easily converted into factual evidence of their inferiority, feeding the perpetuation of discrimination and the underlying prejudices. As Pastor Visser't Hooft has pointed out, tackling prejudice is much more difficult than we tend to acknowledge:

In order to combat prejudices which have entered so deeply into the structure of society and the attitudes of men, knowledge and reason are not enough. They can render great help by exposing the rationalization of prejudices, and supply much-needed ammunition in the battle for racial understanding, but they cannot supply the dynamism required to replace prejudice by a positive attitude towards those of different race. In other words racial prejudice is not just a form of ignorance which can be progressively dispelled by enlightenment or by the proclamation of the idea of racial understanding. Pride can only be overcome by a force which makes for humility. An egocentric will-to-power can only be countered by a deep sense of responsibility for a kinship with those who are in danger of becoming victims of that attitude. [21]

The term *social exclusion* was developed within the European Union to denote the marginalization of individuals through economic deprivation and social isolation. The emphasis on *social* – as opposed to *statal* – exclusion typifies the diminished role of the state and probes the assumed inclusiveness of social policies. Social exclusion could be defined as a denial of human rights, but human rights language is usually avoided in favour of terms like disadvantage or deprivation or vulnerability.[22] One typical feature of the victims of exclusion is their provenance, another – and related – is their race. Most tend to be seen as alien, non-European. Box 13.4 includes an excerpt from Georg Mikes's 1975 best-seller, *Switzerland for Beginners*, in which he described how discrimination is created.

As Sven Lindqvist has put it, 'it is not knowledge we lack. What is missing is the courage to understand what we know and to draw conclusions'.[23]

Notes

1. Commission on Human Rights, Report submitted by Katarina Tomasevski, Special Rapporteur on the right to education: Mission to the United States of America 24 September – 10 October 2001, UN Doc. E/CN.4/2002/60/Add. 1.
2. S. Goldenberg, 'It's gone beyond hostility', *Guardian Weekly*, 22–28 August 2002.
3. S. Mondale and S. B. Patton (eds.), *School: The Story of American Public Education*, Beacon Press, Boston, 2001, p. 5.
4. US Supreme Court, *Meyer v. Nebraska*, 262 US 390 (1923).
5. Information at www.usdoj.gov/crt/ora/main.html.
6. Information at www.usdoj.gov/crt/wviacla.htm.
7. Full text at nces.ed.gov and www.ojp.usdoj.gov/bjs.
8. D. K. Crawford and R. J. Bodine, 'Conflict resolution education: Preparing youth for the future', *Juvenile Justice*, Vol. 8, No. 1, June 2001, p. 21.
9. C. Bonnet, *L'Enfant cassé*, Albin Michel, Paris, 1999.
10. Committee on the Rights of the Child, General comment 1 (2001): The aims of education, UN Doc. CRC/GC/2001/1 of 17 April 2001, paras. 2-3.
11. Final Document of the International Consultative Conference on School Education in Relation with Freedom of Religion and Belief, Tolerance and Non-Discrimination, Madrid, 23–25 November 2001, para. 6 (www.unhchr.ch).
12. F. Pingel, *The European Home: Representations of 20th Century Europe in History Textbooks*, Council of Europe, Strasbourg, September 2000, p. 87.
13. N. Gachesha et al., *Istorija za III razred gimnazine prirodno-matematickog smera i IV razred gimnazine opsteg i drustveno-jezickog smera* (History for 3rd grade pupils of secondary school of natural science–mathematics orientation and 4th grade pupils of secondary school of general and social science–linguistics orientation), Secretariat for Textbooks and

Teaching Tools, Belgrade, Eighth Edition, 2000, pp. 274 and 178.

14. Suh-kyung Yoon, 'South Korea: Lessons in learning', *Far Eastern Economic Review*, 28 February 2002.

15. Performance by thirteen-year olds in the Third International Mathematics and Science Study, reproduced in 'World education league: Who's top?', *Economist*, 29 March 1997.

16. 'Education: Thinking out of the box', *Far Eastern Economic Review*, 14 December 2000.

17. 'Mental health: Suffer the children', *Far Eastern Economic Review*, 9 August 2002.

18. European Commission on Human Rights, *Seven individuals v. Sweden*, Application No. 8811/79, decision of 13 May 1982 on the admissibility of the application, *Decisions and Reports*, Vol. 29, p. 111–12.

19. 'A lesson learned: Spare the rod' (editorial), *Bangkok Post*, 15 September 2000.

20. C. D. Ammon, *Study of Discrimination in Education*, UN, New York, No. 1957.XIV.3, August 1957, p. 10.

21. W. A. Visser't Hooft, *The Ecumenical Movement and the Racial Problem*, UNESCO, Paris, 1954, p. 68.

22. The Social Exclusion Unit, set up by Britain's prime minister in December 1997, defines social exclusion as 'a shorthand term for what can happen when people or areas suffer from a combination of linked problems such as unemployment, poor skills, low incomes, poor housing, high crime environment, bad health, poverty and family breakdown'. London, May 1999.

23. S. Lindqvist, *'Exterminate All the Brutes'*, Granta Books, London, 1992, p. 2.

Index

Abacha, Sani, 10-11
Ablo, Emanual, 14
Abubakar, Abdulsalami, 10
acceptability, 51
access, to education, 51, 88, 99
adaptability, 52
Adventures of Huckleberry Finn, 43
Advocates for Children of New York, 175
Afghanistan: bombing of, 125; refugees, 17;
    Taliban rule, 166-7
Africa: education statistics, 86; educational
    retrogression, 87; fertility levels, 163; SAPs,
    89; school drop-out rates, 69; sub-Saharan,
    85; World Bank study, 76
aid, 2, 15, 64, 72; decrease, 10-11
Albania, education fiancing, 135
Ali, Ahmadu, 109
Altensteein, Karl, 46
Amnesty International, 20, 100, 125
Angelou, Maya, 193
Angola, 15
anti-racism messages, 196
apartheid, 143; global mobilization against, 144
Aqil, Sheikh Abdul-Aziz al, 160
Arab states, gender diusparitry, 158
Argawal, Bina, 169
Argentina, financial crisis, 76
assimilation, 190
austerity policies, 77
Australia Institute, 119
availability, 51
Aziz, Abdul, 160
Aziz, Sartaj, 13

Babangida, Ibrahim, 10
Banda, Hastings, 72-3
Bandanaraike, Sirimavo R. D., 155
Bangladesh, 27
Bannet, Nicholas, 110
Bantu education, 147; 'Bantu Education'. 143-4
Barber, Michael, 114
'Battle of Seattle', 77, 89
Beckendorf, August, 46

Beijing Conference, 166
Belguim, religious schools, 47
Berlin airlift, 40
Benin, education budget, 24
Bidun people, Kuwait, 189
Bokassa, Jean-Bedel, 20
Bolivia, 76; indigenous peoples, 172
Bonnet, Catherine, 193
Boratav, Ferhat, 18
Bosnia, truth commission, 21
Botswana, 158, 166
Brazil, financial crisis, 76
brideprice, 160, 162
Brittain, Victoria, 15
Brown *v.* Board of Education of Topeka, 145-6
Brown, Linda, 146
Brown, Oliver, 146
Buddhism, 155
bullying, 60
Burkina Faso: education financing, 24, 135
Burma, student repression, 116
Bush, George, 114
busing, 147

Cárdenas, Victor Hugo, 172
Cambridge University, corporate sponsorship,
    120
Canada: bilingual guarantees, 176; Supreme
    Court, 55, 152, 177
Cassese, Antonio, 108
Cassin, René, 42
Celal Guzel, Hasan, 167
Central African Empire, scholchildren's protest,
    20
Central Asia, educational regression, 88, 89
Chad, 69
Chang, P.C., 39
Charter on the Rights and Welfare of the
    African Child, 165
'Chicago economics', 108
children: excluded, 125-7; labour, 1, 24, 27-8,
    32, 70, 130; 'learn and earn' 32; mothers,
    165-6; pre-school, 196; rights of, 54; soldiers,

1, 30, 62; with disabilities, 5, 33, 143, 151-4
Chile, World Bank lending to, 108
China, 15, 39, 76, 116, 117; education purpose, 191; education-through-labour, 16; Japanese aggression, 181; Tiananmen Square massacre, 116-17
Cold War, 53, 64, 89; end of, 89; fault lines, 3; human rights paralysis, 36; impact on UN, 41
'collective arbitariness', 84
Colombia, Supreme Court, 112
Commission on Human Rights, 91; Western domination, 39
Committee on the Rights of the Child, 136, 193
conditionality, 80
Convention on the Elimination of All Forms of Discrimination Against Women, 53, 58, 61
Convention on the Elimination of Racial Discrimination, 52
Convention on the Rights of the Child, 52-6, 59, 62, 93, 97
Copithorne, Maurice, 149
corporal punishment, 62, 194-5
corporate sponsorship, universities, 120
corruption, 77; Nigeria, 10-11
Coulby, David, 184
Council of Europe, 89, 184
creationism, USA, 150
Croatia, textbooks, 169
Cuba, 91; education purpose, 191
Czech Republic: government, 152; maths, 194

Dakar Conference (World Education Forum), 94, 98-9, 101, 136; new vocabulary from 100
Darwin, Charles, 150
debt, Third World: relief, 133, 136, 141; repayments, 10, 138; servicing, 86
decolonization, 41
demographics, global, 133
Denmark: Danida, 102; negative stereotyping, 184
development literature, 2
disabilities, semantics, 151
discrimination, 57, 59-60, 76, 143, 152, 195; caste-based, 127; gender, 167; indigenous peoples, 172-3; linguistic, 148; minorities, 128; Netherlands, 168; perpetuation dynamic, 197; teachers, 180
division of labour, ministerial, 1, 24
domestic servants, Gulf region, 189
donor agencies, 11
dowries, 160, 162
Drop the Debt campaign, 134

East Asia, financial crisis, 76
East Germany, former, 11
Eastern Europe, 63, 64, 87, 88; aid promises, 89, 91; countries, 39; educational regression, 89
economic growth, fetishization, 33-4
economic optimism, end of, 84
Education Acts (UK) 47-8
Education for All plans (EFAs), 136
education: alternative models, 2; bilateral aid statistics, 95; budget statistics, 85, 87; bureaucracy cost, 10, 14; commodification, 72-3, 86, 112-14; compulsory, 9, 22, 44; compulsory length, 25-7; constitutional rights to, 69; cost-sharing, 139; girls, 161-3; inequality, 78; international trade, 118; multilingualism, 176; nation-building, 17-18; pre-school, 119; public funding reduction, 3; purposes of, 61, 173, 191-2; reductionsist defining, 34; 'relevance', 29, 32; retrogression, 89-90; right to dilution, 42, 101; Rwanda, 19-20; segregation, 5; social control, 15; social mobility, 29; spirit of, 42; sponsor advertisisng, 120; teacher salaries, 179-80; trade liberalization, 114-15
'educational ghettos', 32
El Salvador, 're-education', 16
employment, minimum age, 24-5
equity, rhetorical notion, 78 80
Ethiopia, 36, 178; student repression, 116; teacher abuse, 179
Eton College, UK, 48
European Central Bank, 85
European Commission against Racism and Intolerance, 184
European Commission on Human Rights, 194
European Community, 117
European Convention on Human Rights, 54
European Court of Human Rights, 148, 175
European Social Charter, 83
European Union, 89, 91, 133, 198; Development Council, 96
evolution, theory, 151

Ferro, Marc, 184
Finland, International Development Agency (FINNIDA), 29
Fontana, Josep, 182
'forgotten aspirants', 30-1
France, 40; 1791 Constitution, 46; headscarf ban, 168

Galbraith, John Kenneth, 84

GATS, 115
Geldof, Bob, 134
gender: discrimination, 5; disparity, 163-4;
  enrolment disparities, 159; equality aim, 158,
  161; inequality, 169; secondary education,
  105
genocide, school incitement, 15
geographical maps, ideological, 183
Germany: Federal Constitutional Court, 154;
  Hitler period, 17; teacher exclusion, 117
Ghana, British missionaries, 44
girls: education, 168; education ban, 166-7;
  school access, 158
Global Campaign for Education, 99
global finance, instability, 76-7
global inequality, education provision, 63-4
Goldberg, Suzanne, 192
Gorbachev, Mikhail, 117
governments: education responsibility, 56-7, 93,
  115, 128, 136; role, 9, 53, 83, 129
Grameen Bank, 81
Great Depression, memories of, 2
Group of Seven (G-7), 80, 96; Cologne meeting,
  133
Group of Eight (G-8), Genoa Summit, 134
Guissé, El Hadji, 183
Gulf War, 189

Haiti, 178
Hamilton, Clive, 119
Health and Morals of Apprentices Act 1802,
  UK, 47
Healy, Jane, 178
Hill, Brian, 15
HIPC-II, 133
hispanicization, 173
history: ideolgical use, 184; rewriting, 183;
  teaching, 155
HIV/AIDS, education need, 162
Hoagland, Jim, 13
Holocaust, guilt about, 2
Honduras, PRSP, 136
Hooft, Visswer't, 197
Hu Yaobang, 116
'human capital' approach, 22, 33-4, 71, 77, 102
'human resource development', 33-4
human rights: Cold War debate, 41; education
  on 32-3; education violations, 190; history
  of, 188; indivisibilty principle, 158;
  international law, 1, 11, 15, 51, 127, 148;
  language of, 99-100, 184; law, 4, 129, 132;
  peer pressure, 36; safeguards, 172-3, 187;
  women, 167
Hutton, Will, 114

Ienaga, Saburo, 181-2
illiteracy, 32, 130; increase in, 86, 139
India, 42, 129; education budget demands, 130;
  education spending, 14; primary education,
  132; Supreme Court, 32, 56; universities,
  118
indigenous peoples: discrimination, 172-3;
  languages, 175
indoctrination, 192
Indonesia, education bureacracy, 14
industriousness, educational aim, 44
inequalities, accumulation, 53
informal sector, 32
International Bill of Human Rights, 52
International Convention on the Elimination of
  All Forms of Racial Discrimination, 58, 61
International Covenant on Civil and Political
  Rights, 56
International Covenant on Economic, Social
  and Cultural Rights, 56, 61, 84
International Labour Organization (ILO), 2, 16,
  57, 167, 177; Convention 10, 24;
  Convention 182, 27; Convention concerning
  Indigenous and Tribal Peoples, 59; Freedom
  of Association Committee, 179-80; Human
  Rights Committee, 181
International Monetary Fund (IMF), 70, 77, 85,
  136, 138, 179
international trade law, education, 112
International War Crimes Tribunal for the
  former Yugoslavia, 108
internment, Japanese Americans, 192
Iran, Islamic revolution, 149
Islam, negative publicity, 149
Israel, 88; stereotyping of Arabs, 182; UNESCO
  withdrawal, 94

Japan: history textbooks, 181-2; maths
  standards, 194
Jason, Pini, 11
Jehova's Witnesses, 148
Joinet, Louis, 183
Jomtien Conference 1990, 3, 89, 94, 98-9;
  Declaration, 93; new vocabulary, 100-1
Jubilee 2000, 133

Kanbur, Ravi, 78
Katari, Lidia, 172
Kenna, George, 64
Kenya, 80-1; colonial policies, 145; primary
  education, 132
Keuakoun, Thonhpaseuth, 109
KinderCare, 119
Kingayo, Johnson, 15

Ko-Yung Tung, 75
Kosovo, 102
Kozol, Jonathan, 114
Kramer, Heinz, 18
Kuwait: education statistics, 188; non-citizens, 189

language: denied rights to, 18-19; discrimination, 148; of instruction, 173-6; power of, 153, 156; segregation by, 155
Laos, 27; education fees, 100; student repression, 109; unilingual, 176
Latin America, 46, 85; *la década perdida*, 85
Lebanon, 42
Lesotho, 158
Lewis, Stephen, 86
Liberia, 36
Lindqvist, Sven, 197
literacy: employment requirement, 135; Korean campaign, 23; rural women rates, 13
Live Aid, 134
Lovrenovic, Dubravko, 21
Luard, Evan, 39
Luther, Martin, 45

Maarifa Ni Ufunguo, 140
Madrid Conference on School Education, 193
Malawi, 74; primary education, 132; primary school fees, 3, 72-3
Malaysia, 108
Mali, 69; education budget, 24
Marcuse, Herbert, 77
marriage, child, 1, 27
Marshall Plan, 64
Marshall, Thurgood, 146
Maru, Essefa, 179
mathematics, gloabl league tables, 194; textbook propaganda, 17
Mauritania, 69; primary education, 135-6
McNamara, Robert, 76
Mehta, V.R., 118
Mexico: financial crisis, 76; student repression, 116
Mikes, George, 198
militarization, boys, 19
military spending, 2, 10-11, 86, 108, 138; Pakistan, 13; statistics, 12
Milner, David, 196
Milosevic, Slobodan, demonstrations against, 116
Mingat, Alain, 33
minorities, rights, 175
Mongolia, 158
More, Hannah, 44

Mouvement ATD Quart Monde, 84
Mozambique: 're-education', 16; PRSP, 135
Mugo, Beth, 80
Mureithi, Mutahi, 80
Musharraf, General??, 13
Myrdal, Gunnar, 70

National Association for the Advancement of Coloured People (NAACP), 146
National Security Council, Turkey, 18
National Union of Nigerian Students, 109
Nepal, 27; dowries, 160
Netherlands, education, 25; Equal Opportunities Commission, 180; first education laws, 47; religious education, 144
New York, education bureaucracy, 14
New Zealand, 115
Newby, Howard, 118
Niger, adult literacy rate, 135
Nigeria: corruption, 10-11; Free Education Jihad, 109, primary education, 132; student repression, 111
North-South global division, 3
Norway, Red Cross, 31

Obasanjo, Olusegun, 109
obediance, conformist imposition, 60-2, 190
Oxfam, 99, 125
Oxford University, corporate sposnsorship, 120

Pahlavi, Shah Reza, 149
Pakistan, education spending, 14; military spending, 13
Palestine, 88
parent pressure, 194
parental choice/freedom, 42, 44, 55-6, 102, 147-8, 163
Pareto efficiency, 78
peace-building, 1
'pedagogy of patriotism', 192
Penrose, Perran, 139
Peru, textbooks, 169
Pestalozzi, Johann H., 46
Philippines, 158; Supreme Court, 148
piety, educational aim, 45
Pinochet, August, 108
Poland, minority languages, 175
Portugal, colonial policy, 144
poverty, 27, 32, 127; ideological analysis, 126; reduction aim, 4, 74-6, 102
Poverty Reduction Strategy Papers, World Bank, 80
Preval, René, 178

pregnancy, school expulsion, 165, 166
prejudice: combatting, 197-8; formation, 195-6
primary education/schools, 53, 56, 63, 85-6, 99, 112, 165; adaptability, 28; enrolments, 69, 135; fees, 72-5, 132, 140; girls, 163; global emphasis on, 22; India, 129, 131; numbers decrease, 83; statistics, 45
private schools, 147; intake, 143
privatization, 33, 71-3, 83, 86-7, 115
'progressive realization', 53
PRSPs (poverty reduction strategy papers), 133, 135-6
Prussia, state schools, 44, 46
Psacharoupoulos, George, 71, 73
public sector employment, 29-30
public-private partnership, 119

race, discrimination, 5; 198; racism, 15
Rajasthan University, 118
're-education', 16
Reinikka, Ritva, 14
religion: freedom of, 148; religious schools, 143-4; US political power, 150-1
'right to be different', concept, 143
right to strike, teachers, 180
Roma children, Czech discrimination against, 152; Slovak discrimination against, 153
Romania, 're-education', 16
Roosevelt, Eleanor, 44
Russia: elites, 131; financial crisis, 76; textbook access, 91
Rwanda, genocide incitement, 19-20; Truth Commission, 21

São Tomé and Principe, education, 25
Sachs, Albie, 143
Samuelson, Paul, 70
Sarajevo, University of, 21
Saudi Arabia, 39, 158; education purpose, 191; girls' education, 160
Saugare, Roman George, 140
schools, sale of, 113
Schuknecht, Ludger, 85
Schultz, Theodore, 34
secondary education, 102; enrollment statistics, 103-5; Korean investment, 23
segregation, 188; racial, 143, 145-6, 148
Sen, Amartya, 14, 33
September 11th attacks, 193
Serbia, textbooks, 193
Sharia law, 166-7
Shihata, Ibrahim, 75
Shiksha Yatra (India Marches for Education), 129-31

Short, Clare, 100
Sierra Leone: elitist education system, 30-2
Singapore, 194; UNESCO withdrawal, 94
Social Summit, Copenhagen 1995, 97
Society for Promoting Christian Knowledge, 47
South Africa, 36, 39; apartheid system, 143; Children's Summit, 162; Constitutional Court, 147
South Korea: Centre for Internet Addiction Counsel, 178; education investment, 22-3; secondary education, 102; violence, 194
Southampton University, 118
Soweto, student uprising, 144
special needs children, notion, 152
Sri Lanka, 127; history teaching, 155
Stiglitz, Joseph, 78
structural adjustment policies, 74, 179; Africa, 89; education cuts, 85
Students Movement for Democracy, Laos, 109
Sweden, 194-5
Switzerland, headscarf ban, 168

Taiwan, 39
Tamil-medium schools, 155
Tanganyika, colonial policies, 144
Tanzania: basic-needs policy, 139; debt relief, 141; maths-books propaganda, 17; primary education, 132; textbooks, 169
Tanzi, Vito, 85
taxation, 4; avoidance, 13; regressive, 140
teachers, 9, 55; bilingual, 175; gender, 163-4; rights, 178-81
textbooks: authors, 188; censorship, 181-2; gender bias, 169; history, 183, 192; in Russia 91; xenophobic, 193
Thailand, 195; student repression, 116
Thirty Years War, 46
Thobani, Mateen, 72-3
Tiananmen Square, student protest, 116-17
Timberlake, Lloyd, 125
Tobier, Emanuel, 14
Togo, 69; compulsory education, 120
tolerance, educational aim, 184
Tolley, Howard, 39
Tolstoy, Leo, 131
trade unions, 180
'transitional bilingual education', 173
Tuathail, Gearóid Ó, 183
Turkey, 46, 88; compulsory education, 17-18; headscarf ban, 167; women's education, 168
Twain, Mark, 43
Tyack, David, 192

Uganda, 136, 162; brideprice, 160; debt

bondage, 137; education bureaucracy, 14; primary education, 132; Universal Primary Education programee (UPE), 138-9
unemployment, 153; graduate, 29-1, 117
uniliguilism, 174
United Kingdom (UK), 40, 42; colonial policies, 144-5; primary schooling, 47; public schooling, 46; special needs learners, 153; stratified schools, 48; UNESCO withdrawal, 94
United Nations (UN), 60, 63-4; agencies, 101; Children's Charter, 162; Commission on Human Rights, 90; Committee on Economic, Social and Cultural Rights, 136; Committee on Israel Human Rights Practices, 183; Committee on the Elimination of Racial Discrimation, 152; discrimination in education study, 196; Economic Commission for Latin America and the Caribbean, 102; High Commission for Refugees, 125; human rights agenda, 62; *instruments*, 36; membership chronology, 37-8; Programme of Action for African Economic Recovery, 86; semantics, 100; UNICEF, 31, 91, 163, 167
UNESCO, 44, 101, 143, 177; Convention against Discrimination in Education, 52, 55, 58, 61; Declaration on Higher Education 1998, 119; ideological debates, 94; Institute for Statistics, 99, 158; Monitoring Learning Achievment Project, 174
United Soviet Socialist Republics (USSR), 62-3; Berlin blockade, 40; *defectology*, 151; human rights proposal, 39; Sputnik launch, 48
United States of America (USA), 4, 40, 42, 64, 70, 117, 118; common school model, 46, 48, 145; education trade liberalization, 115; ideological model, 3; in-school commerce, 113; Islamaphobia, 148; schools 'white flight', 147; school violence, 193; Supreme Court, 15, 48, 150, 188, 192; UNESCO withdrawal, 94; unilingualism, 174; war-against-terrorism, 13

Universal Declaration of Human Rights, 2-3, 17, 36, 38-42, 44, 48, 52, 64; Iran dissociation from, 149
universities: commercialization, 119; differentials, 118; fee-paid, 117; fund starvation, 111; laissez-faire regime, 115; Turkish teacher dismissals, 167
University of Delhi, 118

Venezuela, compulsory education, 120
Verwoerd, Hendrik, 144
Vienna Declaration and Programme of Action, 97
Vientiane University, 109
Vietnam, 27
voucher schemes, 112, 114

Wackman, Harold, 80
Warren, Earl, 146
Weber, Max, 1
Winchester College, UK, 48, 114
Wolde-Semayat, Taye, 179
women: education statistics, 161; rights, 31
Woodhall, Maureen, 71, 73
World Bank, 3-4, 18, 69, 75-6, 94, 99, 101, 115, 136, 138-40, 179; conditionality, 110; education finance, 93; education ideology, 71; education lending, 70, 96; expense of, 81; image promotion, 78; leveraged, 79-80; loans to Pinochet regime, 108; school fees rationalization, 72-4; semantics, 133
World Jewish Congress, 42
World Trade Organization, 114
worldwide web, 178
Wresinski, Joseph, 84

Yadav, Sukhiya, 160-1
Yunus, Muhammad, 81

Zaire, 174
Zambia, 74, 86; FINNIDA programme, 29; primary education, 132

This book is also available in the following countries:

EGYPT
MERIC (The Middle East Readers' Information Center)
2 Bahgat Ali Street, Tower D / Apt. 24 Zamalek, Cairo
Tel: 20 2 735 3818/736 3824   Fax: 20 2 736 9355

FIJI
University Book Centre, University of South Pacific, Suva
Tel: 679 313 900   Fax: 679 303 265

GHANA
EPP Book Services, PO Box TF 490, Trade Fair, Accra
Tel: 233 21 773087   Fax: 233 21 779099

INDIA
Segment Book Distributors, B-23/25 Kailash Colony,
New Delhi
Tel: 91 11 644 3013   Fax: 91 11 647 0472

MOZAMBIQUE
Sul Sensacoes, PO Box 2242, Maputo
Tel: 258 1 421974   Fax: 258 1 423414

NAMIBIA
Book Den, PO Box 3469, Shop 4, Frans Indongo Gardens,
Windhoek
Tel: 264 61 239976   Fax: 264 61 234248

NEPAL
Everest Media Services, GPO Box 5443, Dillibazar, Putalisadak
Chowk, Kathmandu
Tel: 977 1 416026   Fax: 977 1 250176

PAPUA NEW GUINEA
Unisearch PNG Pty Ltd, Box 320, University, National Capital District
Tel: 675 326 0130   Fax: 675 326 0127

RWANDA
Librairie Ikirezi, PO Box 443, Kigali
Tel/Fax: 250 71314

UGANDA
Aristoc Booklex Ltd, PO Box 5130, Kampala Road,
Diamond Trust Building, Kampala
Tel/Fax: 256 41 254867